A Legend of Holy Women

NOTRE DAME TEXTS IN MEDIEVAL CULTURE
The Medieval Institute
University of Notre Dame

John Van Engen and Edward D. English, Editors

A LEGEND OF HOLY WOMEN

Osbern Bokenham
Legends of Holy Women

TRANSLATED, WITH AN INTRODUCTION AND NOTES, BY

SHEILA DELANY

University of Notre Dame Press
Notre Dame   London

Library of Congress Cataloging-in-Publication Data

Bokenham, Osbern, 1393?–1447?
  [Legendys of hooly wummen. English]
  A legend of holy women : Osbern Bokenham, Legends of
holy women / translated, with an introduction and notes, by
Sheila Delany.
    p. cm. — (Notre Dame texts in medieval culture)
  Translation from Middle English of: Legendys of hooly
wummen.
  Includes bibliographical references.
  ISBN 0-268-01294-6
  1. Christian poetry, English (Middle)—Modernized
versions. 2. Christian women saints—Legends. I. Title.
II. Series.
PR1840.B5L4413 1992
821'.2–dc20   91-51117
                                                                  CIP

CONTENTS

ACKNOWLEDGMENTS

My interest in Bokenham began as a spin-off from a study on Chaucer, but it rapidly acquired its own momentum. I was able to develop the project in the close-to-ideal scholarly setting of Berkeley during the academic year 1987–88, thanks to a year's release-time stipend from the Social Science and Humanities Research Council (SSHRC) of Canada. The University Library, the Bancroft Special Collections Library, and the Library of the Graduate Theological Union in Berkeley were rich resources for this and other projects. A President's Research Grant from Simon Fraser University enabled me to consult the unique manuscripts of the *Legend* and the Claudian translation at the British Library in the fall of 1989, as well as the cartulary of Reading Abbey. Renewal of the SSHRC grant for 1989–90 made it possible to prepare the translation, apparatus, and manuscript without sacrificing other work. I am also indebted to the able help, at different points in the work, of my research assistants Ken Christenson and Arlene Cook. As always, Anita Mahoney of Simon Fraser's support staff has enabled the production of the manuscript to go smoothly.

For offering an opportunity to present some of my early speculations about Bokenham and Chaucer, I want to thank Miceal Vaughan and the Medieval Seminar at the

University of Washington (Seattle), with particular appreciation to Michael Curley of the University of Puget Sound for his bibliographical help and his encouragement of a novice in hagiographical studies. Susan Crane offered perceptive commentary on an early version of the material given at the Delaware Valley Medieval Association's "Literature and History" conference in 1989, organized by Betsy Bowden. The University of London's Old English, Medieval, and Renaissance Seminar (LOMERS) and the Cambridge University Medieval Group provided receptive audiences and helpful commentary to my talks there in 1989, and I am particularly grateful to Pamela King, James Simpson, and Jill Mann for their cordial hospitality. My colleagues Paul Dutton of Simon Fraser's History Department, Rhoda Friedrichs of Douglas College, and DeLloyd Guth of the Law Faculty at the University of British Columbia have been generous with friendly advice on Latin and historical sources. At the University of Notre Dame, Edward Vasta of the English Department and John Van Engen, Director of the Medieval Institute, have encouraged and expedited this project. The meticulous and sensitive copyediting of Dr. Jeannette Morgenroth, of the University of Notre Dame Press, was much appreciated. I have felt privileged to work with the Press and the Medieval Institute, and honored that this project was selected to inaugurate the present series.

I am grateful to the Council of the Early English Text Society, which granted permission to use the EETS edition of Bokenham's legends as the basis for this translation.

INTRODUCTION

The Author and His Context

What we know about Osbern Bokenham is pieced together from the internal evidence of his poetry and from
sparse—very sparse—documentary evidence.

In the *Legends* Bokenham informs us of his age, express-
ing the hope that Atropos will not too quickly cut his "fatal
threed. . . Wych lachesys hath twynyd ful yerys fyfty" (line
248 in the Early English Text Society's edition: fated life-
thread. . . which Lachesis has spun out for full fifty years").
This remark occurs in the life of St. Margaret, which the
author says he began on 7 September 1443 (lines 187–91).
His birthday is St. Faith's day (6 October), we learn later
(line 4034), so that if Bokenham is anticipating his "full
fifty" by a month, he was born in 1393.

The unique manuscript of the *Legend* was copied, and
therefore presumably completed, in 1447. This date and
the author's name are given in a note and a table of contents
that are appended to the manuscript. Since the author
had, early on in the work, expressed a wish to remain
anonymous, the *Legend*'s EETS editor, Mary Serjeantson,
inferred that he had died in 1447. She assumed that no one
would flout the author's wish during his lifetime. However, documentary evidence published since Serjeantson's
1938 edition shows that in 1463—at the age of seventy—

Bokenham was alive and well at Clare Priory, signing a document on his patron's behalf, and was elected vicar general for a coming chapter meeting. That is the last we see of him, and we may assume that he died at Clare.

Bokenham declares that in both speech and writing he uses the ordinary "language of Suthfolk speche" (line 4064): presumably Suffolk was his native county, or perhaps he hailed from the village of Buckenham a few miles north of the Suffolk line. At that time a boy could join the Austin order as early as the age of eleven. He would normally go to live in the establishment closest to his place of birth and, as his education advanced, proceed to higher schooling in a larger city; Norwich and Cambridge would be the likely places in Bokenham's case. Then he would proceed to one of England's two universities. On 21 March 1423, Bokenham was made *baccalarius* at Cambridge University, the day after John Capgrave, another Augustinian, to whose life of Saint Katherine Bokenham refers in his own hagiography (6356). Though he received permission to travel to Italy, he did not go then but may have remained at Cambridge to teach or study, and he is likely to have completed his duties for the degree of *magister* in the next two to four years (1425–1427).

There would be later journeys abroad, for as a member and an official in an important international order, Bokenham would need to travel. In the prologue to his life of Margaret he mentions two trips to Italy, in the prologue to Magdalen, a pilgrimage to Santiago de Compostela in Spain. Bokenham was in Venice, he says, about five years before the present writing (1443), hence about 1438. With tantalizing brevity he relates a harrowing experience at the hands of a Venetian tyrant. Though Venice was an important point of departure for the Holy Land, it was not itself a major object of pilgrimage, and one assumes that if Bokenham had been to the Holy Land he would have said so. He may have been in Venice either on chapter business or en route to the convening of the council at

Florence in 1438. His trip to Rome he referred to as "The laste tyme I was in Itayle," but it isn't clear whether this means the 1438 trip. In any case, on the journey back from Rome rainstorms forced Bokenham to stay at the hostel in Montefiascone, about fifty miles north of Rome. Montefiascone had a cult of Margaret, and the pious English friar occupied himself with transcribing the saint's legend, which he then brought back to Clare and proceeded to translate. The pilgrimage to Santiago was performed in 1445, just before Bokenham undertook the life of Magdalen.

By 1427 Bokenham was at Clare Priory in Suffolk, East Anglia. His old Cambridge friend and fellow author John Capgrave lived in the Augustinian convent at Lynn about fifty miles away. Capgrave became prior provincial in Britain (1453–1457) and a prolific producer of religious, and occasionally of historical, works. Also resident in Lynn was the enthusiast and mystic Margery Kempe, who died about 1438: Bokenham can hardly have been unaware of his unusual but respected neighbor, and while no evidence proves that they met, Bokenham would likely have been among Margery's admirers; for Saint Elizabeth, with whose life Bokenham concludes his set of thirteen lives, resembles Margery in several important respects, not least in her being married and a mother, and in her crying and sobbing aloud. Only fifteen miles away was the ancient and immensely wealthy Benedictine abbey of Bury St. Edmunds, whose abbot, William Curteis, sat in Parliament as moneylender and advisor to the king. The abbey's most famous literary inmate was Bokenham's older contemporary, the poet John Lydgate (1370–1450).

Social life in England was turbulent during Bokenham's lifetime, among all social classes. In 1401 the Lollard heresy, which developed a significant following among East Anglian artisans, had been declared a capital offense; thereafter, investigations and prosecutions were frequent, and the burning of books and heretics, if uncommon, did occur. (For civil troublemaking and treasonous behavior, the punishment was to be hanged, then drawn and quartered, with the head set in a public place and the quarters often dispersed to display as a sanguinary warning.)

During the 1430s and 1440s major riots broke out in Norwich and Lynn, some intervening in urban partisan politics, others protesting ecclesiastical interference in urban life. Rivalry among ambitious barons and gentry was intense, often erupting into violence. Abroad, the war with France dragged on. Henry VI, the reigning Lancastrian king during Bokenham's adult life, married a French princess, Margaret of Anjou, in 1445 and attempted to negotiate peace. His effort was opposed by many English who preferred an aggressive foreign policy to protect English territories in France and English commercial interests at sea and abroad. Propaganda of the period was often expressed in verse, and the rhymed "Libell of English Policy" (1436) gives voice to those mercantile interests.

East Anglia was an extremely wealthy area in the high and late Middle Ages thanks to its wool and textile industry, and to England's policy of keeping gold and silver at home. A great landholding abbey like Bury St. Edmunds struck a fifteenth-century Italian observer as resembling a baronial palace in magnificence, and even the parish church at Long Melton, a few miles from Clare, still impresses observers with the obvious prosperity of its donors (some of whom were Bokenham's patrons). Clare, where Bokenham spent his adult life, was the oldest Augustinian establishment in England, founded in 1248 by the Clare family. Joan of Acre—daughter of King Edward I, wife to Gilbert of Clare, earl of Gloucester, and an early donor to the priory—was buried there. So was Prince Lionel of Clarence, son of King Edward III, in whose household the young Geoffrey Chaucer learned courtly habits and acquired a foothold in the civil service. Elizabeth Clare de Burgh founded Clare College at Cambridge in the mid–fourteenth century.

It was, in short, a distinguished patronage whose social life and aspirations the Austins shared. They did so as neighbors and material beneficiaries, as chaplains at the adjacent Clare Castle, and as university men whose training offered not only entertaining and refined conversation to while away provincial winter evenings, but also valuable propagandistic skills in the service of family ambition. It can have been no hermit-like existence that Bokenham led at Clare, and in the *Legends* he names various patrons among the local gentry and nobility. Above all, he boasts of his friendship with two aristocratic patrons: Elizabeth De Vere, countess of Oxford, and Lady Isabel Bourchier, countess of Eu. In the prolocutory to Magdalen's life, Bokenham sketches the celebration at Lady Bowser's (Bourchier) on Twelfth Night, 1445, when the noblewoman commissioned the Magdalen translation. Now Lady Isabel's genealogy (of which Bokenham gives a partial account) goes back through her mother, Anne Mortimer, to the Clares; on both sides it also goes back to Edward III. The importance of this genealogy at the moment of composition is that Isabel's brother—Richard, duke of York—would soon be proposed as a legitimate candidate for the throne of England, then held by the Lancastrian Henry VI, descendant of the usurper Henry IV. Indeed, Bokenham's praise of Lady Isabel modulates into the wish that the royal right passed down through Isabel's (and Richard's) paternal line may be realized by Richard: "the ryht now to the brothir . . . is come, / Wych god hym send, yf it be hys wyl." To be sure, the syntax of the long sentence indicates that the right explicitly spoken of here is the royal title of Spain. Nonetheless, the succession had been an important question in England ever since the 1399 Lancastrian usurpation, which created a good deal of disaffection among all social strata. In 1451 Richard was nominated in Parliament as successor, but there is evidence (see below) that as early as 1445 his claim to the throne of England was taken very seriously indeed.

Beside the *Legends*, several other works can be attributed to Bokenham, whether certainly or tentatively. Indisputably

his is the *Mappula Angliae* (about 1440). This translates
part of the Benedictine monk Ranulf Higden's early four-
teenth-century *Polychronicon*, one of the most famous
books in England. From Higden, Bokenham imitates the
acrostic in which the initial letter of each chapter forms
the writer's (here, the translator's) name. Bokenham's first
name also appears in a concluding Latin distich, and the
work itself contains references to Clare and to Joan of
Acre. The text describes the advantages, marvels, geogra-
phy, cities, administrative divisions, and dialects of England;
it ends with a rather charming "epiloge excusatorie" apol-
ogizing for the writer's linguistic rudeness (specifically the
local dialect of his youth) and revealing the acrostic.

The *Mappula* grew directly out of a previous project,
according to Bokenham: a compilation of saints' lives (not
the *Legends*) that mentions various English places and to
which the *Mappula* is therefore intended as a guide or key.
This earlier compilation may be lost, or it may be the prose
collection called the *Gilte Legende*. This collection exists
in eight manuscripts, all from a version made before 1438
and translated from a French version of Jacob da Voragine's
thirteenth-century *Legenda Aurea;* a version was published
later by Caxton. Scholars remain divided about the attri-
bution to Bokenham.

Probably by Bokenham are two other pieces of apparently innocuous scholarship but with significant political
implications. One is a translation of Claudianus's fifth-
century panegyric on the soldier-consul Stilicho, *De Con-
sulatu Stilichonis.* According to the manuscript, the work
was done at Clare in 1445. The text, a facing-page translation, gives the English in Troilus stanzas. The translation
is preceded by a short prologue that begins by compar-
ing to the heroic Stilicho "the high prince. . .which of al
Engelonde is namyd the defense." Richard, duke of York,
is meant, and the poem ends with fulsome assertion of
Richard's divine guidance, perhaps even divine right:

ffor now the parlement pierys where thei goo or ryde
Seyen the duke of yorke hath god vpon his side
Amen. amen. blissed Ihesu make this rumour trewe
And aftir. feele peryles. this prince with Ioie endewe.

For now the Parliament peers, whether [or: wherever]
    they walk or ride,
Say the duke of York has God upon his side.
Amen, amen, blessed Jesus make this rumor true,
And after many perils, this prince with joy endow.

In 1445, then, either Bokenham or another inhabitant of Clare strongly supported the descendant of his priory's founder. It would be another five years before popular support of York came to violent display in the 1450 Cade rebellion in Kent, and six years before Richard was (unsuccessfully) nominated in Commons as heir presumptive in the absence—temporary, as it turned out—of a son to King Henry VI. Some historians of the period are reluctant to believe that Richard's royal ambitions could have begun any earlier. Yet given his pedigree as a prince of the blood, and his family's history, it is difficult to see how Richard could ever have lacked a clear awareness of the possibility of succeeding to the throne, and, in the troubled times preceding 1450, the desirability. But whatever Richard's intentions, the Clare document suggests that to some Englishmen in the 1440s, Richard seemed the obvious candidate to defend the national interest and to restore order in a troubled kingdom, in whatever capacity. Bokenham's Magdalen prolocutory, also dated 1445, makes an even more open bid on Richard's behalf.

The other work possibly by Bokenham is a "Dialogue at the Grave" (1456), which recounts the genealogy and descendants of Joan of Acre, a founder of Clare Priory buried at the establishment. But this pedigree is also the royal descent and hereditary claim to the throne of Richard, duke of York. In 1460 Richard himself formally laid claim to the throne. The House of Lords devised a clever compromise to his petition: acknowledging the validity of his claim, they insisted it not be implemented while Henry VI lived. Richard died in a military skirmish at Wakefield, at the end of December, 1460.

In addition to these extant works, Bokenham mentions in the life of St. Anne (lines 2080–82) a Latin stanzaic verse treatment of Anne and her three daughters. This has not been located.

What else do we know about Bokenham? That he wore spectacles. That at the age of fifty he considered himself old and expected to die before he could complete the work in hand. These last two details are recounted by the author (lines 897, 245–46), and indeed we are constantly kept aware of the author's age, mood, plans, and social environment; his worries about illness and death; his difficulties in working (especially in translating Ambrose on Agnes); his aesthetic principles; sometimes even the length of time a given translation took (five days for Katherine [line 7367]). Nor is his the only physical presence we may notice. There are several references to the red or bloody flux, the disease of choice for minor characters in this work. The persecutor-villains all suffer from "melancholy" (a superfluity of black bile believed to produce depression and insanity), while the martyrs, by contrast, maintain a good, healthy color and cheerful disposition throughout their ordeals. This contrast is not uncommon in hagiography, but it receives special emphasis in Bokenham's legendary. We have, in short, a very embodied figure of the author, who gives us a distinctively embodied cast of characters. He even personalizes his pen as a snouted animal tired from its exertions, telling the author it wants time to rest and get repaired (lines 898–908).

This embodiedness seems consistent with a stylistic earthiness that coexists with the elaborate latinity of syntax in the *Legend*. "Not worth a flykke!" (line 2957: "not worth a flitch" [of bacon]) says the persecutor Julian of

a magician's tricks. Exhausted from work after completing the Margaret, the author feels like a tired-out pilgrim
desiring only a little food and drink, and then "his bonys
aftyr in a bed to beyke" (line 887: "to beak his bones in
bed"): here Bokenham borrows from rural or artisanal life
the term for straightening a piece of unseasoned wood by
heating it. In Magdalen, the naked abandoned child is seen
"On chyldryns wyse besyle pleying, / And smal stonys on-
to the see castyng" (lines 6056–57: "playing busily as children do, throwing little stones into the sea"). Perhaps all
this is the plain Suffolk countryboy speaking alongside the
Cambridge student of Latin classics. Perhaps it is the master
in theology and the ecclesiastical administrator well aware
of the new theology of the body: the international trend
in late medieval devotional literature, art, and sermon that
dwelt on the embodiedness—what Leo Steinberg has called
the "humanation"—of Jesus. And, not least, it is certainly
the poet making space for himself within the narrow room
of hagiography.

The Legends and Their Context

What is a "legend"? Most literally it is a thing to be read
(legenda). The legend was originally, in the early Christian
period, a tributary biography or memorandum compiled
by a church archivist from local memory and testimony as
to the holiness of a deceased member of the community.
It would be read aloud in church as part of a liturgy commemorating the anniversary of the individual's death. If the
saint grew famous, or the church or abbey prospered, then
the service might become more elaborate, the legend more
detailed. At first the word "legend" carried no implication
of fictionality, although over the centuries many saints'
legends were compiled of fictional material from folktale,
classical myth, and romance. A collection of martyrs' lives

would be a "passionary" (from the Latin, *passio*, suffering); a collection of nonmartyrs' lives (holy hermits, virgins, or functionaries) would be a "legendary," but this distinction collapsed fairly early on. Eventually, during the eleventh century, the centralized ecclesiastical bureaucracy at Rome took over the process (and indeed invented the concept) of canonization, which thereafter became quite complex, costly, and vulnerable to political influences.

Bokenham's legendary is composed in several verse forms. The meter is rugged, slipping between four- and five-stress lines and often irregular within the line. When Bokenham apologizes for his lack of polish, he is to some extent indulging in the conventional "modesty topos," for his management of rhyme and rhetoric is skilled enough; but his metrics surely warrant the disclaimer. On the other hand, the quality of Bokenham's metrics is not unlike Lydgate's, about which scholars have spilt much ink. Possibly with Bokenham, as with Lydgate, method guides apparent madness (though I have not yet discerned it).

Bokenham uses three verse forms in the *Legend*: rhymed couplet (opening prologue, prolocutory to Mary Magdalen, life of Katherine, prologue to Cecelia, life of Agatha, and part of the prologue to Elizabeth); Troilus stanza or rhyme royale, a seven-line stanza rhymed ABABBCC (lives of Margaret, Anne, Ursula, Faith, Agnes, Dorothy, Magdalen, and part of the Elizabeth prologue); and Monk's Tale stanza, an eight-line stanza rhymed ABABBCBC (prologues to Margaret and Anne; life of Christine; prologues to Agnes, Magdalen, and Lucy; life of Elizabeth). The stanzaic forms, originating in French courtly lyric, were popularized in English by Chaucer. Certain elaborations and variations on these schemes were explored, for example a great deal of rhyme-linkage between stanzas in both of the stanzaic forms. To report a consistent metrical illustration of the Christian principle that "the last shall be first" would be pleasant, but the link is not necessarily between immediately adjacent last and first lines. Another variant: the Anne prologue uses a double-reverse Monk's Tale stanza for a sixteen-line unit. Some, though not all, of these complexities were highlighted by the scribe, who drew brackets in red ink to connect rhymed lines, a not uncommon scribal practice in fifteenth-century manuscripts.

From internal evidence it is possible to reconstruct the four-year compositional process of the work, which was not written in exactly the order the manuscript presents. The explicit to the manuscript gives 1447 as the date when Bokenham's "son" (this could mean either godson or young friend), Friar Thomas Burgh, had the text copied, in Cambridge, at a cost of thirty shillings, and then gave it to an unnamed convent of nuns. If we assume that the work was copied just after completion, then 1447 is the date of completion.

The main prologue tells us that an inspiration for the author's translation of one legend—that of Margaret—was the request of a dear, but unnamed, friend who was particularly devoted to that virgin (lines 175–80); perhaps this friend was Thomas Burgh, who is named a few lines further on as recipient of "this symple tretyhs" (203–21). After some deliberation, the author says, he began the project on 7 September 1443. Margaret's story falls into two parts: the life proper; the history of the saint's remains. Between these sections the poet takes a ten-day rest, until Michaelmas (29 September), presumably completing the work another two or three weeks later, in October of 1443.

The next explicit dating in the text occurs in the Magdalen prolocutory: on Twelfth Night (5 January) 1445, Isabel Bourchier, countess of Eu and sister to Richard, duke of York, commissioned a translation of the life of Mary Magdalen, to whom Isabel bore a special devotion. In recounting their conversation the author reveals that he had already translated several other lives: not only Margaret's (done two years earlier) but also the accounts of Anne, Dorothy, Faith, Christine, Agnes, and Ursula with the eleven thousand virgins. He had also recently begun a life of St. Elizabeth of Hungary at the request of another noble patron, Elizabeth Vere, countess of Oxford (5045–55). The author asks his noble patron for a delay until he can complete a pilgrimage to Santiago de Compostela in Spain; assuming this journey was taken soon thereafter, we can safely date the Magdalen and its prologue to 1445.

Which would leave, therefore, the lives of Katherine, Cecelia, Agatha, and Lucy for 1445–1447. We cannot know the order of composition of these last four, though we do learn that the fairly lengthy and important life of Katherine was done in only five days.

Of the total of thirteen lives, three were commissioned: Margaret, Magdalen, and Elizabeth, which become the first, middle, and last in the completed set. Magdalen is not the precise numerical middle, coming eighth rather than seventh in the sequence, but if lines are counted it straddles the midpoint of the work—a positioning of particular importance in medieval and renaissance poetics. Elizabeth, though finished, or at least started, before Magdalen, was relocated after it.

What about the ten others, then? Why this particular selection and arrangement? There was a large number of female saints from which to choose and several possible methods of arrangement. The collection is neither alphabetically nor chronologically arranged. Unlike Jacob da Voragine's immensely influential *Legenda Aurea* (our author's primary source) or John Mirk's well-known *Festial*, Bokenham's martyrology does not follow the liturgical calendar starting with Advent (December), nor, as in the *South English Legendary*, starting with the calendrical new year. Unlike the *Scottish Legend Collection* the order is not hierarchal, progressing through degrees of sainthood from apostles and gospel saints down through early martyrs. As for women saints who are not included: The author did not choose to write a life of Monica, mother of the claimed founder of his order. He did not include the Virgin Mary, whose cult at the prosperous Augustinian shrine of Walsingham (Norfolk) was famous throughout England (although admittedly his choice of Anne permits him to pay a little attention to Mary). Not a single English saint is represented in the collection, despite a plentiful number available and despite such precedent as John of Tynemouth's *Sanctilogium Anglia* (revised by Capgrave) or other, shorter patriotic collections. Bokenham did not write about the recently canonized St. Bridget of Sweden, whose *Revelations* was a standard devotional tract in fifteenth-century England and whose newly established convent of Augustinian nuns at Sion monastery was supported by King Henry; nor even about Barbara, whom Bokenham claims, along with Faith and Cecelia, as his "valentine" (line 8278).

My hypothesis is that Bokenham's poem is modeled on Chaucer's *Legend of Good Women*, and that this imitation provided, to some extent, a principle of selection and of arrangement. The compositional history outlined above might seem to preclude the possibility of any such coherent structure or deliberate modeling, dependent as it is on apparently chance commissions. On the other hand, we cannot know the literal truth about the commissions and whether the author himself might have proposed a subject; nor can we know at what point an organizational structure suggested itself, whether from the start or partway through. Chaucer's great work-in-progress, *The Canterbury Tales*, is another instance of that sort of evolution toward coherency: a group of short pieces incorporated at some point within a broader structural framework. What comes clear about Bokenham's legendary is that the correspondences with Chaucer's mock-legendary are consistent throughout the first ten lives, that their order follows the order of Chaucer's *Legend*, and that their number is statistically far beyond coincidence.

Bokenham was, we know, an attentive reader of Chaucer. He several times praises the trio of Chaucer, Gower, and Lydgate, but this is virtually formulaic homage by fifteenth-century writers. He appropriated Chaucerian verse forms, as did many other writers of the century. Nor is it atypical to find secular influence permeating pious literature composed by ecclesiastics. Hagiography itself is a deeply syncretic genre, over the centuries incorporating oriental and western folktale, classical myth and legend, adventure story, political propaganda, biography, travel literature, and romance. Capgrave brings into his *Life of St. Katherine* echoes of Chaucer's *Troilus* and other secular literature. It is not impossible that at least some of Chaucer's works were held in the library of Clare Priory. We do know that John Bury, one of Bokenham's colleagues at Clare, donated to the inmates of another house a collection of material that included Chaucer's translation of Boethius's *De consolatio philosophiae*. Other, larger, houses—such as the Augustinian library at York—possessed a fairly wide range of historical and morally edifying literature, including Geoffrey of Monmouth's *Historia* and other Arthurian material; Aesop's fables; Dares and Dictys on the Trojan War; virtually everything by Ovid, Juvenal, Horace, and Virgil; and a good many works on medicine, natural science, and astronomy. Colledge has suggested that the Brigittine nuns at Sion were familiar with the *Troilus*. Still, it is not extremely likely that a contemporary, vernacular, and courtly work like Chaucer's *Legend* would be part of a monastic collection, so that a more plausible source for Bokenham would be the loan of a volume from a noble patron.

The legendary echoes several Chaucerian passages: Bokenham's "yive feyth & ful credence" (line 7875) and Chaucer's "yive . . . feyth and ful credence" (*LGW*, F 31; not in G); or Bokenham's wish to "forge and fyle" his rhetoric (line 408) and Chaucer's Cupid who is seen to "forge and file" his arrows (*PF* 212: this sounds like an alliterative formula, but *MED* lists only these two occurrences before 1450). Bokenham's Margaret has "bent browes blake" (line 450), as Chaucer's Alison has "browes . . . bent and blake as any sloe" (*MilT*, 3245–46). For Agnes, Jesus is

"To me...a wal inpenetrabyle" (line 4327), as for
Criseyde Troilus was "to hire a wal / Of steil" (3.479–80).
There are the Sicilian pilgrims who travel to Saint Agatha's
shrine:

> Whan thorgh the provynce . . .
> The gloryous fame dyvulged was
> Of the blyssyd virgyn seynt Agas . . .
> Whom for to seken wyth an holy entent
> On hyr festful day mych peple went
> From every plage of the seyd Cecyle,
> And specyally from Syracuse.
>   (Lines 9019–28)

The passage evokes their famous English counterparts, as a
comparison of syntax and vocabulary shows:

> Whan that Aprill . . .
> Whan Zephyrus eek . . . , etc.
> Thanne longen folk to goon on pilgrimages, . . .
> And specially from every shires end
> Of Engelond to Caunterbury they wende,
> The hooly blisful martir for to seke.
>   (*Canterbury Tales*, 1–17)

Other instances could be cited, but a more significant influence than verbal borrowing is the structural alignment
of Bokenham's hagiography with Chaucer's *Legend*. I will
give a brief outline of this alignment; a fuller discussion will
be published elsewhere.

The first object of the poet-narrator's devotion in the
Legend is the daisy, Eros's "relyke" (F 321), to which
Chaucer devotes probably the most powerfully moving passage in the entire work (F 68–96). The first life in
Bokenham's series is Margaret's. Flower and woman share
a name: in French, "marguerite." Both flower and woman
are, moreover, apostrophized as muse of the work just
begun: Chaucer's "marguerite" to preside over "my wit . . .

my word, my werk" (88–89), Bokenham's "Marguerite" to illumine "My wyt and my penne" (333–36).

The second object of Chaucer's devotion in the *Legend* is Alceste, companion to the God of Love and sponsor of the legends to follow. Alceste's fame was due to her willingness to die in her husband's place; she descended to the underworld and was rescued by Hercules. Bokenham's second life is of St. Anne, mother of Jesus' mother, hence in lineal contact with the God who is love. The prologue to this life is full of imagery of the underworld. The author anticipates his own death. He mentions Proserpina (line 1457), who, like Alceste, was rescued from the underworld. He tells of Orpheus (lines 1461–62), who also journeyed to Hades. He addresses Mary as "Lady of erthe and empresse of helle" (line 1503). The point of contact is imagery recalling the salient feature of Alceste's story.

The third female figure in Chaucer's legend, and the first of the actual legends, is Cleopatra, who kills herself by jumping into a pit of serpents and who was associated with three Roman leaders (Julius Caesar, Octavian, and Marc Antony). Bokenham's third saint, Christine, is also exposed to snakes as a means of death, but instead of biting her they turn against their handler (lines 2931–68). She is associated with three Roman officials, her persecutors: the prefect Urban (her father), his successor Dyon, and the judge Julian. Both stories contain an important sea scene: the sea battle of Actium for Cleopatra; the ordeal by drowning in which Christine walks on water.

The story of Thisbe, Chaucer's second tale, narrates the engagement of a young couple, together with the circumstances that prevent the marriage and lead to the couple's death. The same outline constitutes the plot of Bokenham's fourth story, that of Ursula and the eleven thousand virgins.

Chaucer's third tale, the life of Dido, focuses on the bed as key image and locus dramatis. Dido and Aeneas spend a great deal of time in bed, separately and together; it is the site of major speeches, dialogues, and laments.

Repeating the image is Bokenham's fifth life: St. Faith is
bound to a bed or grill of brass and roasted; the bed is her
traditional emblem. As Dido is paired with Aeneas, so Faith
is paired with her convert Caprasius—who, however, rather
than abandon her as Aeneas does Dido, comes in from his
cave to share her martyrdom. (We recall too that it is in a
cave that Dido and Aeneas first consummate their lust.)

Like Chaucer's fourth legend, Hypsipyle and Medea,
Bokenham's sixth tells of two women: Saint Agnes and
her devotée Constance. The motif of the wealthy lover is
important to both narratives; Jason, the Chaucerian se-
ducer, is constantly associated with wealth and treasure
(he seeks the Golden Fleece, for instance), while Agnes
declines marriage on the grounds that her lover, Christ, is
far wealthier than any prospective groom.

The stories of Lucrece, Chaucer's fifth, and Dorothy,
Bokenham's seventh, share the image of feet as a mem-
orable detail: Lucrece covers her feet in modesty as she
dies; Dorothy is hanged by the feet. (The central incident in Dorothy's story is the roses and apples produced
miraculously in winter; there is no parallel to this in the
Chaucerian tale.)

Chaucer's legend of Ariadne, number six, opens in
Athens. The prolocutory to Bokenham's number eight,
Mary Magdalen, contains an extended reference (lines
5029–34) to Minerva, or Athena, patroness of Athens.
Minerva enters Bokenham's text not as goddess of wisdom
or of war but as patron of the art of weaving. Thread plays
an important part in Ariadne's story, for she helps Theseus
to escape the labyrinth by giving him a ball of thread to
guide him back out.

Chaucer's seventh legend, that of Philomela, is about
speech and silence. The raped and maimed heroine,
tongueless, communicates in weaving the hideous story
of her victimization. The life of Katherine, ninth in Bokenham's set, is also about speech and silence. Its central
episode is the heroine's debate with fifty sages and orators;

its climax, the silence to which she reduces them. "Be ye tunglees?" the emperor rages at his scholars—an unusual image, present only in the Middle English *Seinte Katherine* but retained here in order, I suggest, to underscore the Chaucerian parallel.

To the legend of Phyllis, Chaucer's eighth, I have found no particular correspondence in Bokenham.

Hypermnestra, Chaucer's ninth and last heroine, is a newly married woman keeping a secret from her husband. So is St. Cecelia, Bokenham's tenth. In both stories the secret is revealed, and it eventually brings the couple closer together. In both, the secret proceeds from a male authority figure who asserts priority over the husband: Hypermnestra's father; Jesus.

With St. Cecelia, Bokenham must perforce end the alignment of his work with Chaucer's. His last three lives— Agatha, Lucy, and Elizabeth—form a peroration whose thematic point is to restate an orthodox Augustinian position on the body, particularly the female body, and on physical nature in general. I won't develop this assertion here, nor account in the fullest literary-ideological sense for Bokenham's intention in appropriating, for at least part of his work, the Chaucerian structure: these and other questions are dealt with elsewhere. From what I have written here, though, it should be clear that Bokenham's attitude toward his great precursor was ambivalent: given Bokenham's theological rigor, necessarily so. His parallel is at once homage and critique; his strategy, to replace the mock-hagiography with a real one. *Caritas* replaces *cupiditas*, and instead of suicides we have martyrs; instead of erotic passion, the *passio* (suffering or acceptance) of faith and its consequences; instead of seduction, conversion. If he does less than full justice to Chaucer's own moral seriousness, Bokenham does nonetheless succeed— quite outstandingly, I think—in making a strikingly original contribution to a very specialized literary genre.

Bokenham's *Legend* is unique in the history of hagiography, for it is the first all-female hagiography in any language. There were, to be sure, partial models and antecedents. Classification by sex was common in early Latin collections, and the Anglo-Saxon scholar Aldhelm, following this taxonomic convention, divided his treatise *De Virginitate* (c. 680) into male and female virgins. During the late thirteenth or early fourteenth century the Franciscan friar Nicholas de Bozon wrote, in Anglo-Norman couplets, the lives of nine female saints, though there is no evidence that they were intended as a set. And in 1405 the French courtier Christine de Pizan compiled stories about a group of women saints as a short portion (about one-seventh) of her otherwise secular *consolatio, Le Livre de la Cité des Dames*. Christine's work was well known in England and could have been known to Bokenham.

While it might therefore be overstating the case to claim that Osbern Bokenham invented the female legendary as such, nonetheless it is certainly fair to say that he reinvented it—not as a system of classification, not to illustrate the value of virginity, not subsumed within another form, but as a free-standing, carefully crafted instance of the demanding genre of hagiographical verse.

The time was ripe for such a project. The previous century had witnessed the efflorescence of the *devotio moderna* and the development of a new tradition of affective piety among laypeople and religious, emphasizing a personal, passionate attachment to Jesus and his saints. These trends remained strong in the religious life of the fifteenth century, not least in East Anglia, where Bokenham might have met both Margery Kempe and Julian of Norwich, exemplars and products of the new piety. Norwich itself had more hermits and anchorites (enclosed solitaries) of both sexes than any other town in England, and it is the only English town known to have had communities of devout laywomen resembling the continental *béguinages*. Lollardy, though a heresy and capital crime, was particularly strong in East Anglia and attracted a large proportion of women.

The time was ripe in a more specifically political way as well. In the dynastic dispute that had been simmering since the 1399 Lancastrian usurpation, and that would during Bokenham's lifetime erupt into the series of armed conflicts known as the Wars of the Roses, the question of woman's role and of female character generally was a latent but important dimension to the debate between rival claims. Already in 1406 Henry IV had sponsored a parliamentary statute entailing the succession to his male descendants. But the statute was repealed when it was pointed out to the king that his own claim to the crown of France depended on a female ancestor. Some years later, the tutor of the young Henry VI, Bishop Beckington of Wells, wrote a treatise attacking France's Salic law, which excluded women from succession there: the bishop's apparently prowoman position was required in order to defend the English claim to the French crown.

Domestically, though, and dynastically, the shoe was on the other foot, for the Lancastrian right to English rule was claimed through a male hereditary line, while the competing Yorkist line descended at several points through women. The capacity of women to succeed to rule or—more to the point—to transmit the right to rule therefore became a significant component in public debate.

Sir John Fortescue was a close advisor to the reigning Lancastrian Henry VI, chief justice of the King's Bench from 1442 to 1462, and a prominent Lancastrian propagandist. In several English and Latin tracts upholding the Lancastrian claim, Fortescue argued against the right of women to succeed or to transmit the right to succession. His *De natura legis naturae* (about 1462) is a veritable thesaurus of misogynistic arguments drawn from Scripture, classical philosophy, English legal principle, and Christian authorities such as St. Thomas Aquinas. Here are a few excerpts:

From the discharge of higher and public offences, which are fit for men alone, as are the offices of Constable and Marshal of any kingdom, Nature hath excluded women; wherefore such offices cannot descend to them, so long as everything that descends tends only to its natural place. And if such offices be not allowed by nature to descend to women, how can the office of King, which is public . . . how can it descend or be suited to the woman, whom nature hath subjected to the man?

The Lord often among the weighty words of his threatening, says [to idolaters] that he would not leave of them *mingentem ad parietem* [anyone who pisses against a wall: 1 Samuel 25.22, 34]. Now this action is the action of a man, and not of a woman, the Lord thus distinguishing the sons of those wicked men from their daughters, as the male dog is distinguished from the female, a distinction which He certainly would not have made if the female, like the male, could have succeeded to those kings ordained to destruction.

Nature works nothing except with suitable and the fittest instruments; art, therefore, which imitates nature, works not otherwise. Who ever hunts hares with cats? Nature disposes greyhounds for the fields and the pursuit of hares, but cats for staying at home to catch mice. It is a shame, as though a man should hunt game with cats, to draw away from home, for the purpose of governing nations, the woman whom nature has fitted for domestic duties . . . . An artificer is not so inconsiderate as to cleave wood with a mattock, nor a sailor so careless as to entrust the oar to the hands of one with palsy . . . . Behold, then, a sufficient cause clearly set forth why a woman cannot succeed in a kingdom.

[As for exceptional women who have ruled], what profit do these facts and events that have happened bring to us who are disputing about the decision of reason? It is reason that corrects facts, but facts never change reason; for facts may show what has been done, but it is reason alone which informs us what ought to be done. Therefore, if the arguments

which we have urged are valid, they cannot be disproved by
bygone facts.

In a number of ways Bokenham's *Legends* refutes this
general position, though obviously, because of the dates
of the works, it cannot have been a direct response to
Fortescue's treatise. I do find it interesting, however, that
Fortescue had already established himself as no friend to the
Austins (who were, by and large, of Yorkist sympathies): in
1441 Fortescue had represented the crown in a tax suit
against another Augustinian monastery, at Eddington in
Wiltshire (the decision is not recorded). In any case the
ideas were far from novel, and the position is likely to
have circulated in less formal ways than the treatise quoted.
Social historians have noted the tremendous increase during the fifteenth century of propaganda in various forms:
handbills and broadsides, pamphlets, letters and bulletins,
chronicles, and, of course, verse by lay and ecclesiastical
writers commenting on many issues and incidents of the
period. When we think of propaganda we usually think of
an item destined for a mass audience. Clearly, Bokenham's
legendary would not have much broad appeal: its genre,
length, and style would ensure a limited readership, and
the existence of only a single complete manuscript confirms
this. Yet even though intended for a relatively small circle
of provincial nobility, gentry, business people, and ecclesiastics, the work has its politics. To those who identified
their fortune (in both senses) with that of the Yorkists, it
would be, I think, a welcome, if modest, affirmation of
their hopes.

The Austin friar gives us not only an all-female hagiography—an authorial decision significant in its own right—
but a gallery of powerful, articulate women who are indu-
bitably worthy to do God's work. Some of them are well
educated; some give sound political advice to a monarch;
some preach, converting hundreds and thousands to Christianity; some walk on water or perform resurrection. Nor

are they pacifists: on the contrary, they call for divinely in-
flicted vengeance and approve violence in their cause. Thus
Margaret uses physical force against Satan, and Christine
exults in her father's death, as do the Christians when a
thousand pagan bystanders are killed at the destruction of
Katherine's wheel by an angel.

Now these traits are not original with Bokenham or
unique to his legendary. However, as other hagiographies
both earlier and later prove, the givens of plot do not auto-
matically produce a prowoman text. The tonal or attitudinal
dimension may vary tremendously according to literary
treatment: dialogue, description, authorial comment, omis-
sion of some material, addition or invention of other. While
working within a narrowly defined genre with well-known
stories, Bokenham is no mere copyist. He does not simply
transcribe his main source, the thirteenth-century *Legenda
Aurea*, nor only imitate English collections such as the
South English Legendary. Everywhere Bokenham reworks
the material, reshaping it according to his own vision.

The major incident in Margaret's life, for instance, is her
victory over a dragon that appears in her prison cell. This
dragon is a devil who, when returned to his own shape, is
in some versions bitterly ashamed to have been defeated by
a mere female, and a slender young one at that. "If a man
had vanquished me," Lydgate has the devil say, "I could
have tolerated it" ("The Legend of Seynt Margarete").
Bokenham omits the misogynist lament, making the demon
completely subservient to the saint.

Similarly for Katherine, the central episode is the contest
for which the emperor Maxence has hired fifty scholars to
debate with the aristocratic young woman. In Capgrave's
version, one scholar is reluctant to come: "He nedeth not
his labour on a woman spende, / he shal on-to hir his
discipulis send" (4.1000–1001). The emperor whips up
his team with a great deal of misogyny and machismo,
exhorting them to virile courage and to "Lift up your
hearts, men!" Though Bokenham knew Capgrave's text,

he omits all this: one of his scholars does comment that "for so smal a matter" (line 6705) any one of the fifty would have sufficed; but this is not linked to the opponent's sex.

On the other hand, Bokenham does have the emperor indulge in misogyny when the latter says that Katherine is

> by natur
> A wumman. . ., & a frele creatur,
> Wych is evere varyaunth & unstable,
> Fykyl, fals and deceyvable,
> As we wel knowyn by experyence
> (Lines 6629–34)

> by nature
> A woman. . ., and thus a frail creature
> Always variable and changing,
> Fickle, false, and deceptive,
> As we know well by experience

and therefore he need not believe her theology, and would not even were she an angel. This tirade serves as foil to Katherine's calm refutation of misogynist slander, not only by her own example, but also by her calling into question the philosophical underpinning of the position. It is not the senses that provide a basis for proper judgment, not appearances and superficials, but reason. Only by following reason and justice can a man deserve the title of king, whatever his lineage (lines 6636–55); biological sex is one of those superficials irrelevant to ultimate truth. This antiessentialism is perfectly orthodox as far as it goes, but it is easy to see where it might lead if rigorously followed: to the ordination of women as priests, or to the justification of female rule. But Bokenham does not follow it out, either in the ecclesiastical or the political sphere. Were he to have done so, his candidate for the throne would have been his patron Isabel Bourchier, for she was older by several years than her brother Richard. Nonetheless, and despite its limitations, the contemporary dynastic application of Katherine's message is clear.

The story of Elizabeth's humility might have remained a misogynistic mirror for wives, but Bokenham explicitly generalizes it into a mirror for both sexes and particularly those in religious orders (lines 9838–48).

In these and other ways the sadistic sexual politics of hagiography—the torture of women, and of men—is met by the affirmative sexual politics of women's moral strength and spiritual victory. It is not, to be sure, a liberationist credo, scarcely to be expected in a fifteenth-century context. Even Christine de Pizan had told tales of tortured women. Committed to refuting misogynist slander, Christine went no further than asserting the moral and intellectual capacities of women much as her primary source, the humanist Giovanni Boccaccio, had already done. Despite its limitations, then, Bokenham's legendary is nonetheless a significant example of the contradictory or ambivalent nature of much literature of the period, reflecting what David Aers has called "cultural heterogeneity in late medieval England." Indeed that heterogeneity was evident in the Yorkist stance itself: on the one hand, as monarchic and cult-ridden as any feudal faction; on the other, responsive to the mercantile, expansionist, and nationalistic interests of the urban and provincial commercial and business groups— the "new middle classes"—who tended to support it.

The Translation

The text exists in a unique manuscript, Arundel 327 in the British Library. It has no title, but the title I use translates Mary Serjeantson's *Legendys of Hooly Wummen*, which the EETS editor extrapolated from the author's description of his work as "dyvers legendys . . . Of hooly wummen" (lines 5038–40). The present translation was made from

Serjeantson's EETS edition (o.s. 206, 1938) and checked against the manuscript, whose distinctive features Serjeantson describes. The explanatory notes are mine, except where attributed to EETS. In lines 6347–48 of the prologue to Katherine's life, Bokenham apostrophizes "all tho that redyn or here / Shal this tretyhs" ("all those who shall read or hear this treatise"), suggesting that he anticipated separate circulation of individual lives for recitation at home or convent. The existence of a fragment of the life of Dorothy (in BL Add. 36963) would seem to confirm this inference.

I have wanted to be a conservative translator of Bokenham: it seemed the best gesture of loyalty to a writer whose work I enjoy, to a style sometimes frustrating in its blend of tedium and vividness, and to a language from which our own evolved. I have therefore produced a literal translation, neither entirely word-for-word, nor, at the other extreme, entirely free; I stayed as close as possible to the original vocabulary and imagery, but occasionally altered an onerously complex sentence structure or unnecessary archaism for the sake of modern English usage and readability. Explanatory notes are gathered at the end, listed according to page number.

Bokenham's can be a ponderous and wordy style at times. For instance, a Christian never simply kneels; rather she kneels down on the ground on her knees—and usually on both two knees at that. A saint never prays except devoutly, humbly, and with entire heart devoted to her lord, etc. Sentences may be extremely long, strung together with appositives and subordinate clauses such as "where . . . who . . . wherefore . . . thus," or with modifiers strewn Latin-style throughout the sentence at some distance from their object. These are the kinds of stylistic idiosyncracy that I have felt free to adjust from time to time, especially since much of the superfluous verbiage or contorted syntax is present in order to eke out a metrical line or supply a rhyme. On the other hand, I have not wanted to replace Bokenham's style—a fairly typical one, after all, for the fifteenth century—with something deceptively terse; and by "deceptive" I mean untrue both to author and to period. Poetry was different then from what it is now, and I think it important to maintain that sense of difference. To that end, I have preserved medievalisms as much as possible, and imagery, and the hypotactic structure of sentence and line.

The most obvious major change is that I have translated into prose—reluctantly at first, but I soon recognized the futility of attempting to duplicate Bokenham's rhymes in modern English. "Unrhyming"—translating from verse to prose—while common in late medieval France, was relatively rare in England: coincidentally, the *Gilte Legende* unrhymes its verse sources. However, I have preserved stanzaic divisions with paragraphing, while sections in couplets have been paragraphed as if they were prose, i.e., according to sense and narrative structure. The reader will doubtless notice how much more fluent and lively Bokenham's writing is in the flexible couplet form than in the more technically demanding stanzaic sections.

Some of the lesser changes are these: The second person singular (thou) has been replaced throughout with second person plural (you). The gender-specific noun "men" has been replaced with "people" or an equivalent where the meaning is plainly gender-inclusive; similarly, "apostoless" for Mary Magdalen has been replaced with the gender-neutral equivalent "apostle." In some cases, the avoidance of a gender-specific pronoun has required the use of the hybrid form (first used in the mid–sixteenth century) of the singular antecedent coupled with a plural pronoun, for example, "whoever" paired with "they" or "them." "Januence" has been modernized into Jacob da Voragine, and most other historical names into their contemporary versions. Pronouns and nouns pertaining to God (e.g., lord) have not been capitalized, though "God" has been capitalized to distinguish Christian deity from pagan; actually, none of these terms was regularly capitalized in Middle English transcription.

Osbern Bokenham's
Legends of Holy Women

PROLOGUE

Two things every writer ought to announce in beginning a work, if he wants to proceed in an orderly way: the first is "what," the second is "why." In these two words, it seems to me, are included the four causes that, as philosophers teach us, people ought to look for at the beginning of every book. According to philosophers the first is called efficient cause; the second they call material cause; formal cause is the third, and the fourth is final cause. The efficient cause is the author, who according to his ability works to complete the material, which itself is the second cause; and that it may be clearer, the formal cause sets the material in due order passage by passage. These three things belong to "what": author, matter, and orderly form. The final cause declares fully the reason behind the work: the final intention of the author, and what he meant. Thus you may see how in these two words "what" and "why," people may discern the four causes of each work, as philosophy requires.

But to our purpose. If this treatise be interrogated as to "what" or "why," then as for the first, whoever wishes to hear, the author was an Austin friar whose name I will not just now reveal, lest the unworthiness of his person and his name make the work be scorned. So, because of personal dislike and malice, few would have the pleasure of reading it and the work would be thrown into oblivion's corner. But I think it would be a pity if my work were hated because of

me, for I'm sure everyone knows that no one throws the
rose away though it grows on a thorny stem; and who is so
foolish as to cast away good grain because it grows in chaff?
People also drink ale and leave the dregs, even though the
ale ran through the dregs. And gold, as all wise people
know, grows in foul black earth, yet gold is a precious thing
collected in many a coffer. A marguerite pearl, according
to the philosopher, grows on a shell of little value, yet it
is precious; and no wise man would despise the powerful
crapaude stone, even though a toad's head was its first nest.
And with these manifold natural examples Scripture agrees;
for, as the Old Testament bears witness, the son shall not
suffer for his father's wickedness unless he actively follow
it, and if he do, then it is appropriate that he be partner
in pain as he was in blame. So that if my work is good,
let not disdain for the author disfigure it, I beg; for only
a fool, as I just now showed, would kill the child for the
father's offense.

The material I will write about, though I can compose
only crudely, is the life of blessed Margaret, virgin and
martyr, whom the love of Jesus inflamed so fervently in her
youth that for all the rage and tyranny of false Olibrius, she
would rather die than forsake Christ, as her legend clearly
declares and as they shall hear who will listen.

The formal structure is by no means poetical, following
the school of the clever writer Geoffrey of England in his
innovative work entitled *Poetria Nova*, which is so plentifully embellished with colors of rhetoric that nothing like
it was ever seen in any May meadow mottled with flowers
on green grass; for neither Tully, prince of eloquence, nor
Demosthenes of Greece had more wealth of rhetoric than
this Geoffrey. But since I never did pore over that clever
work, I now refuse it and will simply tell about the birth
and upbringing of Saint Margaret, according to the story,
and how she came first to the faith and then to martyrdom,
as close to the legend as my wit can manage. Then I will
tell how, by whom, and how often she was translated, and

where she now rests, as I learned both in writing and orally the last time I was in Italy. The story is by no means unknown at Montefiascone—whoever doesn't believe me, let him go there and he can find out—fifty miles or more this side of Rome; there they entertain weary pilgrims with Tribian wine instead of Muscatel. There, when I was delayed by heavy rain on my way home from Rome, I visited this blessed virgin, and I wrote out the whole story, and brought it with me back to Clare, and now intend to tell it in English.

But whoever would ask me, lastly, about the reason for translating it into our language, I reply that two causes mainly moved me to do it. The first cause is to stimulate people's emotions to take pleasure in loving and serving this blessed virgin, so as to preserve them from all misfortune, according to the intention of the saint's prayer before she died, as you shall shortly hear. Let no one be surprised that I work to please the worthy excellence of this holy maiden, for very near where I was born, in an old priory of black canons, there is one of her feet, both flesh and bone. There, through a bright, pure crystal, one can behold each feature of the foot, except the great toe and the heel, which are in a nunnery called Reading. As for the foot, many a miracle has been shown there to learned and laymen alike. And especially if people touch the foot with a brooch or ring before leaving, and take the item with them, if they fear any danger, let them promise to bring back and leave the same item that touched the foot, and they shall remain healthy and safe if they do it with good devotion. This is my considered opinion. For in fact I had experience of it myself only five years ago, when a cruel tyrant drove me out of a barge into a swamp just outside Venice, with five other men. I thought I was in serious trouble until the grace of God relieved me through the blessed mediation of this virgin. For soon after I had promised the ring with which I had at parting touched her bare foot, I was quickly relieved. Now blessed be that holy virgin who is willing to turn her ear to sinful prayers! And this is one reason why I am impelled to translate her life, as I said before.

Another cause that moved me to make this legend was the importunate request of one whom I love with my whole heart, one who has a particular devotion to this pure-minded virgin. He whose request is a commandment to me begged with humble will that if I loved him I would do it. I dared not hastily agree, well knowing my own inadequacy, until I had thought about it for a while. And then in the year of grace 1443, in the vigil of the nativity of her who is the gem of virginity, on the seventh day of September, when I began to remember his request, I thought it would be contrary to charity to deny his desire any longer. And yet I was afraid of envy, which is always diligent to slander secretly others' true intent. Therefore, to prevent their malice I will not tell my name here, as I said before. Therefore I pray and request you, son and father, to whom I direct this simple treatise, that you not display it where villainy might have it, and primarily at Cambridge in your establishment, where many capacious and subtle wits would soon discern my ignorance. Therefore, kindly keep it as private as you can for a while. If nonetheless you should let it go out, don't admit who it comes from but say you believe it was sent from Ageland from a friend of yours who sells horses at fairs and who dwells near the castle of Bolingbroke in a town called Borgh where you first took the name Thomas. And thus you will excuse me and make sure that people won't find a way to suspect me. But, to draw this long tale to a conclusion, I beg you, friend, that you vouchsafe to pray for me to this virgin, so that before I die I may purchase through her merits a pardon of grace for my wrongdoing, and that I may have a fuller remission of my old and new transgression, and that after the end of this outlawry I may, with her above, magnify God in his blissful eternity, where felicity never ends. In that place the lord who harrowed hell grant the both of us to dwell.

THE LIFE OF ST. MARGARET
VIRGIN AND MARTYR

Prologue

Of Saint Margaret the pure virgin, who is likened to a precious marguerite (deservedly so, as is written in old texts), I am now delighted to translate the life—if Atropos will delay a while and not too quickly cut my life thread that Lachesis has spun for fifty years.

This glorious virgin may suitably be compared with a marguerite which is white, small, and powerful. White she was through virginity; through meekness, small; and most especially powerful through her outstanding charity, plentifully demonstrated in the working of miracles.

Didn't she love virginity and preservation of chastity when Olibrius proposed that she should be his wife and be called a princess and have great wealth—indeed outstanding pleasure, wealth, and fame—but for the sake of chastity she set no store by his offers?

Great meekness she had for Christ's sake when in youth she forsook the title of her birthright and chose to be his handmaiden, ignoring her father's enmity. She chose instead to dwell with her nurse in poverty and in low degree, minding her sheep diligently.

And to speak of charity, certainly she had abundance of it as she showed in her suffering; for as her legend recalls, she directed the people to repentance and always strove to win them to God; and when she was to die, with great constancy she made a charitable prayer.

Moreover, as I find written in a book called *The Golden Legend*—and this statement is taken in turn from writers on nature—the marguerite helps to stanch hemorrhage and will protect from cardiac disease and comforts the spirits wonderfully.

Because of this threefold property of the marguerite, Saint Margaret may well be compared to that gem; for all three properties were appropriate to her. As for the first, I guarantee, when her blood ran out copiously, she was so enflamed with heavenly heat that she endured it steadfastly.

As for heart palpitations, that represents, as writers declare, the temptation of our spiritual enemy who always aims to entrap humankind and won't desist from bringing people to sorrow and care. Yet he never hurt her, although he was sly, nor might catch her in his snare, but instead she always had the victory over him.

That the marguerite comforts people's spirits is seen in our Margaret, who all her life was pure and clean in her spirit. Through her cleanness many people are quickly comforted and through her teaching they are directed to abandon sin and folly.

Thus for this sixfold property of the marguerite which duly pertains to Margaret by congruity of similitude, we may understand that she was strong in six virtues: chastity, meekness, and charity, constancy in enduring wrong, in spiritual comfort, and in victory.

These six virtues are represented indirectly in the six-winged cherubim that Isaiah saw standing above the high throne, in his vision and with his spiritual eye. For our purpose they now signify that this blessed maid Margaret worthily rose up to heaven through these six virtues, there in joy to dwell perpetually.

Now, blessed virgin, who in heaven above are crowned in bliss full gloriously, be ever propitious to them on earth who serve and love you, and especially vouch of your special grace, lady, so to illumine my wit and my pen with ability and eloquence that I may adequately complete your legend now begun.

The Life

Once, as the story teaches us, in Antioch, that great city, there was a man called Theodosius of great status and dignity. He was the patriarch of paganry, the ruler and governor to whom all priests did obeisance.

This Theodosius had a wife suitable to his rank, with whom he had a fair daughter called Margaret (as God provided). Just as a rose fair and good grows from a sharp thorn, so sprang Margaret from heathen blood.

For though her father and mother were born and raised in idolatry and ended their lives that way and miserably went to hell-pain after their death, yet she was so illumined by grace that she was both christened and martyred, and went to heaven, that glorious place.

Her father was very glad of her birth, hoping she would be his comfort in old age. Many people came to his celebration, both men and women, joyfully thanking their gods that their patriarch had such fine offspring.

I don't recall that I ever read what rites the heathen used in namegiving, but I imagine it was done with solemn ceremony, and particularly for children of high rank.

Afterward, as was the custom in those days and still is among nobility, they hired for their daughter a nurse not far from home, who was to devote every effort to nurture the child in all tenderness.

This nurse dwelt only fifteen furlongs from the city of Antioch, and secretly she was a Christian, pure and clean in her dealings with others, as was seen in what followed: for

she raised Margaret in all virtue and taught her the faith of
Christ Jesus.

But when her mother passed away while she was still
quite young, Margaret had set all her affection so firmly on
her wise, good nurse that she forsook all her high lineage
and decided to stay there, for she would not return home
to her father.

And because she worshiped and loved Christ and would
not return to paganry, her father hated and reproved her
and didn't care what happened to her. But the sovereign
lord on high filled her with such great virtue that in spite
of everything in a few years she grew perfect.

She was excellent not only in grace but in nature as well.
There was no creature so fair in the whole country around,
for shape and color and each feature were proportioned in
such balance that she could be the mirror of all beauty.

If I could forge and file the craft of description as well
as Boethius in his *Consolation of Philosophy*, or as Homer,
Ovid, or else Virgil or Geoffrey of England, I would com-
pile a clear description of all her features one by one.

But truly I lack both eloquence and ability to amplify
such matters, for I never dwelt with innovative rhetoricians
like Gower or Chaucer, nor with Lydgate (who is still alive
unless he died recently), so that I fervently beg everyone
to excuse me though I do crudely.

This virgin had not only a singular abundance of the gifts
of nature, but she was also inwardly endowed with virtues,
for she had faith, hope, and charity—the divine virtues—
and also the four great cardinal virtues.

When she had arrived at the age of fifteen and heard how
cruelly Christian blood was being shed through the fierce
rage of tyrants, she prepared herself to die for Christ, all
the while keeping her nurse's sheep in the field every day.

Now to Antioch there approached from Asia a tyrant,
the prefect of that country, and Olibrius was his name. But
as he came, wherever he saw any Christians, he destroyed
them cruelly and without mercy.

It happened that he rode near where Margaret was pasturing her nurse's sheep, when suddenly his eye fell on her, so demure of countenance. Immediately her beauty so strongly lured his heart that he stood still and looked again.

And when he saw her forehead lily white, her curved dark brows and grey eyes, her ruddy cheeks, her straight nose, her red lips, her chin that shone like polished marble and was cleft in the middle—he was so astonished by that sudden event that he scarcely knew where he was.

He looked no further than her face, where there was a plenty of natural gifts. He thought that never in one small place had he seen more to attract his heart as the magnet attracts iron. When he suddenly awoke from his trancelike swoon, with a serious face he said to his men,

"Go over there, where you see a fair maiden keeping her sheep, and find out whether she is serf or free, and let me know. If she is free, I will wed her with a ring and bring her to great honor and endow her with many a castle and tower.

"If she be a bondswoman and in serfdom, then—because I don't want to wrong another man—I will give her lord a good fee and receive her as my paramour. Hurry, don't be long, for I won't leave this place until you bring me an answer."

When this was said, hastily his men hurried to where she was and told her the situation. At once the blood drained out of her face for fear, and devoutly to God she prayed:

"Have mercy, lord Jesus, on me and destroy not my soul through merciless men! Help me, lord, to joy in you and to praise you with your servants, amen. And send me an angel to teach me wit and wisdom to answer this wicked prefect when I am all alone.

"I see myself, lord, like an innocent sheep surrounded by ravenous wolves. Help now, good lord, and keep me from them, if it please your sovereign majesty." When they heard this they fled as from a witch, and in a moment came to their lord and said,

"Lord, whom fortune has enhanced and set in a position of great dignity, in no way may your power be shared with her to whom we were sent; for she worships Christ as her god, lord, and she will do no service to our gods but blasphemes them amazingly."

When Olibrius heard these words, he changed color and expression, and behaved like a madman and stood in doubt about what to do. After thinking it over he ordered them to fetch her, and when she came he interrogated her thus with a pale face:

"Tell me, damsel, of what family you come and whether you are bond or free." "Servitude has nothing to do with me, for I am Christian, sir," she said. "I ask of what family you come," he said. "I serve," she replied, "that sovereign godhead that has preserved my maidenhood so far."

"Then it follows obviously that you call Christ your god," he said, "whom my ancestors did crucify." "Nothing truer could be said," she answered; "your forefathers nailed up on a tree Christ, whom I worship with my whole heart, and they suffer sharp pains in hell."

When Olibrius heard this conclusion from maid Margaret, he nearly went insane. He ordered her to be shut up in a prison nearby, still considering in his disturbed mood by what deception he might take her virginity.

After this, he ceremoniously entered the city of Antioch and made sacrifice to his gods as was the custom of that country. On the next day he commanded Margaret to be brought into his presence and thus addressed her:

"What is the reason and the cause why, Margaret, in your cruelty, you have no mercy on yourself and will ruin your great beauty? Leave this folly and consent to me, by my advice, and I will reward you with great abundance of gold and silver."

Said Margaret, "If you, O wicked man, knew how little I value all your offers, you wouldn't concern yourself about me, truly. For I never will depart from the ways of truth, but I worship him whom every creature fears and whose reign shall endure forever."

"Margaret," he said, "listen to what I say. If you will not worship my gods, you shall die by my sword. Trust me, it will be so. But if you will meekly obey me, it shall be to your benefit, for I will love your body exceedingly."

"My body," she said, "I offer readily to God's sacrifice, so that I may rest with holy virgins, whenever you please to exercise your tyranny against me; for I want you to know very clearly that I in no way fear dying for the sake of Christ who died for all humanity."

When he heard this, he cruelly commanded that she be hung high in the air and be beaten with rods; and when she was tormented thus, she lifted her eyes devoutly heavenward and said, "In you, lord, I trust, and in your mercy. Let me not be tortured endlessly."

And while she was occupied thus in prayer, the tormentors scourged her so cruelly that her blood ran out as plenteously as water in a river. While they beat, a beadle called, "Believe, Margaret, I advise you, and you shall be happier than all maidens."

And not only this beadle but also the men and women who stood nearby shouted, weeping, "Margaret, we sorrow for you now! Olibrius in his ire will soon kill you. Believe him, we advise, and live!"

When Margaret heard these words among her sharp strokes of torment, she said, "O wicked counselors, men and women, what are you doing here? Go to your work! For without equal the lord who sits in high throne is my helper—this I trust well.

"Also, I want you to know and think about this: that when Gabriel blows his horn in the day of the great last judgment, when people arise in body and soul, then my soul shall be saved by this torment from that hard judgment.

"So if you want to be saved then, I advise you faithfully to forsake all false gods and believe in my God who is mighty in power and hears everyone gladly who prays to him purified from vice. He opens to them the gates of paradise.

"Quickly forsake all false gods, then, by my advice, which are nothing else, I guarantee, but gold or silver, stone or wood, manufactured by people; they can neither walk, speak, hear, nor see. If you don't believe me, test it,

"And you shall prove empirically that they have feet and can't move, ears not hearing, and eyes not seeing, for in them is neither spirit of life, nor flesh nor bone to their bodies. To such godhood no wise person ought to pay attention.

"If you will follow my advice, my soul for yours, you shall be saved. But you, tyrant, who will not do so, and who persevere in the work of your father Satan," she said, "and against the majesty of the one God bark like a shameless dog, in hell your pain shall be endless."

Olibrius, hearing this, fell into a rage like a man out of his mind and ordered his tormentors to rip and rend her tender flesh, hoping to kill her. Meanwhile she lifted her eyes to heaven and said,

"Besieged am I with wicked counsel, and many dogs surround me, fierce and cruel against me. So comfort me, lord, I pray, and send down from heaven by your grace a white dove to help me, before I die in this place.

"And also, lord, if it please you, I beg with all my heart that I might once see my adversary who fights with me and would pervert me, and that I should hurt him badly, and give an example by my victory for all virgins to trust in your mercy."

During her prayer they ripped her flesh on every side so maliciously that her blood flowed to the ground faster than a river. The pitiless prefect hid his eyes with his cloak and couldn't bear to see so much blood running out.

When he saw her display such steadfastness in suffering, "Margaret!" he loudly cried, "Consent to me and with heartfelt meekness worship my gods, so that you won't die horribly." "Your advice," she said, "I completely reject, for if I should have mercy on my flesh, my soul would perish, as yours certainly will."

When he saw this, he ordered the tormentors to take her down from the high gibbet and place her in a dark prison. As the clock struck seven she entered that awful place blessing herself, and said meekly,

"Behold me, lord, who am my father's only daughter, and he has forsaken me because of you, and I him. Hereafter you will be my father! Grant that I may see my enemy face to face, who fights with me and against whom I know not what I have done.

"Of all things, lord, you are judge. Between him and me judge rightfully. And since you are my only refuge, I complain against him that I am hurt and wounded grievously. Yet if you, lord, be not angry with me, I set no store by his enmity."

While she was thus occupied devoutly in prayer, a huge dragon, glittering like glass, suddenly appeared from a corner of the prison with horrible aspect. Its hairs were gold, its beard was long, its iron teeth were mighty and strong;

Out of its nostrils it blew foul smoke, its eyes glittered like stars at night, it threw its tongue over its head, in its claws was a sword burnished bright. Immediately the prison was full of light from the fire that ran out of its mouth and burned everywhere.

When Margaret saw it, she grew pale and for fear forgot that God had heard her prayer, in which she had cried, "Show me, lord, my enemy once before I die." Then she said, "Let not this dragon, lord, harm me."

This horrible beast put its mouth over her head while she spoke, and laid its fire-red tongue under her heel, and swallowed her instantly. But when her cross expanded in its mouth, it burst in two, and she escaped without harm.

And when she thus had victory over it, through grace of God, to her left another devil suddenly appeared who looked at her with hateful expression. Finally he burst out with sniveling voice, saying,

"Just now I sent you my dear brother Ruffin in a dragon's likeness, and when he swallowed you whole, before he knew it, his life was ruined by your witchcraft. For with the sign of the cross you broke him whose death I am now come to avenge."

As soon as he had spoken these words, Margaret caught him by his long hair and threw him under her right foot, saying, "O you pathetic wretch, leave this cursed and unruly effort to tempt my maidenhood, for truly my help is Christ, whose name endures endlessly."

At this, a great light suddenly illuminated that dark prison, and a bright cross appeared in heaven. Down the cross a dove descended and, with a sweet sound, said, "Margaret! All the saints in heaven are waiting for you, and the gates of paradise are opened wide."

Then Margaret, after thanking God duly, turned to the fiend and said, "Tell me where you come from, foul thing." "Servant of Christ," said he, "I pray you remove your foot from my neck and I will tell you everything I do on earth and in hell."

Then, out of courtesy, she removed her foot from his neck and when he felt himself relieved of that distress, "Thanks," he said, "and by your leave I will now, lady, answer your question briefly as you command.

"My name is Belchys. Satan is our ruler and king. In the books of Jannes and Jambres, our offspring, are plainly written our rules and operation. But to your purpose: if you wish to hear, I will tell how we come here.

"Solomon, wisest king there ever was of the children of Israel, once shut many thousands of us, as stories tell, in a vessel of brass; and when the Babylonians entered the place, thinking they'd found great treasure, they broke the vessel and released us.

"When we were released, we spread out all over the earth, seeking whomever we might trouble and harm, for that quality has always belonged to us." "This behavior is bad," she said, "so go, Satan, home to your kin." And with that word the earth swallowed him in.

The following day, fierce Olibrius commanded she be brought to his presence, and gently he said, "Consent to my decision, I counsel you, and, kneeling, offer frankincense to our gods, and I will love you more than any other woman."

"Labor," she said, "no more in vain, but take this answer as final: I will never worship your gods, nor do I care anything for your love; for you shall die soon and after your death be buried in hell, so don't meddle with me."

When Olibrius heard this, he began to shout, "Tormentors! Tormentors!" as if he were mad. "Hurry! With glowing firebrands burn and sear this witch's sides as long as you find any flesh there! And when she is well warmed this way, baptize her in clear cold water."

As he commanded, so it was done. It was pitiful to behold how on both sides, down to the bone, her flesh was burnt with many brands and then, afterward, how she was bound and flung into cold water so that the sudden change from heat to cold should increase her pain.

But God, who will never forsake his servants, nor suffer them to fail, suddenly caused an earthquake which quenched the fire that grieved her. In the water he relieved her so that unbound and without harm she came out, which amazed those who stood about.

On account of this miracle five thousand were converted there and martyred too, and when Olibrius saw things go this way, considering what was best to do, and fearing that more people would turn to her if she lived any longer, without further delay sentenced her to decapitation.

Of this sentence she was glad, having full trust in God's goodness. When she was brought to the place where she was to receive the judgment, she, with humble expression and filled with charitableness, asked Malchus the time for a short prayer.

He granted it. She kneeled down and, lifting her face upward to heaven, began to pray: "O lord ever reigning in eternity, have mercy on me. And for your great pity,

O blessed Jesus, forgive the trespass of those who persecute me.

"Moreover, lord, I humbly beseech you on special behalf
of those who read or write or teach my passion, or who
make a church or chapel to me, or pay for a devotional
light: lord, from your great grace, grant them repentance
before they pass hence.

"Also if women in labor be oppressed with pain and
trouble, and they devoutly pray for help to me, grant them
a quick and safe delivery. And generally, lord, in any ill
fortune, if people call and cry to me for help, grant them
quick comfort and remedy."

When she had thus ended her prayer, suddenly from
heaven this voice came down so loud that everyone heard
it: "Your prayer, Margaret, is heard and granted, so that
whoever in any discomfort prays devoutly to you, for your
sake that person shall be heard."

And with this word she turned her face to Malchus and
said with joy, "Brother, perform your duty now as Olibrius
commanded, for I have nothing further to do here." And
Malchus then smote off her head with one stroke.

But scarcely had her body fallen to the ground than her
soul was in heaven's bliss. Now, glorious lady, let your pity
abound to bring our souls where your soul is, for then we
never shall lack joy, where the holy trinity may bring us.
Let everyone say amen, for charity.

Lo, son, now I have accomplished briefly, as I promised
you in the prologue and according to the legend, the birth,
upbringing, and events of the life, and finally the passion,
of Saint Margaret the blessed virgin who committed her
heavenly grace to illumine my wit and pen. And now I
ask of you leisure and rest for a while, for I am like a
pilgrim who stumbles along the road desiring neither to
joke nor play nor talk nor sing nor be entertained until he
approach his shelter where he may rest and be comforted
with food and drink according to his need and afterward
beak his bones in bed, wearied and weakened with work.

But when he has supped a good meal and slept enough and rested well and rises early the next morning, then he finds himself strong enough to achieve his journey. So it is with me, for my hands tremble, my wit dulls, and my eyes would be blind were it not for the help of spectacles. My pen also begins to resist and wishes no longer to run on paper, for I have so often blunted its snout on my thumb that it is nearly useless. As it goes along it blots and makes many a spot in my book, signifying thereby that it were best for both of us to rest, until it and my wit can be restored with some care. Therefore, son, grant us both a vacation until Michaelmas. That isn't far away, for today is Saint Matthew's eve, only ten days before Michaelmas, after which I will try, if God of his grace grant me the time, to achieve the remainder of my promise, for I won't ask a longer delay. This granted, farewell! Now I am free for nine days from now to pleasure me.

Now that Michaelmas day has come and gone, I will hasten to fulfill the promise I made, according to the strength of my ability. That is, to tell how the translation of Saint Margaret from Antioch to Italy was done, how and when, from whence and whither, and by whom, and also in what circumstances. And that I lack no truth in this action, I lowly beseech him who is truth and who teaches truth, the lord who sits above the sky, that he vouchsafe to guide my wit and my pen in truth to the land of the sweet virgin and blessed martyr, Saint Margaret. I beg everyone to say amen.

From the time of the incarnation of Jesus Christ nine hundred and eight years, by true computation, when Sergius was universal key-keeper of holy church and Berengar had sole empery, the following occurred which I shall here touch on rather than narrate.

The second year of the aforesaid pope, and twelfth of the indiction, as I understand from chroniclers, there developed a grievous quarrel between the patriarch of Antioch,

Eusebius, and him who was then, by tyranny, prince of their polity.

Andronicus was that prince's name who, during Eusebius's absence, by tyranny usurped the princehood of that place. From this, serious trouble befell, for through the debate and strife of these two, many a man lost his life.

To tell everything would take too long; many details are required to reveal fully what great wrong this prince did, and to what misfortune he brought the city through misgovernment, and by what treason he did in his son-in-law Siniardus at night.

I won't tell what legal action he contrived to persecute the patriarch, and by what pretenses he drew many people to his cause. So, to eschew prolixity, I will abandon all digression and proceed to the conclusion.

When through his pride the city of Antioch was nearly destroyed with fire and sword, he burnt many a church, which was a pity to see. Among them was Saint Margaret's, of which he left neither stick nor stone.

In this church was a solemn abbey of monks, whose abbot, the chronicles say, was a good and observant man named Augustine, of noble blood, born in Pavia in Lombardy.

When this Augustine saw the great damage to the city and his abbey and the impossibility of relief, his spirit nearly left him; he thought he might as well die. And when he had long stood dismayed, at last to himself he said:

"I am a foreigner in this country and have no friends here to help me. So I think it best to return to Italy where I have good friends to rely on, for there my relatives live, especially in Pavia."

When he had decided to return to his own country, he planned to carry out of Antioch the bodies of two holy virgins, Saint Margaret and Saint Euprepia, for the good of the church and also in honor of Saint Cyrus the confessor, in Pavia.

For he had secretly learned from a dying priest, Ubald— a man of great devotion—how he could find the body of Saint Margaret and where it rested in a coffin of gold and silver.

And because he couldn't do alone what he wished to do, he secretly called two of his men, Lucas and Robert, and asked if they would be loyal and go home with him to his own country.

And if they would, he promised them abundance of gold and treasure, and that he would make every effort to advance them that they might have gilt spurs and ride with spear and lance. So they swore on Scripture and seal to keep his secrets.

"Fellows," he said, "my intention—taken in sheer devotion—is to translate some relics out of this place which is burnt and brought, as you see, to great desolation; and especially the relics of that blessed and holy virgin Saint Margaret, and enshrine them in Pavia."

When they heard this, they cheerfully approved his intention and said that whenever he wanted to go ahead with it, they would agree. "For here," they said, "the relics will only be destroyed. So we believe that God has inspired you to act on this holy decision."

Soon after, they all three came secretly one night to the place where Augustine had learned the relics of Saint Margaret were hidden, and they dug in so deep that finally they found a chest strongly bound with iron and brass.

On the outside of the chest was written: "Herein rests the body of the pure virgin Saint Margaret." Without delay they broke the chest, and there in a silver vessel, decorated with gems, they found the blessed body.

They were delighted to see it and reverently raised it up and took it secretly to the house of a man whom Augustine the abbot loved—Crisper, who dwelt nearby. They stayed four days, though they wouldn't tell Crisper what they brought.

Meanwhile they prepared their journey. They broke the silver ark and tied the body in a wooden box so that no one would suspect any treasure. Then they took leave, went to ship, and God of his grace sent them a rapid voyage.

They arrived at Brindisi, and, when they had refreshed themselves there, they bought three horses and hastened to Rome where diligently and devotedly they worked to get holy pardon.

After fifteen days they had expiated and cleansed themselves with devout hearts and visited many a holy station. Suddenly an attack of red flux troubled Augustine so badly that he thought he would die of the illness.

So, seeing no hope of cure, he took leave of his host and paid his expenses. Next day, when he had commended himself to Peter and Paul, he took horse and arrived that night at Sutri.

They went with great effort to the Church of Blessed Victory of the Virgin, which stands, as one can see, along the main road near Venus-hall. There he was decently received, at the moment when the first dedication and solemnization of the church was about to occur,

On October 7, and Augustine offered up one of Margaret's ribs in a rich cloth. When the people saw it they received it gladly and dedicated an altar in her honor.

From there, they moved on despite Augustine's great illness. Within two days they came to the Palantes Valley and a house of black monks devoted to Saint Peter. The abbot, Boniface, received Augustine worshipfully and charitably.

When Augustine saw his illness grow worse every day, he sent for the abbot Boniface and, weeping, declared his intention in the presence of the entire convent:

"Alas!" he said, "as a stranger unknown in this place I must inevitably die here, for my infirmity increases. Nonetheless I will make a virtue of necessity, and commend my soul to God and to you.

"Moreover, I want you to know the two precious relics I have with me here: the body of Saint Margaret, and the head of the virgin Euprepia, in a wooden coffin, which I have brought from Antioch and intended to take to Pavia.

"But since I see death approaching fast, and I have very little time left to live sound of mind, I give these relics to this holy place, asking you only this favor: that you will pray for me specially and observe every year the anniversary of my death."

When they heard this they thanked God and Augustine, and granted him what he so devoutly desired. Then all the monks together sang Te Deum Laudamus and rang the bells solemnly.

The cloaked abbot with all his monks, with torches and candles burning, bore these precious relics to the high altar and set them there; and eight days later they made a joyful celebration that many people came to observe.

Meanwhile this blessed man Augustine, who had given the holy relics to the place, performed his rites, commended his soul to God, and passed away on the sixteenth calend of November, Saint Luke's Eve.

When they had said his Dirige properly, they bore his body to their church and buried it worshipfully beside an altar of Saint Blaise, then busied themselves solemnizing the translation of these holy relics.

For though Calixtus's day (he was martyr and pope, and his anniversary falls on October 13th, as the old records testify) was the first day of this ceremony for the revelation of translation of Saint Margaret's body, they celebrated for another eight days.

During these eight days God worked many great miracles there, as I have seen written. But I won't narrate them because of my haste, and so that I may move on quickly to other things, and also to eschew prolixity—even though suspense is "stepmother of favor" according to a line in Matthew of Vendôme.

But since nothing is perpetual in this world nor stable in one condition, this same abbey was desolated a few years later in the great wars that occurred in the area and the contention between cities. The abbey's inhabitants fled for fear.

When it was blown about by the trumpet of Fame and widely known that the abbey was in such desolation, the neighboring Ruvillians met. All their clergy gathered in a procession from Our Lady's Church, and with great reverence fetched Saint Margaret's body from the abbey back to their own church.

When they had solemnly brought the body into Our Lady's Church, they enshrined it in slabs of marble curiously carved, along with Saint Felicity, whose feast falls at the time of Saint Clement's and, as I recall, is the ninth calend of December.

When these two virgins had lain enshrined together for over a hundred years, such trouble came to Ruvillian that it was beaten flat, and it remained that way so long and was so overgrown with trees and wild bushes that hardly anyone knew where it was.

But when it pleased the sovereign goodness of God, who sits in heaven above, to deliver out of that wilderness these two virgins whom he loved, so that they could help and comfort many people, he then chose a foreigner to be minister of their translation.

In the year of grace 1405, the first year of Pope Urban II, when Henry III was alive and ruled the empire, the following revelation was made, as you shall hear.

Between Naples and Terracina, in a forest belonging to the marquis of that country, dwelt two hermits, whom God vouchsafed to illumine with grace to live there and serve him. John was the one to whom Saint Margaret appeared, saying,

"John, God's servant, go as fast as you can to Montefiascone on my errand. Go to the prior of Saint Flavian's, who is called Burgundio. Tell him that God wishes him to do his duty and that neither Saint Felicity nor I are to be left any longer in isolation."

"Who are you," said John, "that speak to me and ask me to do what I can't do?" "I am Margaret, God's handmaiden," she said, "who in Antioch took martyrdom under fierce Olibrius, the prefect then. But when that city was nearly ruined with schism, a man called Augustine brought me from there to Tuscany."

"Lady," said John, "I don't know that place, nor in what country it is." "Never mind," she said, "for while God's grace guides you, you can't go wrong; for wherever you go it will instruct you, and whatever you require will be provided by God and me."

When John heard this he immediately called his companion and set forth on his journey, trusting that God's grace would guide him aright. And so it did, for soon he came to Montefiascone, where she again appeared to him and said,

"Go, tell the prior to send quickly to Ruvillian, which is wilderness now, and to the place where St. Mary's Church was; and there, if they dig industriously, they will find, in carved marble tablets, my body and Felicity's, I assure them."

John went to the prior, and told him by whom and why he was sent, and begged the prior to do it right away so that he could go home. But the prior gave no credence to his words, so that John went away weeping.

He was sorry that, as he thought, he had wasted his efforts. As he went home, Saint Margaret appeared to him right in the road and said, "John, don't be sad, but go to him again and do your errand."

"Lady, he won't believe me," John said. "But go!" she said, "and before you return, he shall be so inspired with grace that he shall happily assent to do as you say, and believe you, or else he will regret it."

"Lady," said he, "in this matter I would think it best— saving your reverence—that you appeared to him yourself and showed him your meaning; then he would have to believe." "No, John, God doesn't wish it so, but through you he wishes the message done."

When John heard this, and many others standing nearby had heard this conversation, they said they would go with him to the prior and bear witness to all these words.

When they did, the prior believed John's message and sent men to search so that he could test it out. They labored digging in the church pavement from morning till evening but they found nothing.

Angrily they went home again and said to John, "You have made us labor in vain, for no fruit has come from our labor." "Sirs," said he, "if you will come again with me, by God's grace I will bring you to the right place."

They agreed and returned, and though he had never been there before, "Here is the spot," he said, "—where the brambles and thorns are growing. I expect no labor will be lost here." There they dug and within an hour they found even more than they had sought.

For with the bodies of the two virgins, Felicity and Saint Margaret, they also found three ribs of Cosmas and Damian, smelling very sweet; and an epitaph was written in the marble: "Lo! here in this chest the bodies of Margaret and Felicity rest."

When they saw this, they joyfully sent word to Montefiascone. The prior gathered a procession to bring the bodies home, and all the people followed, singing and praying devoutly.

While they were singing, night suddenly overtook them, and the procession lost its way. The clouds grew blacker, the people trembled with fear and loudly cried, "Saint Margaret, have mercy on us now!"

As soon as they had prayed, a great brightness spread over them as though heaven had opened, and it led them to Montefiascone. As they walked the light accompanied them until they came to the town.

When they passed in front of the house of a man called Benencasa, the relics grew so heavy that they couldn't carry them past his stables, so the people thought that the relics wished to remain there.

Together they said to Benencasa, "Since God wills that a church should be made here for these relics, give up your house for it willingly. If you won't, we'll buy it or give you a better one."

Benencasa said no. Suddenly a thunder and lightning storm began that lasted for three days without interval. When Benencasa saw this, he decided to take another house and release his own, and when he did, the storm ceased.

Then the people solemnly bore the relics into the house and as best they could they made a church there, in which to this day rest the bodies of the two sweet virgins, Saint Felicity and Saint Margaret.

Many a miracle was shown there at the time of the translation and after, which would take much work to write, for I estimate that if they were written, the material would continue longer than all the rest before.

This second translation of the sweet virgin and blessed martyr Margaret, as I recall, was the 17th of November and the 15th calend of December, which is named in honor of glorious Hugh, bishop and confessor.

Now, blessed virgin, who lie at Montefiascone enshrined in a fine altar, grant me the boon I now ask: first, that I may purchase pardon here for all my sins, and then be partner in joy where you dwell, a joy so great that no tongue can tell. Amen.

THE LIFE OF ST. ANNE
MOTHER OF ST. MARY

Prologue

If I had knowledge and eloquence to dilate my conceits skillfully, as formerly did the fresh rhetoricians Gower,
Chaucer, and now Lydgate, I would occupy myself in translating the life of Saint Anne into our language. But I fear
to begin so late, lest people ascribe it to dotage. For I
know full well I am advanced in age, and my life's term
fast approaches, and the fierce rage of cruel death—as my
inevitable fate wills—has stopped his cart at my gate to
carry me off; and I neither may nor can, though I hate
him, resist his force.

Therefore I think, and it's true, it were best for me to
quit writing and to reform what's amiss in my living. That
is a supreme knowledge: for a man to know his trespass
in order to amend, as far as God will grant him grace.
While a man still has time in this world, before death
embraces him, if he will ransack his life in every detail,
make a reckoning with his conscience and set right what is
wrong: then he cannot fail, when he leaves this life, to go
to bliss.

Nevertheless I trust the sovereign goodness of Jesus and
of Mary his generous mother to accept my intention in

striving diligently to clarify, according to the story, Mary's mother's life and genealogy: to stimulate people's devotion.

For I assure Saint Anne and her daughter Mary, that if I could perceive in my opinion any error against good manners, or any heresy against the faith, I would apply all my wits with all diligence to reform and correct it.

But before I proceed further in this matter, I lowly beseech all who read this story that they seek no elaborate speech, for Tully never taught me, nor did I ever sleep on Parnassus where Apollo lives, nor ever sought

Flowers on Aetna where, as Claudian tells, Proserpina was ravished; nor did I ever taste of the sweet Heliconian spring to doctor my rudeness (for the muses were always hostile to me), and Orpheus, cruel wretch, who sought his wife in hell, never took heed of me, nor taught me a note of his harmony to arrange rhymes in musical proportion.

But in spite of all that, and for your sake, my friend Katherine Denston, I won't delay starting this story, if grace will illumine my pen. Pray to the blessed virgin, the daughter of Saint Anne, to allow a beam of her special grace to shine on me. Pray that I may have leisure and time, through the help of divine influence, to conclude for our comfort this legend now begun before death untwine the thread of our fatal fabric, which is quite thin spun. Pray that she save us both from endless pain, and here on earth preserve us from shame and sin.

O peerless princess, singular gem of virginity, who are always ready to help those who cry out to you in need: Listen, lady, in your womanhood to my prayer, and help me who aim to say something about your kindred and especially in honor of your mother who was root of you, sweetest flower, and who fostered and fed you with her milk for three years and then led you to the temple to offer you. Now, lady, grant me the reward of seeing you both in eternal bliss.

The Life

According to the rules of interpretation, "Anne" is the equivalent of "grace." This appellation suitably belongs to her, for within her womb she bore her who is the well of grace, Lady of earth and empress of hell.

I mean that blessed and holy virgin, mother of Jesus our savior, Mary, best medicine for sinners after her son, and special help in all distress. Of this flower so redolent and sweet the gracious Anne was stem and root.

She is praiseworthy for three things especially. First, for her noble and royal family descending lineally from David; also for perfect living; and finally for plenteous fruit. Her father was called Issachar, and Nasaphat was her mother's name.

As for the first, know, by the teaching of Scripture that does not lie, that David had in Jerusalem four sons by Bathsheba, who was formerly the wife of worthy Uriah. The third son was called Solomon, and the fourth Nathan.

Know too, as Jerome and Damascene testify, that it is not the custom of Holy Scripture to record the genealogy of women; so that, just as the line of Mary is known only through Joseph, so is Anne's through Joachim.

For even clearer understanding of this genealogical descent, you must know that old law permitted no intermarriage among different clans; therefore Joachim took Anne from the family of his relatives, and Joseph was constrained to marry Mary.

These data I interpret as follows: From Nathan descended Levi long after, whose wife Estha (Damascene says) bore two sons, Pantar and Melchy. Pantar had Barpantar, and he had Joachim, husband to Anne the mother of our solace.

On the other side descending from Solomon to Matthan came Jacob, according to the gospel of Matthew; but as

Damascene says, Melchy (of Nathan's line, Pantar's brother and Levi's son) wedded Jacob's mother and begat Eli.

So Jacob and Eli were uterine brothers, though Jacob was sired by Solomon and Eli by Nathan. When Eli ended his life without issue, Jacob, to restore his brother's seed, took his brother's wife (as the law commanded at that time) and begot Joseph, Mary's spouse. So ends this double genealogy.

And if moral interpretation pleases to draw out the names of the progenitors of Mary—that chief gem of virginity—we shall find sweet-smelling flowers of healing doctrine, if we can properly approach those names in order according to etymology.

According to the instruction of the holy doctor Saint Augustine, "David" signifies "the sovereign heavenly progenitor," and "Solomon" means "peaceable," according to etymology, while "the prince of peace" truly means him whom the Father sent down to make perfect peace when he took on our nature.

By "Nathan," David's son through whom the line descends to Levi, is also signified "gift" or "thing given" and also "taken up" or "applied." In this we are symbolically assured that through them our nature shall be taken up by the second person of the trinity.

But the assumption of our frail nature—which was nearly ruined with sin had not our wound been healed—was not sufficient, and he vanquished what caused the wound. Thus in the order of our restoration descent is then to Jacob, tokening "supplantation."

Jacob supplanted his brother Esau, which means "rough" or "hairy," and it signifies that our lord Jesus supplanted the devil, our rough enemy, when he was shamefully hung naked on the cross, fastened with nails and pierced to the heart with a sharp spear.

After Jacob, next (as the text says) in genealogical descent stands Joseph, which means "increase." He is spouse of Anne's daughter Mary, mother of Jesus; her name signifies "a bitter sea" and "salvation," which is moralized thus:

Joseph, increasing in goodness, must wed Mary, the bitter sea of penance, in constancy and stability. And if Anne be penance's mother which is called "grace" and "charity," then Joseph shall by humble virtue conceive salvation, indicated by the name Jesus.

Now I have shown this noble pedigree more succinctly than it ought to have been done, except that I follow my source closely and hope to avoid prolixity. Since my wit is short, as you can see, I will hasten to the second part of my work and describe Anne's life.

This blessed Anne of the royal blood of King David was born in a city called Bethlehem. She was raised in all virtuous habits as diligently as her father Issachar could do, and her mother Nasaphat also.

And when she had arrived at the age of discretion—I don't know what age that was, according to their laws, but probably not too young—she was wedded ceremoniously in a country called Galilee to a man appropriate to her degree, that is, Joachim, who dwelt

In the city of Nazareth and descended from David's house, a rich man of high position whose life had always been virtuous, simple, righteous, and merciful, commendable before God and man. To him Anne was extremely well suited,

For according to the philosophical doctrine of Jesus Sirach (whoever can read it), like always approaches like: sheep to sheep and person to person, partridge to partridge and swan to swan: so virtue is agreeable to virtue and Anne to Joachim was a suitable wife.

For since they both were well-bred in youth, so in marriage they grew even more steadily in virtue, and here is why: as a poet long ago said, whatever new contents a vessel hold, it still is redolent of the old.

Because they wished to live in conformity with God's pleasure, they divided their property in three. The first they gave with devotion to the temple, the second to sustenance of pilgrims and poor old people, the third they kept for their household.

Thus righteous to God and man they lived twenty years without issue, in chaste marriage without vice. Though no fruit grew of their seed, they continually appealed to God thrice annually at his temple with offering and with devout prayer

And vowed that if God would send them any fruit through his special grace, they would present it to him, whether it were man or woman, in the temple, that holy place, there to cense themselves clean and pure as long as they were able.

Long after, on a festival day called the Dedication of the Temple, Joachim went in his best array to Jerusalem to make his devout offering as was his wont, along with other burgesses of his city as was appropriate to each one's position.

At that time Issachar was bishop in the temple, as the story relates. And when he noticed Joachim standing there with the others, he rebuked him and asked why a man barren and fruitless dared appear in that place.

"Your gifts," said he, "are unworthy, and unacceptable to God. You ought to know that barrenness is offensive to God; cursed and condemnable (as Holy Scripture tells us) is the man who brings forth no fruit in Israel.

"Therefore, Joachim, I instruct you never to have the presumption to offer here until you are absolved of this legal curse. And when you have got absolution from this curse and have fertility, then shall your gifts be acceptable."

When Joachim had been thus rebuked publicly by the bishop, he was so ashamed that he would not go straight home, lest his neighbors at home should reprove him again; and so he took another way.

He went to his herdsmen who were pasturing his sheep in the wilderness. These sheep were his main concern, for with the surplus of their offspring he and his wife would feed the God-fearing poor.

While Joachim was busy with his sheep in the wilderness, and his spouse Anne had heard no news of him for five months, then with great sadness, oppressed and prostrate she began to pray, saying,

"O sovereign everlasting majesty, who have ever been and shall be reigning in stable eternity, whose reign may neither bend nor fall, and whom every mortal creature must obey—now, lord, out of your nobility pity me in my need!

"Ah, most mighty lord of Israel, since you have given me no children, how have I trespassed against your mercy that thus you take my spouse from me? Five whole months have passed since I have had news of him, whether he is dead or alive.

"Now help me, lord, I beg you, and grant me grace to have some information about where to seek my husband, for if I knew where, I would without delay look for him if he were alive; and if he were dead I would take proper care of his burial.

"For, lord, you know how affectionately I love him and always have done since we were first joined by law: past all creatures. Lord, help me! and if the knot of our marriage now be untied, I know no one but you, lord, that may be my comfort."

When she, sobbing for woe and sighing in heartfelt bitterness, had said these words and many more which I can't express, she went into an arbor beside her house and there prayed again.

When she rose from her prayer and casually lifted up her eye, in a fresh green laurel she saw a sparrow feeding her young in a nest made of moss and clay. She fell down suddenly on her knees and cried:

"O lord almighty, who has sovereignty over all and who has granted to every creature—fish, fowl, beasts both large and small—by natural engendering to enjoy their like, and

in their offspring, each after its own nature, to worship your
name endlessly!

"I thank you, lord, that you have done what pleases you
with me, excluding me from the gift of your benignity:
such is my lot. Yet if you had liked to favor me with son or
daughter, I would humbly have offered it to your service."

When she had mournfully said her mind, suddenly an
angel appeared before her, clad in light brighter than the
sun. With cheerful reverence he spoke:

"Be not afraid, Anne, though I appear unexpectedly in
your presence, for I am sent down from heaven to encense
you with glad tidings: how the fruit of your body shall be
held in honor and reverence, and remembered through all
generations to the world's end."

When the angel had thus briefly performed his mission,
he vanished away. She was so astonished and disconsolate
that she was speechless and returned to her chamber, where
without bodily comfort or help she lay a day and a night
in prayer.

Then she arose, all wept out from her prayer and called
her maid. "Since you saw me lying here so long without
comfort or help from anyone, what is your excuse for not
visiting me even once?

"Alas, lord, that it should be said that you have with-
drawn all human comfort from me, even help offered by
my handmaid who ought, I should think, to have been my
comfort! But you do all this, lord, so that I should trust
only in you, and put all my hope only in your mercy."

To Anne the maid grudgingly replied, "Your God has
shut your womb with barrenness, and taken away your
husband: do you imagine I can repair that damage? No,
I can't." Then Anne, despondent at this answer, fell down
and wept disconsolately.

Meanwhile an angel in the likeness of a handsome young
man appeared to Joachim in the green hills, as he was
walking among his sheep. The angel asked, "What is the

reason, tell me truly, why you do not return home to your wife?"

"Young man," said Joachim, "I will tell you how it is. I love my wife as deeply as any man does his, but for the last twenty years that we have been together, the seed I've sown has been lost.

"I lack the proof of manhood, and when men are counted I am left behind; for I can have no children, neither son nor daughter of my species, and since I find no fruit in my field, it is useless to till it any longer.

"For he that sows his field annually with great diligence, and waters his appletree daily, and nothing grows, he is like one who drinks salt water to stanch his thirst, or beats the winds, or sows in gravel, or plows the shore where nothing will grow.

"So I have labored in vain for twenty years, and when I think of the shame I felt when the bishop ordered me out of the temple and despised my offering, I want to mourn.

"All these things considered, whatever happens I won't go home again but will stay with my herds and with good will I shall send to temple and wife and poor men the portion that belongs to them."

When he had thus declared his intention, the young man answered calmly, "I am an angel of the heavenly king. I appeared today to Anne your wife as she wept continuously, and now I am sent to you to let you know that your prayers and alms are heard by God.

"I have also witnessed your shame and the hateful reproof of barrenness leveled against you through no fault of yours. Know that God is avenger of wickedness, and when he shuts the womb of his wellbeloved, he opens it the more wonderfully.

"Sarah, the princess of your ancestry, was barren until the age of eighty, and then she had Isaac to whose seed the blessing of the people was promised. Barren was Rachel until she had Joseph, who became governor of Egypt and saved many people from hunger.

"Who among dukes was mightier than Sampson? Tell me! Or who among judges was holier than Samuel? And both their mothers were barren. Your wife is similar now, for she bears a daughter

"Whose name shall be called Mary. She shall be offered from the moment of her birth to God's temple by the vow of both of you, and from her mother's womb she shall be filled with the holy ghost. Therefore go home quickly now to your wife, for blessed is her seed whose daughter shall be mother of everlasting bliss, by God."

Joachim, startled by this announcement, worshiped the angel and said, "Sir, if I have found grace in your sight, come sup with me, I beg you, in my tabernacle here by the road, and bless your servant." To whom the angel kindly responded,

"I would have you say fellow servant, not servant, for we are both servants of one lord above. Because my food is invisible and my drink celestial, it cannot be seen in this mortality; so urge me not to your tabernacle, but whatever you would give me, offer it up to God in a burnt sacrifice."

As soon as this word was said, Joachim ran to the sheep-fold and brought a clean lamb. As the angel bade he burnt the lamb; and right before his eyes, before he knew it, this handsome bright angel flew to heaven with the smoke.

Joachim fell down prostrate and afraid; he lay on the earth from noon until night as if dead. When his herdsmen, thinking him dead, prepared to carry him to his grave, he came to himself again.

And when he was recovered from his trance, he told his servants the cause, and they advised him to obey the angel's instructions immediately.

As Joachim considered what to do, sleep closed his eyes and the angel appeared to him again, just as he had done when Joachim was awake, and gave this message:

"I am your guardian angel, assigned by God. The purpose of my coming is that you should go home right away.

Your prayers are heard, and therefore you shall have such a child as never was born of woman, nor ever shall be again."

When Joachim awoke, he readied himself immediately, thanked God, and homeward took his way. He took herdsmen and beasts along for company, and as they walked, of God's goodness they spoke and talked.

When they had spent nearly thrice ten days on their journey, an angel was sent to Anne. He commanded her to go to Jerusalem where at the Golden Gate she would see her spouse, the joy of her household.

Out of her prayers blessed Anne then arose, and hurried to Jerusalem; and when she saw her husband and his herdsmen at the Golden Gate, she began to run as fast as she could.

She saw nothing else but only him, for she was overjoyed at his arrival. She embraced and kissed him, caring for no other joy since she had him back, and she cried, "Welcome, dear spouse and thanks to God!

"I was a widow and now I am none. I was barren and blameworthy, but now barrenness has left me, and God's eternal providence has enabled me to conceive; for the goodness he has showed to me, may his name forever magnified be."

When this miracle was blown about the country by the trumpet of Fame, everyone who knew or loved them was full of joy at the news, especially their relatives. Then they went home to await patiently God's promise.

After the ninth month, when Phoebus had nearly run his course in Virgo (I mean September eighth), a new sun appeared to the world and from Anne's womb sprang the oil-tun of gracious health for all sick who seek it with devout heart;

That is, on this day was born the glorious gem of virginity such as was never like before nor ever like will be; whose singular privilege was that she would be both a virgin and the messiah's mother; and her name was Mary.

To praise this lady rightly, according to the merit of her worthiness, surpasses my wit though not my will. I fully acknowledge my own rudeness. Whoever would know her praise, let them look at John Lydgate's book on our lady's life.

But whoever wishes to know the praise of this lady rhetorically expressed in Latin, he must seek the ten volumes entitled "Of the Wedding Songs" in elaborate verse. In these two works the reader will find everything I omit.

When Phoebus (who daily changes his residence, always on the move and resting nowhere stably) had in due order passed the twelve signs of the zodiac three times, and resided in Virgo once more, then blessed Mary was three years old.

Joachim prepared himself and his wife Anne to fulfill their vow and offer their daughter to the lord of life, to dwell in the temple as long as it pleased his blessed will; and so they went to Jerusalem at the next festival.

Before the entrance to the temple were fifteen stairs of grey and brown marble (as old writings say). Mary was set down at the lowest, and she climbed right up to the top with no help except grace.

It was marvelous to see that all the while she was climbing up from step to step, despite her tenderness of age, she never once turned her face nor called for father or mother until she had climbed up all the stairs.

Right up to the top she went, erect in posture, her eyes lifted to the temple and never on anything else. When Anne her mother saw this marvel, full of the holy ghost's grace, she said,

"Our lord God, supreme in power over all others, is always blessed for he remembers his holy word and has conferred his grace on me that I shall no longer be reproached for barrenness. Worship him for his goodness!

And not only from shameful barrenness has he delivered me, but also his people who were in distress he has visited so mercifully that through my fruit—thank the lord—not I alone but all mankind shall find eternal comfort."

Together Joachim and Anne presented little Mary in the temple, humbly praying that God vouchsafe to accept their gift.

When this was done they left her there and returned to Nazareth and lived in holiness. How much longer Joachim lived I can't say, but I know that Anne had three daughters, each called Mary;

But whether by one husband or by three I will not specify, for I have already chosen some of this material to compose in Latin ballade-rhyme. Thus I turn to conclude St. Anne's life, beseeching her with lowly heart:

O gracious Anne, who worthily has the name of grace, out of whom sprang the woman who brought forth into this world the well of grace and of eternal life: grant, at my departure in due course from this mutability, that I be established in eternal bliss.

Provide, lady, too, that John Denston and his wife Katherine may have (if it please God's grace through your merits) a son before they die, as they already have a beautiful small daughter called Anne in honor of you. And convey them all three to eternal bliss. Amen, lord, for charity.

THE LIFE OF SAINT CHRISTINE

Once beside Lake Bolsena there stood a city called Tyre, powerful and worldly as old stories tell. It lacked nothing but God's grace, for it would not receive Christ's faith; instead, the cruel emperor Diocletian persecuted the faith everywhere.

In this city a worthy man (in terms of worldly position) was prefect. His name was Urban, and he also commanded knights. He had a wife of suitable rank, daughter of the imperial blood, but they both were heathen, of the sect called pagans.

But just as from a sharp thorn often springs a lovely flower, and from foul earth grows good grain as well as gold, silver, and precious stones, so from these vice-ridden heathen who led their lives in idolatry was born a fair and gracious maid whom they called Christine.

When Christine was twelve years old, she was not only physically beautiful but also wise, prudent, and sage beyond all women of that city. She intended to love and serve only the omnipotent lord of heaven and earth, but kept this holy intention secret from father and mother.

Urban, considering the great beauty and fresh complexion of his daughter, had a high and gloomy tower built in which she was put with twelve maidens; for he would not have her seen in public, fearing the perils that might befall. He ordered golden gods for her to worship and to call.

43

Wooers came desiring to have her in marriage, but her
father sent every one of them away, citing the tenderness of
her age. He added that he knew her concern was to serve
the gods, and that she would not deviate from this duty
for anything or anyone, even under threat of death.

But this blessed Christine was disposed in quite another
way than her father imagined or could guess. Her heart was
entirely committed to God's service, so that she would not
sacrifice to idols as her father had commanded, but heartily
despised all his gods forged of silver and gold.

So the gums and frankincense that he had ordered her to
offer in honor of his gods, she set in a window facing east.
From this window she could see the sun and moon and stars
passing in due course, whereof she marveled and said,

"Great is that God, and most worthy to be magnified,
who through his grace and for no other reason has ordained
all these for human solace. But my father's gods with their
golden faces can't do this as far as I can see. So let the
name of God—whose dwelling is above the firmament—
be glorified everywhere.

"Him only will I serve and no other while I live, though
I may be threatened with death, and I shall never deviate
from this for my father or mother or anyone else. Maintain
me in this, lord, and suffer me never to change; for though
I see not with my bodily eye, yet I trust only you, lord,
and no other."

So for seven days Christine would not sacrifice to others
but only to heaven's God. Then the twelve maidens whom
her father had appointed to Christine's service came to her
and knelt with great reverence, saying,

"O lady, whose face is imperial and most worthy to
rule, to whom no one may be compared in beauty, we
wonder why—though we do not want to complain—you
have, apparently unreasonably, strayed from your father's
religion.

"You worship a god we don't know, nor none of our
ancestors knew; and if this rumor comes to your father, we

are lost. We'd be better off unborn, for he will say it's by our suggestion you've been brought to that opinion.

"And if he accuse us of that, where shall we flee? What shall we do? Alas, we are ruined! Have mercy on yourself first and foremost, we beg, and then on us, and don't allow, for a little folly, yourself and us to perish thus."

When these maidens had thus piteously complained, Christine seriously and kindly replied, "Why speak you so, maidens? Do you want me to ask these idols for help which can neither hurt nor help me?

"No, damsels, I think it best to worship and serve him who can and will comfort body and soul here and in eternal joy, where there is never night but always day a thousand-fold brighter than here. Him I will worship wholeheartedly as long as I live."

While they were talking, her father came in to see whether his daughter had made her offering properly, as he had commanded. She would not listen to him but, opening her window, looked upward to heaven, wept devoutly, and prayed to God in her heart.

When Urban saw Christine's mood, he called her to him and said, "Dear daughter, why do you not approach my gods and sacrifice to them as I've taught you to do since you were born? Come here and do as you have done before.

"Don't you realize, daughter, with what labor and weeping and trouble, and with what reverence and honor I obtained you through the goodness of my gods? Then don't let it happen that they in wrath avenge your unkindness. Come here and with all humility sacrifice to them, I beg you."

Blessed Christine, inspired with grace, replied modestly to her father, "Do you think, judge, that I do wrong to worship God in heaven on high?" "No, daughter," he said, "but I do consider it foolish that in your heart you uphold and cherish one god so affectionately that because of him you despise all others."

"Do you then consider my devotion futile—please tell me the truth—when I worship father, son, and holy ghost?" "No, but then," he said, "since you worship not one but three, as you yourself acknowledge openly, why won't you worship other gods along with them?"

"Now I see," said Christine, "that you require wit and understanding, and lack the influence of divine grace to know the high mystery of this thing, how three persons have only one substantial being. You would cleverly bring me to the false conclusion that I should worship more than one god.

"That won't be. I know your will and how concerned you are to deceive me, but you won't fool me with the number of a trinity. Try no more, for it won't be. I shall never worship more than one God, yet I admit there are three distinct and separate persons in him.

"Him I will love and serve, with true and heartfelt subjection, who can preserve me from all evil and protect me in every need; not your gods who can neither hear nor speak nor understand nor move from their places without the help of a human hand.

"So order me new frankincense that I will offer with cleanness of heart to his sovereign reverence who reigns in heaven and always has. Also order me clean clothing in which, stripped of my old clothes, I may pray his forgiveness for the offences I committed when I was young."

Her father quickly did as she asked, ordered her a new garment and new incense for sacrifice. When it came she dressed herself, went to her window, and humbly made her offering, saying to her lord and love:

"O lord who dwells in heaven above, O savior sent by your father for humanity's love into this world and who suffered hard judgment for his sake; O blessed Jesus, accept the intent of your handmaid and make me strong enough never to forsake you whatever torment is determined for me."

When she had prayed, an angel stood in front of her and said, "O Christine, full of grace, our lord has heard your prayer. Be strong in him and be cheerful, for you will be examined by three judges. But God will not forsake you, so that his virtue may be glorified in you."

"Now lord God," said Christine, "be my helper so that no one may conquer me." "Your desire is granted, Christine," said he. With that she noticed a loaf nearby, white as snow and sweeter than honey, and when she had tasted it, she thanked God:

"Thank you, lord full of goodness, who has sent me a loaf of immortality as token of forgiveness of my sins, through your pity. Thank you, lord, for your charity that has preserved me alive; for through my father's great cruelty it is twelve days since I saw any bread."

That evening Christine broke all her father's gods of gold and silver. She threw the pieces out a window into the street and called poor men to come and get this charitable distribution, not fearing her father's persecution.

Next day when Urban came to see his daughter and found his gods broken and gone, in his angry passion and full of cruelty he called his daughter's maidservants and harshly spoke: "Where are—tell me quickly—my glorious and immortal gods?"

At this the maidens fell down, so afraid were they of his cruel mood, and said, "Sir, you are our ruler and may do with us as you will; we can't escape; so we tell you that your daughter threw your gods out this window."

When Urban heard these maidens' words, he slapped his daughter hard on the cheek, and said, "Tell me where are my gods, before I punish you with more torment." "If they are gods," said she, "let them speak for themselves openly and prove their godly worth."

When she had said this, he sentenced the maidens to be beheaded in her presence, and the sentence was executed. Christine said, "O pitiless tyrant, why do you slay these innocents without reason? I warn you, this blood shall damn you and God's vengeance shall follow you shortly."

When Urban heard this, he furiously commanded she be beaten with rods. She was scourged so cruelly that it was a pity to behold. Yet her tormentors were more pained than she, for they fell down weary. Urban went nearly mad seeing this, and threatened them and called them cowards.

But while blessed Christine was thus tormented, she changed neither color nor mood, for she was filled with heavenly comfort and said to her father, "O you, hateful to God and humanity both, what can your pain and threats do? Don't you see your servants overthrown here, and your father the devil, and your own wits too?"

Then Urban commanded an iron collar to be placed around her neck with chains on her hands and feet and she was put in prison. Which done, he returned to his palace and fell down prostrate, sorrowing that he was so despised by his daughter.

When Christine's mother heard how she had suffered such torment from her father, she tore her clothes like a madwoman, poured ashes on her head, and went to the prison. There, falling down and weeping piteously she spoke to her daughter:

"O my daughter Christine, have mercy on me your wretched mother, for I have only you and no more to be the light of my eyes. Think, daughter, that I bore you ten months in my body and brought you with great pain into this world. Is this respect, daughter, to worship so eccentrically a god we don't know?"

But she whom grace illumined answered her mother, "Is there any of your kin called Christine?" "Not that I know of," her mother replied. "Then you trouble in vain," said Christine, "to call me daughter, and you waste your labor, for I want you to know in plain words that I have my name after Christ my creator.

"He is my father, he is mother also, who has called me to heavenly chivalry. I will serve and worship him who has assured my victory against all those who, blinded by idolatry, do not worship the omnipotent God. He encourages me to defy the idols in whose service you mistakenly toil.

"So go away and worry no more. Don't call me daughter; I forsake you here." The mother went home and told all this to her mate, so that he began to tremble for anger and swore by his gods that the next day, if he lived, he would take vengeance on his daughter's words without delay.

Next morning he had Christine brought publicly to the high court. When women saw this fair young girl treated so cruelly, among them was many a weeping eye, and with a loud voice together they prayed, "O god of this girl, help her, we pray, and don't let her die so shamefully who flees to you in her tender age."

When Urban saw her he said (sitting on his throne), "Christine, what is the reason why you refuse to sacrifice to our gods according to the custom of this country, gods who could help you in this error into which you have fallen through recklessness? And if you won't, I shall assail you with torments and never call you daughter again."

"For sure, cruel tyrant," Christine said, "you do me a favor if you never call me your daughter. I don't know what more you could do for me." He then commanded her to be hung on a gibbet, and the torturers came to her and tore her sides with instruments of iron.

While these torturers so cruelly tore Christine's flesh, she threw a chunk of it into her father's face as if she were playing, and said, "O old shrew who pass evil days, since you wish to eat flesh, seek no farther and in no other place. Feast on your own!"

When impatient Urban heard this, he had his dear daughter taken down from the gibbet and set on an iron wheel, and ordered a great fire to be made under it. So that no pity should appear in him, he cruelly ordered oil to be thrown into the fire. She lifted her face to heaven and prayed,

"O God who have your dwelling place in heaven, father of Christ Jesus who is ever blessed, forsake not me your handmaid here in this great struggle. Show your might and power on this fire made for my torment, so that they who know you not will know that you alone are lord omnipotent."

When Christine had ended her prayer, suddenly the fire jumped out and burned a thousand and five hundred of them who sacrificed to idols. Urban called Christine and said, "Tell me who taught you this witchcraft—foul befall him!"

Christine answered thus: "O cruel tyrant, full of unpity, why ask who taught me witchcraft, when I told you that Christ is my father and none but he, who gives me patience to endure. He is light to the blind that may not see, and joy of them that suffer tribulation.

"He is my master, and only he taught me fear of him and all righteousness. Nowhere is there so perfect a master as he, through whose doctrine I have overcome your insolence and the cruelty of any torment you can devise. That's why I despise your power and that of Satan your father."

With these words, Urban, stormily troubled and dismayed, thought how to destroy her. He shut her in a dark prison into which she entered gladly, singing and thanking God there.

As soon as Christine had entered that horrible and ugly dungeon, three angels appeared in front of her bringing her bread as white as linen and other food, and they cared for her wounds. She, looking heavenward, made her prayer with steady heart, saying,

"O lord Jesus Christ be thanked, who of your grace and goodness promised not to forget me, but who have sent me through your nobility heavenly food with your angels: such food as I dare say no one on earth gets."

That same night the cursed man, the cruel and unpitying Urban, sent five servants to the prison. He bade them tie a heavy stone to Christine's neck and carry her to the sea and throw her in. As he commanded they performed his cruel decree.

When they had thrown Christine into the sea, tied to a heavy stone, these men rowed home again. But a great company of angels uplifted her, with whom she walked on the water with no sign of injury; and then she prayed to God:

"O lord, who accompanied your servant Moses across, and who drowned Pharoah in the salt sea when he pursued your people, and guided Peter in the raging storm, now by the same power save your handmaiden and grant me the washing of immortality here in this water, O blessed lord Jesus, and with the light of grace now illumine me."

And while blessed Christine prayed thus, she saw God's majesty approaching, a golden crown set on his head. His clothing was a robe of pure purple; before him passed many angels smelling sweetly of incense, and after him went thousands of angels with harmonious hymns and psalms.

When Christine saw this glorious sight, she fell down flat on the water, for she was astonished with fear. And the good lord, approaching, lifted her up and said, "Be of good cheer, Christine, dear daughter! I am your savior whom you love and serve with whole heart. I come to deliver you from idols' error.

"I am Jesus, lord of the heavenly host, light, granter of grace to them who humbly call my father and me in the holy ghost and who heartily despise all false idols." With that, he baptized her with his own hands in the salt sea, and when she arose from the water he set her in the middle of the city.

Christine, kneeling, thanked God for his grace, lifted her eyes and saw heaven open and Jesus in procession. She fell on her face in reverence to Christ, then went to her father's palace, continuing in prayer until dawn.

When day came and Urban found Christine praying in his high court, he was astounded and blamed his servants for deceiving him. He sent Christine back to prison and called for her the next day.

"Christine," he said, "what enchantment do you practice, that the sea may not drown you?" "Damaged in intelligence and blinded in your wits, you are without understanding," said she, "otherwise you would realize that last night my God baptized me. So your father the devil and you with all your false gods I despise."

These words so angered Urban that he sent her to prison again, planning to slay her the following day for certain. What are you doing, Urban? You labor in vain, for she will be victorious over you and two more, as was told her in full revelation. And so she prayed:

"O lord Jesus Christ, who came down from heaven to me for my solace, and baptized me in the salt sea with your own hands through your special grace, behold how Urban threatens to slay your handmaid tomorrow. Lord, let him pass away according to his deserving and frustrate him of his will, I beg."

This prayer done, as the story tells, she entered prison magnifying God. That very night there occurred to Urban the revenge she prayed for. The devil vexed him with such torment that he cried aloud, for his entrails swelled and he died horribly within the hour, and according to his merits went to the devil in hell.

When people told Christine of this, she kneeled and devoutly prayed: "Lord God, well of all goodness, many thanks for showing your power over Urban, who was alienated from your promises. Everyone's honor and praise is appropriate for you, lord, who with your only son and the holy ghost live and reign, one God, forever, amen."

Not long after God's righteousness had thus taken vengeance on Urban and delivered Christine out of distress, the emperor appointed a new prefect who loved to persecute Christians wherever he could hunt or catch them. His name was Zyon.

The case of Christine was soon presented to him by officers of the city, and when he read it, with a pale face, he was astonished by the information. He asked where she might be and was told that she had neither hidden nor fled but still dwelt in that city.

He reflected: "Since torture couldn't convert her to sacrifice to our gods, how shall I manage to terrify her into agreeing with my opinion?" He sent officers to arrest her.

When she was brought before him, he began to assault her with fine talk and said, "O well-born damsel, too often distressed in jail, I would like to know what good it does you to forsake the ever-living gods who shield you with their godhead, and to worship one who can't help.

"Don't do so, my daughter, but instead according to my advice come forward and sacrifice to our gods, and I shall inform the emperor of the dignity of your birth and you shall be married to some well-placed courtier. You shall rise to great respect, as your birth and your beauty demand."

"Judge, cease these words," said Christine, "for your trouble is all in vain. Know that neither you nor your emperor shall make me forsake my creator Christ Jesus, king of heaven, to honor these idols that were made by human hands."

"Damsel," said he, "you're mistaken to provoke me so soon, but I shall teach you a new game that will make you sweat blood." He ordered her to be beaten with rods by his tormentors, but even so she wouldn't stop rebuking him:

"O cruel tyrant, full of melancholy, aren't you ashamed to assault me with so little pain? Don't you know I've endured this and more? Your brother Urban couldn't force me to worship or serve these idols. Take this for an answer: you won't either, though you kill me."

Zyon, aggrieved with this answer, had them bring a heated brass vessel full of pitch, rosin, oil, and grease, and had the young woman thrown into it, assigning four men to prod her with iron staves that she might die more quickly.

When Christine saw this vessel, she raised her tearful eyes to heaven and said, "O God, lord of all, I pray with lowly heart to you who quenched the fiery furnace's flame for the three children: be present now to your handmaiden and let me not die with this horrible and cruel torment."

When she had thus offered her heart's desire to God, she went voluntarily to the vessel before the tormentors approached and placed herself in it joyfully. The fire hurt her not a bit, for she was enbalmed with heavenly dew as if she lay in a fresh arbor among flowers and green grass.

"Christine," said Zyon, "I see that this fire hasn't harmed you. Take my advice and duly thank our gods, through whose power and special operation you are preserved; make them an offering with frankincense as you know how to do."

"Sir judge," said Christine, "what is your name?" "My name, if you wish to know, is Zyon, which Fame's trumpet has spread afar in many countries." "I believe this name is rightly yours, for this is a name of blind idols, dumb and crooked, which to overthrow is no great thing."

Zyon, hearing this, commanded that her head should be shaved and burning coals spread on it. When the women of the city saw this, they cried, "O judge, your decree is wrong and unrighteously done, for in this maid you destroy all women utterly."

He sent her again to prison, and early the next morning had her brought in and exhorted her: "Christine, let us now go to the temple and there worship Apollo's high reverence; he shall deliver you from all this woe."

Blessed Christine, placing all her trust in God and inspired by the influence of divine grace, entered the temple with the judge and all the people following. Standing amidst the crowd she addressed the heathen: "See now the truth of God's working, and behold how I shall sacrifice."

And while they waited to see the result of her intention, she prayed, "O my light, Christ! O my hope, Jesus! O only begotten of God! O my blessed lord! Hear the prayer of your handmaiden and destroy this idol through which many damnably err; break it to dust!"

When she had prayed, the idol fell down from its place and broke into dust as everyone could see. The judge fell on his face for fear, and after he had lain there for some time he arose and said, wondering, "Christine, you have done a great wrong. Your witchcraft surpasses our knowledge."

When Christine heard Zyon say this, she began to sigh, and again she said loudly, "O cursed tyrant, enemy of God in heaven and of everything holy, you say that Apollo is a god, and yet he was made by human hands and through him many souls err grievously.

"I don't think such a one is a god." She looked about at the people and said, "Sirs, behold here your god to whom you were accustomed to bow. Look where he lies; his eye has fallen out. Try to raise him up now; and if you can't, know that such godhead is foolishness."

At these wise words, many a pagan was converted and began to cry: "O God and lord in every place and of your servant Christine, grant us grace to love and dread your holy name. And forgive us, lord, our trespass in caring about idols.

"We were deceived for lack of instruction, and so our error in idolatry was prolonged, but now with the help of this blessed virgin we receive the true belief. To keep it, lord, make us strong; let us never forsake it though we die, and with spiritual joy and heavenly song your holy name always glorify."

At that time three thousand pagans were converted. When Zyon saw this, he fell down and died on the spot for fear, because of Apollo's desolation and the people's transmutation. And when this was told to Christine, she thanked God, saying devoutly,

"Thank you, lord, who are ever ready for them that trust in your goodness and who often show how mighty you are to repress their enemies." When she had finished her thanks, one of the judge's officers sent her to prison until a new judge should come from the emperor.

When Christine entered that horrible tower, she kneeled, saying, "O father, creator, reigning in bliss with Jesus Christ your only begotten son, with whom the holy ghost equally lives and reigns, yet all three, substantially distinct in persons, are but one God in trinity.

"Thank you, lord, for now I trust that the time is near when you will take me to your mercy and bring me above the stars. For two judges have died here in a short time, as everyone knows. Now, lord, show me your good cheer in eternal bliss where you reign, amen."

After Zyon went where God's righteousness intended him to go, a new judge, called Julian, was sent to Tyre. He was a pagan too and a cruel man, whose pleasure—like that of his father Satan—was to pursue Christ and Christians.

To that end he was curious about the acts of judges preceding him, and soon the life and teaching of Christine was presented to him, and how she swore to judges that her will would not change. Julian sent his officers to arrest her.

When she was brought in, "By your witchcraft you have performed many wonders," he said, "but don't doubt it: you won't overcome me. I advise you to sacrifice to our immortal gods, or I shall apply such pains to you as would frighten your Jesus, born to Joseph and Mary."

"Hold your peace," Christine loudly cried, "O cruel tyrant without discretion, and at least go insane like a man! This insult no wise man's ears may hear, that you, barking like a dog without intelligence, blaspheme the holy name in whose honor every knee bends in heaven and earth and hell."

When Julian heard this he was angry and commanded her to be shut for three days in a fiercely burning oven. But Christine, trusting in the trinity, with the sign of the cross marking her forehead, entered the furnace where she praised God with devout song.

When the soldiers outside heard her praise God within the oven, they ran to Julian, saying, "We beg you humbly, sir, don't get angry with us, for when we saw Christine, whom we had shut in the oven, glorifying God, we fled for fear."

Julian, astonished with this new event, commanded the oven to be opened. There was Christine, bright as the sun; she came out all harmless, preserved by the grace of God's power, and with hymns and melodious song she exalted and praised her lord Jesus.

Then Julian ordered her before his court and demanded: "Why do you prevail? By what enchantment are you not burnt up? Tell me, or else your tender body shall be torn apart with various pains and tortures."

Christine said, "Hold your peace, miserable tyrant, devoid of goodness. Don't ask such things, which you ought not to know because of your cursedness. I care nothing for your threats and malice, for I faithfully trust in Jesus's mercy and I fear not what anyone does to me."

With this answer Julian went mad. He summoned a snake charmer, ordering him to bring out two horned serpents and two snakes. When they came, "I believe," said he, "that all your enchantments will not prevent these serpents from hurting you."

"You never learn," said Christine, "O fool, even to this extent. Do you imagine my God is like yours, with no power? No, for he who has been helper in all my torments and never forsook me can, if he wishes, defend me now and make me victorious over all your serpents."

He threw the serpents and snakes on her head, imagining that they would hurt her; but as soon as the serpents came to her, they clasped her heels and licked the dust from her feet, and clung to her breasts like infants who know no evil.

This sight stung Julian's heart with sorrow, and to the snake charmer he said, "Your craft is not worth a flitch! You must have converted to this witch's error." The snake charmer did all he could with incantations to force the snakes to bite her, but they left her and killed him instead.

When those present saw the snake charmer dead, they were so afraid of this incident that not one of them would dare approach Christine nor touch either serpent or snake. Christine, seeing this, turned her face to heaven and her prayer did make:

"O lord God who dwells in heaven and sent your son to take on our nature and called Lazarus back from hell, hear me your handmaiden who as best I can beseech you on behalf of this dead man. Revive him, lord, through your mercy, so that all reasonable people seeing this may glorify your name now and endlessly."

When she had ended her prayer, this voice came down from heaven loudly: "O blessed Christine, my dear daughter, trust me steadfastly, daughter, and persevere as you already have. For I want everyone to know that I am with you in all your works, and what you ask is granted."

Suddenly the earth roared and blessed Christine crossed the body crying, "In the name of Jesus Christ, man, rise!" And he rose and humbly fell before Christine and said, "Eternal thanks to your most worthy God, who raised me from death to life again."

Julian was sorry to see this, and said to her, grimacing, "Now since you have publicly displayed all your witchcraft here, return to our gods, thanking them that have tolerated you so patiently so long." To which Christine answered readily,

"O witless man, without fear or understanding of God and sadly blinded in your soul, don't your eyes, looking wide about, see the works of my God, the heavenly king, and those of his son Christ Jesus, which he has wrought in the sight of everyone through the might and grace of his power?"

Then Julian in his melancholy commanded her breasts to be cut off, and it was cruelly done without mercy or pity. "O estranged from truth, Julian," she said, "since you cut away my breasts, look—as a sign of clean virginity, milk for blood comes out."

And looking to heaven she said, "With all my heart, lord, thank you, king of all worlds and Christ Jesus, that you have allowed every physical hindrance to be cut away from my body. Now I know that through your protection I am ready to end my mortality and assume the crown of incorruption."

When her orison was ended, Julian, blinded with anger and melancholy, commanded her to be sent to prison without delay. There she, kneeling with holy will, magnified our lord God and continually blessed his name.

The next morning he called for her again and, when she came, asked why she would not assent to her prince's decision. "Come forward," he said, "and now offer incense to our gods, or else I will kill you; let your God, whom you serve, defend you if he can."

"Know you not, wretch," said Christine, "that God's patience still awaits your penitence and would gladly hear you? But through your stubborn negligence you always misuse his blessed patience. Plunged in the mire of cursed custom and deliberately resisting, you are accumulating vengeance for the day of judgment."

Julian, angered with what Christine said, commanded her tongue to be cut out, but she prayed first: "Lord Jesus Christ, who preserved me from my birth and never forsook me, keep me now, your handmaid, and grant me to end my battle in you, for the time of my rest draws near."

There was heard a voice in the air saying, "Because you have suffered much pain for me, dear daughter, and have always been patient in adversity, therefore the gates of heaven are opened wide to you; come in merrily and rest in peace and tranquillity and receive the crown of bliss endlessly!"

Notwithstanding this heavenly voice, Julian bade them do his command, and they tore out her tongue cruelly. While she was in this torment, she spit a piece of her tongue

with a mighty effort into his face, and it struck his eye so
hard that the sight was blinded, and she said,

"Julian, wretch, you grossly desired to take an organ
of my body and wickedly pulled the tongue out of my
mouth that always praised God's name while it could. Yet
I still have speech, but you deservedly have lost the sight
of an eye!"

Hearing this, Julian charged his hunters to slay Christine
immediately. They struck her pitilessly, making wounds on
her body. "Through your mercy," she prayed, "lord, take
my spirit unto your grace." With that word, her soul passed
out of her body into heaven,

And angels began immediately to torment Julian in various ways, so extremely that he cried, "Alas! What shall I
do? I see clearly that this is happening to me because of
Christine, whom I have slain pitilessly." When he had long
been tormented, he died and went to eternal torture.

When Julian was dead and gone, one of Christine's relatives who loved and feared God, hearing of it, came there.
Because he hoped to have heaven as reward, he made
a memorial in Apollo's temple, brought Christine's relics
there and buried them ceremoniously.

Examined under three judges was this blessed Christine
in the time of the emperor Diocletian, as her legend states.
First by her own father, Urban; then by Zyon, a cruel
tormentor; but last and worst was Julian, under whom she
ended her labors.

Thus her martyrdom lasted fourteen years under these
three judges, whom she overcame with her constancy in
Tyre, then a great city, where she was martyred on the
ninth calend of August (as we read in her legend) which
fell then on a Thursday.

Now I beseech you, O blessed Christine, who reign
with Christ in his heavenly tower as you deserve, mercifully
incline your pitying ears unto the translator who compiled
your legend, not without labor, in the English tongue; and

help, lady, that in the last hour of his mortal life he may be victor of his spiritual enemies.

Grant also, lady, to all who worship and serve you with special affection, that they repent before they die and make confession with full satisfaction before they depart this out-lawry, and afterward in heavenly religion eternally praise and magnify God with you. Amen and thank you Jesus.

HERE BEGINS THE LIFE OF
THE ELEVEN THOUSAND VIRGINS

Whoever is moved with devotion and enjoys hearing the life, progress, and passion of eleven thousand virgins all together, and the cause and occasion thereof according to *The Golden Legend*, let them listen attentively a short while here.

Once in Brittany, there lived a worthy king called Maurus, or Nothus, as the story says; and so much more was his noteworthiness that he believed only in Christ and reproved all false gods.

This Maurus had a beautiful young daughter, Ursula, who loved God first and then virginity. She was prudent and wise as well, so that her name was blown wide in every country by the trumpet of Fame.

When the king of England heard of her—he at that time was a fortunate and powerful man with many countries subjugated to his empery—he thought that nothing would increase his dignity more than if this maid were his son's wife.

This was not only his desire but his son's also; so they sent a solemn embassy to the maiden's father and, so that Maurus would make no excuses, they first promised and then threatened if the ambassadors should return home with nothing.

When Maurus heard their message, he was confused. To marry his fair young Christian daughter to a king's son who was heathen he considered unworthy.

He also supposed that when Ursula realized their purpose she would never assent. Moreover, he feared the English king because of our cruelty, which caused him great sadness.

But when Ursula considered the matter, incited by a heavenly inspiration she said, "Father, be of good cheer and grant what they ask, on this condition: that they will obey certain requirements that I will specify.

First, I ask that they send me ten of the choicest maidens, the fairest and worthiest in their country, and then assign each of us a thousand to attend us, and order ships for us, and give me three years respite to sanctify my virginity.

During this time I also ask that the king's son forsake idolatry, convert to my heavenly God, be baptized in Christ's holy name and fully instructed in my belief. With all this done, I promise to love him above any creature."

But her motive in asking all this was that either the difficulty of the conditions would make him give up and not consent; or else that she would win the maidens to Christianity and, through them, many more. This answer given, the messengers went home.

And when they had declared everything to the king, his son accepted all the grace-inspired conditions. Soon afterward he was christened and immediately asked his father to perform the rest right away.

They sent hasty word back to Ursula that everything she had specified had been performed, and so that their trouble should not be wasted they urged her to proceed to the aforesaid consecration of her maidenhead.

Then from each county in England were gathered the fairest maidens, wherever they might be found, and they were sent over to Ursula. When the extent of her request was fulfilled, they ended the gathering.

Meanwhile, on the other side, Ursula's father dutifully provided suitable means for the company, to serve and support them appropriately as his dear daughter intended and to cheer and comfort her.

When this new miracle became widely known—so many virgins assembled—many a bishop came to see the spectacle. Among them was Pantulus, bishop of Basel, who would convey them to Rome and back, and would later die with them at Cologne on their way home.

Saint Gerasina also came to visit them when she was informed of this gathering. She was sister to the martyr bishop and also to Darya, Ursula's mother. As queen of Sicily, she turned her cruel husband from a wolf into a lamb.

With her she took along her four daughters Babila, Juliane, Victoria, and Aurea; also her youngest son called Adrian, who went because of his sisters. Leaving the kingdom in her other son's hands, she sailed to Brittany and to England.

When Saint Gerasina with her five children came to Ursula, she was extremely friendly to her and the assembly to confirm them in their new grace; she too guided them to Rome and back, and died with them in Cologne.

When all was ready for their holy journey, and by Ursula's instruction the whole company was converted to Christ, they went to sea, shortly arriving at Tiel, a French port, and thence took their way to Cologne.

There an angel appeared to Ursula while she slept. He told her to be glad, for she would return to that place with her entire company and there win the palm of victory and glory through martyrdom.

"So," he said, "keep to your purpose and hurry to Rome." At his advice they went by water to the city of Basel and from there to Rome on foot to purchase their souls' health and salvation.

To Pope Ciriacus it was greatly interesting to know whence they came, for he was also born in Brittany. As he learned from their stewards, he had many a kinswoman in the assembly and therefore strove to receive them with great honor.

The same night he learned by heavenly revelation that he would be martyred with these virgins. He thanked God heartily but kept the revelation secret; and many of the virgins who were not yet christened he baptized then and there.

When the nineteenth pope after Peter had governed Christ's church for a year and eleven weeks, he called a meeting of clergy and revealed his plan. Before them all he renounced his estate and his position.

Against this they all protested, especially the cardinals. They blamed him for foolishness and for being so bestially stupid as to forsake his pontifical glory to run after a few silly women this way, without reason.

Nonetheless, he would not be moved from his purpose for anyone. He arranged for a holy man, Ametos, to be ordained in his place and to occupy the papal see; this done, he hastened to join the blessed virgins.

And because he forsook the papal dignity against the clergy's will, they unanimously ordered his name to be erased from the list of popes. Also the favor that this company of holy virgins had had in the papal court before was utterly lost henceforth.

Meanwhile, as the story tells, two princes of the ruling Roman chivalry, Maxim and Africanus, fierce and cruel, envied these blessed virgins since they saw their company daily increase.

They feared that Christianity might increase through the virgins' teaching, and paganry wane and decrease and all their own heathen rites cease. So the princes plotted by what tricks they might kill the virgins.

When they learned that the virgins would return home via Cologne, the princes sent secret messengers to their cousin Julian, prince of the Huns, asking him for the sake of them all to slay the virgins when they arrived because they were Christian.

When Pope Ciriacus went forth with these virgins, he was followed by a devout cardinal called Innocent, and by a Briton called Jacobus who for seven years had governed the bishopric of Antioch.

And since he had visited the pope at Rome and was returning home again, when he heard tell of such a multitude of virgins from his own country, he left his journey to join their company, intending to live and die with them.

The same did one Mauricius, bishop of the city of Lugnano, and another named Sulpicius, bishop of the great city of Ravenna, and both were considered very holy men. And they accompanied the virgins from Rome to Cologne.

Also Marculus, a bishop from Greece, with his niece Constance, daughter of King Dorotheus of Constantinople —she was to have married a king's son, but he died before the wedding and she had vowed her virginity to God. By heavenly revelation these people were urged to join this congregation.

When all these virgins and bishops returned from Rome with Ursula, an angel bade Ethereus, her spouse, to advise his mother to be christened; for his father had commended his soul to God's grace the first year he was a Christian.

This sweet angel advised King Ethereus not only to baptize his mother, but to go quickly to Cologne to meet his wife Ursula and greet her, so that together they, with many others, might go by martyrdom to heaven's bliss.

Obeying God's counsel he baptized his mother, taking her, his young sister Florentine, and a bishop named Clement; the four of them hastened to Cologne to join the company.

There at Cologne Ethereus and Ursula met. They found the city beset with Huns who were waiting to show these virgins their tyranny, as Prince Julian's two cousins Maxim and Africanus had asked.

When these pagans saw the blessed company approach, they cried aloud with one voice. As ravenous wolves among a flock of sheep, so acted these tyrants among this company of holy virgins and slew them.

They spared not one, neither high nor low, man nor woman, but threw down all with dint of death. It was pitiful to say and hear how cruelly they killed this multitude, excepting only Ursula, as the story tells.

When Julian, prince of the Huns, noticed her beauty, "Cheer up, woman," he said, "for if you will consent to me I will defend you from all discomfort and even wed you with a ring and bring you to wealth and honor."

But she would in no way assent to him, wherefore in his great melancholy he bent a mighty bow and smote her with a sharp arrow through the body: it fell to earth but the soul went to eternal joy.

Yet one maiden, Cordula, according to the legend hid herself in a ship and survived the massacre. No one found her, but when next morning dawned she offered herself to martyrdom, illumined by God's grace, and was martyred.

But since this blessed virgin did not suffer the pain of martyrdom along with the rest of the group, her feast is not held with theirs. That is why she appeared long after to a holy recluse and asked that her commemoration should be held right after theirs.

Thus this multitude of virgins was martyred the 21st of October and the 12th calend of November, at Cologne. Their bodies rest in a nunnery and their souls dwell above the sky.

And so that there should be no obstacles to belief in this matter, God has showed their holiness by different miracles here over the years, of which whoever wishes to hear I will tell two that their legend narrates.

Once there was an abbot in Cologne who, as their story tells, requested the abbess that he might have the body of one of these virgins for his spiritual comfort. He promised faithfully that within a year he would arrange to have it enclosed in a silver coffin.

When he had the body on his high altar, he placed it in a wooden coffin and let it remain for a whole year with no effort to improve it. Because he had reneged on his promise, the body wished to remain there no longer but wanted to return home again.

So, soon after, when the monks were gathered one night at matins, this virgin, seeing them all present, came down from the altar and bowed to God almighty, walked among the monks and returned to her first resting place.

The abbot ran to the coffin and when he found it empty, he was, as well he ought to be, a sad man. The next day he went to the nunnery to tell the abbess what had happened, and they found the body in the same place where it had been at first.

The abbot wanted to have it, or another one, back again, but he couldn't: "For know this," said the abbess, "sir abbot, since she has voluntarily come home, she won't as far as I am concerned be removed again, I assure you." And so the frustrated abbot went home sorry.

Another miracle is also told about a religious man who was devoted to these virgins. He happened to fall grievously ill, and a beautiful maid appeared to him, royally dressed and amazingly fresh of face, and asked if he knew her.

This man, astonished by her sudden arrival, answered that he did not know her. "I want you to know," she said, "that I am one of that large assembly that you have long loved and busily served. I come to teach you what can help you and how you can please me and my companions.

"If you wish once before you die to worship God and honor others, say eleven thousand pater nosters. Your reward for this labor shall be that I and my sisters shall attend you in the last hour of your life to comfort you against all your enemies."

When this was said she vanished away, and he began, as devoutly as he could, to say these pater nosters. He never stopped until he had completed the number she required; which done, he sent to his abbot,

Saying, "Father, with humble will let me be anointed quickly." As soon as he had taken the sacrament, he loudly began to wail: "Flee hence, I beg you all, and yield place to these holy virgins who come here by their grace."

The abbot asked what he meant, and he told him the revelation; so they quickly left the chamber as he asked, and when later they returned he had passed away with this company of blessed virgins to God's mercy.

Lo, in this way and in many more than I can now tell or narrate, has been shown long ago the holiness of this fellowship of good and wise people. Therefore I counsel everyone to rise out of sin and before they die say eleven thousand pater nosters in worship of these virgins.

Whoever will do so, if he be also contrite and clean shriven, will be helped, through these virgins' merits, at the end of his life. Who wishes to know how to perform this entire number in a year, the calendar shows the right way.

Three hundred and sixty-five days are in a year, as is calculated by arithmetic, on which principle I estimate that thirty pater nosters each day, with an extra one on Sundays, makes up the entire number plus two.

Now, holy Ursula, with your fellowship, vouchsafe to defend and keep from all mischief those who love and serve you, and maintain them in chastity; and so that none of them may die in deadly sin, obtain for them the grace of true repentance before they pass away. Amen and thank you Jesus.

HERE BEGINS THE LIFE OF
SAINT FAITH

Once, when fierce Diocletian exercised his cruel tyranny along with his cursed colleague Maximian, he caused many a Christian to die; for where they noticed any Christians the decree was to kill them without mercy or pity.

Therefore they sent cruel ministers of iniquity into every country throughout their empire to inquire about Christ's servants, and, if they heard of any, they sent the Christians to their emperor or slew them with various torments.

Dacian was among them, too, one of the cruelest (as I have read), for so full of Satan was he that all his pleasure was to shed the blood of Christians. He offered large rewards to all who would bring him any news of Christians.

This cruel tyrant in his madness whirled from country to country making everyone kneel and bow to his false gods, and whoever would not readily obey his commandments he had killed with harsh torture.

When he came to Spain, he entered a city called Agen, where he was informed about a maid named Faith living there, who would not honor the gods but despised them.

This maid was born of the noblest blood in the city, as far as her natural gifts were concerned; and though she was lovely she was also good, in all her behavior chaste and pure, serious of countenance and demure in expression, neither wanton nor foolish in word or deed, for she hated nothing but vice.

No wonder: for she was well trained in Christ's school in her youth, and solidly edified in the faith by wise and good people, so that no violence could move her heart from it, for her life was according to her name.

Faith was her name, and faithfully she always trusted in Christ Jesus, loving with a dove's simplicity and a turtle-dove's chastity. Because she wished not to lose her virginity she chose to be Christ's wife only and no other's, even if she should lose her life for it.

For she knew full well that even if she lost her temporal life for Christ's sake, it wouldn't harm her at all, for she would have eternal and immortal life instead. In order to achieve this, she would refuse no earthly pain.

She set no store by worldly opinion and she despised wealth as dung, for all her thought was to serve God. She would value no fleshly lusts but forsook them, and would not call their idols "gods" but called them all "devils' dens."

When this melancholic tyrant Dacian heard of her, he ordered her to appear before him. His men searched her out, but she went voluntarily, and though they dragged her out fiercely, she was not afraid of them.

Just before she came into Dacian's presence, she made the sign of the cross to protect herself, and devoutly she prayed with mouth and heart: "Lord who reigns in heaven above, keep me steadfast now in your love!

"Give me abundant eloquence, lord, when I am brought before this tyrant, and strength and constancy in your faith, and let me care nothing for his tyranny, and, though he assail me with grievous torment, let me neither in word nor thought consent to their desire."

When she was brought to the tyrant, standing before him with attractive and serious appearance, he asked her name and she answered, "I am called Faith and always have been from the time of my birth." "Faith," said he, "what is your faith and your belief? Tell me quickly." "I am Christian. I am truly Christ's servant and have been since I first had any intelligence. I have made myself his spouse and will never forsake him for another."

When Dacian heard this, with simulated expression, half smiling as if he intended a joke, "Fair Faith," he said, "don't be obstinate, but listen to me. I will suggest another way more suitable to your beauty, your youth, and your noble birth.

"If you wish to preserve physical chastity, first forsake Christ and offer yourself to serve Diana, whose nature is like yours, and wear black clothing in her temple. I shall make you so exalted in respect and riches that people will crawl to you."

"For your promises and your fine talk I care nothing," she said, "for as the holy fathers' doctrine teaches, your gods are nothing but devils. So I am surprised that you advise me to despise the true God and his true faith and to sacrifice to false gods."

With the answer he grew very angry and particularly that she called his gods "devils." He swore an oath that unless she would fall down prostrate and sacrifice to all his gods, he would have her killed with new tortures never seen before.

But Faith, who was grounded in stability and strengthened by the examples of many glorious martyrs, and had security through hope of everlasting bliss, steadfastly gave this answer: that she would gladly suffer such torture for Christ's sake, and also death.

He was furious with this, and overcome with the rage of madness, he commanded that she be led to a brass bed, or grill, and be spread out there in four directions, and be bound to it with chains and a great fire made beneath, to dismay her.

When she was brought to where this brass torture device stood burning hot, voluntarily Faith went onto it. Some bound her to it, some brought pans with coals, some threw in oil and grease that her pain should increase.

Some turned her back and forth on the griddle with forks of iron, some blew so hard that the flames sprung up all around her. None had compassion on her except those standing next to her, who hid their faces for pity.

And many cried thus: "O fierce and cruel tormentors, we cannot conceive why you assail this blessed maid with such sharp blows, and why you trouble yourselves to kill her with such terrible pain, except that she serves God in heaven.

"O unpiteousness! O unjust judgments! and O perverse will! To us it seems absolutely unreasonable that this servant of God, this innocent, should be slain with such torment, without consideration of her tender age or the worthiness of her lineage.

"If you wish to know what we will do, we utterly forsake all idolatry, and we will turn to Faith's God for whom we are ready to die with her. We defy all your false gods, who can neither help nor harm anyone."

When this was told to Dacian, he instantly ordered all of them beheaded. Many bodies were thrown to the ground headless, and, to dismay Faith the more and increase her torment, it was done before her eyes.

On that side of the city where Phoebus's meridional arc throws the shadow of every tree, tower, and wall—that is, in the septentrional region toward the polestar that guides shipmen—stands a high hill next to the walls.

This hill is craggy and cavernous, lacking a road or path to guide people, and full of trees and bushes so thick that it is difficult to climb the hill. Whoever is on that hill can see whatever is done publicly in the city below if they look carefully.

In large caves in that hill, many people from the town hid out, fleeing the persecution of cruel Dacian. Many of them, when Faith suffered her torment, stood and witnessed it.

Among them was a young nobleman called Caprasius, and when he saw Faith tormented thus, he kneeled down and lifted his visage upward and with devout heart prayed, "Lord, for your mercy, give Faith the victory over Dacian.

"And also, Lord, if it offend not your goodness, I desire more: Since Faith suffers such great violence of pain and is so badly tortured, what reward will she have for it hereafter, and does she feel any comfort or remedy during her torture?"

When his prayer was done, a white dove from heaven appeared before his sight, bearing a crown of bright gold set with gems brighter than the sun. He thought the dove flew to where Faith lay covered in torments.

As the dove hovered fluttering over her it began to shake its wings gently. With the dew that fell from them the red coals grew black, and therewith Faith's pains grew less; with the dew that fell on her, all her wounds were perfectly cured.

She was immediately clad in a snow-white gown and mantle, and then the dove set the glorious shining crown on her head. When all this was done the dove took flight, returned to heaven, and was seen no more.

Seeing all this, Caprasius arose from his prayer and thanked God for these signs through which he realized that temporal pain, if suffered patiently, is the way to eternal joy.

As he arose, he suddenly smote the hill with his right hand, and there sprang out a well full of bright, clear water of such efficacy that to taste it will heal anyone, through this martyr's merits, of whatever illness he feels.

Then he ran down from the hill. Unperceived by anyone he approached the place where Faith suffered her passion, and he publicly confessed that Christ is God and none but he, and that all other gods are devils.

The tyrant commanded he be presented; asked his name, birth and kin. Caprasius answered fearlessly,

"First I acknowledge the most important thing, that I was christened by a priest at a stone font, and was called Caprasius. Therefore I will worship no false gods, but I serve him who united Jews and pagans against him, Christ Jesus, for whom you persecute this virgin."

"I am sorry for you," said Dacian, "that you err so badly in your belief; and because you are so handsome a young man I should be reluctant to harm you. That you err I prove thus: for Christ was betrayed by his disciple and assaulted with torment to die on a cross.

"To place confidence in one who was tortured for his sin I consider a great error. So leave it, repent of your misbelief, and learn better behavior from those wiser than you. Worship the gods that didn't die, and reject this crucified Christ.

"If you agree to my advice and behave as I tell you, I will present you to the emperors so that through their acquaintance you shall come to great dignity, to worthy estate, and to high honor, and be lord of many a castle and tower."

But Caprasius cared not a fly for all these high offers of worship, wealth, and dignity that Dacian promised—so well rooted was he in Christ's faith. "I prefer to dwell in the palace of him who made all things and who redeemed mankind at high price.

"Him I love and serve alone. But you, Dacian, inebriate with vain hope, care nothing for him, deluded by your goddess called Diana who can't help at all; for it would be surprising if a stick or stone should grant life when it has none itself.

"Since you advise me to do wrong, I will reciprocate with sounder advice, through which you may eschew the endless pain that is certainly ordained for you. Worship my God and forsake sin, and you shall have endless joy."

"Leave this folly," said Dacian, "and hasten to worship my gods, or else I promise you truly that I will apply to you the same pains you see this rebel Faith suffer. But follow my advice, and I will enhance your reputation."

"I care nothing for your great offers," said Caprasius, "for I trust my lord Jesus is best able to advance me. He is true in words, and in works holy; he promises his servants in joy to dwell, and his rebels the pain of hell.

"And Faith whom you torment here shall rejoice and be glad everlastingly, while you shall wallow in hellfire and forevermore weep and be sorry. From her example I am ready to suffer temporary pain and be sure of endless joy for it."

Dacian understood the steadfastness of Caprasius's heart, and knew he could not pervert him from Christ's faith for anything, neither by promise nor threat. "I will no longer," he said, "employ this technique nor permit that in such verbal battle I should be overcome and he prevail.

"Therefore, tormentors, I charge you to assail this rebel with pains: spare him not for being young and tough, but make his blood rain out on every side." They beat him till they dropped, and in all his pains he cheerfully cried, "Jesus, thank you."

And to the people nearby he preached, saying, "Sirs, dread not this tyrant, I advise you, nor obey him whose power lasts only a little while and shall pass away, no one knows how. Fear only him who can throw your body and soul into eternal pain."

At these words of exhortation, the people wept; seeing this cruel examination they cried loudly with one voice: "O pitiless and merciless men, why do you trouble with such cruel torment this blessed man, this holy innocent?"

For Caprasius had a special faculty: that he was beloved by everyone who looked at him, for he was bright of hue and neither pale nor wan in color. And what especially irked the cursed Dacian was Caprasius's constancy, for no pain could ever make him complain.

While Faith and Caprasius were thus cruelly tortured, two brothers, Primus and Felicianus, stood in the crowd. When they saw the others meekly endure their pain, the brothers turned to Christ, rejecting all false gods,

And aspired to join the two. They ran to them and spoke their minds and instantly they were tortured as well. Thus these four united had the victory over furious Dacian.

When he saw them comfort one another in their pain and virtuously exhort one another to perseverance, he went nearly mad with melancholy. He had them led to a temple nearby, to sacrifice or to be beheaded.

At the temple they refused to sacrifice but were ready to die in the service of him who made all things. They were beheaded forthwith and so went to everlasting joy.

When they were beheaded, the cursed pagans left the bodies in the field to be devoured by animals; but when night came, Christians secretly managed to bury them with great respect.

It was only a simple place where they lay for many years. When paganry had ended in that country, through God's grace, and Christ had brought his faith into the light, a bishop, stirred by devotion, desired to make their translation.

He thought it appropriate to the common good of the city to found and build a church to be hallowed in honor of Faith. But he deferred the work a long time, believing himself unworthy to perform such a holy thing.

This bishop's name was Dulcidius, a man of particular perfection. In his sleep he was thus admonished: "Defer your intention no longer but execute it quickly, for by that deed you may obtain grace for yourself and your city."

Quickly he assembled monks and priests and told them his revelation. They advised him to perform the deed, and they helped him, and soon it was done.

When it was completed, he took up Faith's body and reverently translated it there, founding a house of black monks where for Faith's sake God has showed many miracles and still does to this very day.

Now, blessed Faith, obtain for all who serve you both true faithfulness and perseverant steadfastness of faith, and preserve them from all trouble always. Allow them never to die in sin but when they are to pass from this outlawry, grant them to die in final grace.

And especially, lady, because of your passion, show the grace of special favor to him who, from pure devotion, was translator of your legend into English. Grant him, lady, in his last hour of living to be cleansed from sin, for he on your day to live did first begin. Amen and thank you Jesus.

SAINT AGNES'S LIFE

Agnes sacra sui pennam scriptoris inauret
Et det ut inceptum perficiatur opus.

Prologue

Saint Agnes's life I plan to write in English according
to my ability, as Saint Ambrose teaches me: he wrote it in
high style. Now, blessed virgin, pray God to confer grace on
me so that I may adequately fulfill my promise and acquit
myself.

Moreover, as humbly as I can manage I beg every reader
not to despise it, though it be rude, for Pallas has never led
me into the motleyed meadow of Tully's *Rhetoric* to gather
flowers of skillful eloquence; but whenever I hurried that
way, with great disdain she ordered me away.

Still I prayed her with humble reverence that she might
show me some favor, and she answered me plainly: "You
come too late, for the freshest flowers are already gathered
up by three people, of whom two have already finished their
fate while Atropos still favors the third: they are Gower,
Chaucer, and John Lydgate."

So, since Pallas berated me and drove me away
so harshly, I will never argue with her nor presume to

81

approach Tully's meadow. Therefore I will speak and write plainly according to the language of Suffolk speech, and whoever doesn't like it, let them look for better wherever they like.

Agnes was derived from "agna"—so says Jacob da Voragine. "Agna" is a lamb, a very meek and simple animal. These qualities belong suitably to Agnes, for she was so grounded in them that no adversity could budge her from meek and simple innocence.

Agnes is also derived—as this scholar says—from knowledge; and appropriately, for she knew the way of truth while she was young; which truth, as Augustine says, is contrary to three vices that Agnes vanquished in her living: falsehood, deceit, and vanity.

By faith she overcame falsehood, and by hope she despised all vanity; by perfect charity she removed all deceit. To these three we find good correspondence in her life, but to avoid prolixity—which often causes boredom in the hearer—I won't describe it now.

O holy lamb of God, O blessed Agnes, who were so enflamed in your youth with the fervent heat of God's love that no fierce rage of pain could change your courage nor bend your heart from him—obtain me wit, lady, and language to complete your life now begun.

Here Begins the Life of Saint Agnes

I servant of Christ, Bishop Ambrose, send greeting to you holy virgins, exhorting you to arrange a festival to hallow a young maiden; in which festival all people may rejoice with sweet-sounding psalms and Christ's poor may be glad.

Let us all now rejoice in our lord, and to the edification of virginity we record how blessed Agnes was martyred while she was young, for in her thirteenth year she lost death and found life because she loved only the author of nature.

Though she was young by annual computation, in her soul she was mature enough, and so she was in contradictory condition: young in body but wise of soul. And though she was lovely in her bodily visage and endowed with great beauty, yet she was even fairer in her soul because of faith.

While this gem of virginity was coming home from school one day, she was desired by the prefect's son who asked her friends about her. He offered much and promised more, bringing precious ornaments with him, which Agnes valued as dung.

But this lively young man was even more provoked to love her and, imagining she wanted better ornaments, he brought many a ring with him and bright shining precious stones; both he and his friends conveyed his affection to the maiden.

Riches he offered in great plenty, solemn and stately palaces, large landholdings and retinue and all the ceremonial glory of this world—on condition she would not refuse to be joined with him in marriage. To him this wise Agnes said,

"Go away from me, you encourager of sin and opponent of every good intention. Go away from me, for you need to know that I am expected by another lover who has sent me preciouser ornaments and has warranted me with the ring of his faith better than you with your family and wealth.

"He has arrayed my right hand with a precious ring of gold and girt my neck with incomparable precious stones. He has given me innumerable pearls and surrounded me with bright shining gems on every side.

"He has set a special mark in my face that none but he should be loved, and he has clad me in a mantel of golden weave in which are set many precious brooches. He has showed me incomparable treasure to draw me on if only I have perseverance in his love.

"Therefore I can pay no attention to you, who have such a lover in contempt, a lover to whom I am bound in charity, whose kindred are higher than yours, whose power and strength much stronger, his love sweeter, face fairer, and innocence far more graceful—

"My chamber is prepared for this lover, whose organs have made melody for me and the singing of whose maidens is real bliss. I have taken many a kiss of his mouth, sweeter than milk or honey. Often he has embraced me in his arms without blemishing my virginity.

"His body is united with mine and he has decked my cheeks with his blood. His mother is a virgin and his father too; angels serve him humbly; the sun and moon marvel at his beauty, and his odor reinvigorates the dead, I dare say.

"His riches never slip away with fortune's fickle transmutation, so I keep faith with him and always will with hearty devotion. Listen now to my conclusion and take this for my plain answer: I shall never love anyone but him."

When this young man had heard blessed Agnes's answer, he was sad. Blind love pained him so badly that he sickened, anguished in body and soul, and lay down in bed. But his deep sighs revealed him to the doctors, who told his father the situation.

When he saw that his son's affection was set on Agnes, the prefect repeated and even increased the offers. But his labor was lost, for she said plainly that she would never reject her first spouse's offer.

Because he occupied at that time the high position of prefect, he thought that no other creature could be preferred before himself in respect, so he wondered who it might be that Agnes boasted of and who made such a show of treasure.

While he said this, one of those flattering jokers stood by who said, "Sir, this maiden has been a Christian from youth. She is so deluded in the witchcraft taught and practiced in Christian doctrine that she imagines Christ is her husband."

The prefect was glad to hear this and sent a troop of constables to bring her in. As soon as she arrived, he made her a flattering private sermon with many great promises, and then menaced and threatened.

But Christ's maiden would be deceived neither with flattery nor terror, but with steadfast expression and healthy color she stood before him. Because she was rooted in Christ's amour, she inwardly despised the prefect's threats and promises.

Seeing such constancy and steadfastness in this young maid, the prefect spoke to her father and mother. Because of their noble estate he could not attack them with open violence, but, wishing to trouble them another way, he accused them of Christianity.

Next day he commanded Agnes to appear, and he spoke of his son's love and how he was nearly dead for her sake. But Agnes scorned his words and when the prefect saw that, he brought her to his judge's bench where the law was executed.

Said he, "Unless the witchcraft of these Christians' superstition is taken out of you somehow, no one will be able to remove the madness from your heart nor will your ears attend to wise counsel.

"So my judgment is now to send you to the goddess Vesta where, if the pursuit of virginity please you, you may attend to it, and no one will blame you if you are humbly occupied night and day in Vesta's service."

"If I chastise your son for Christ's sake and won't have him—your son who is troubled with foul love, even though he is a living man with intelligence and reason—then do you believe I am going to worship dumb idols and injure divine grace by bowing my head to useless stones?"

"Indeed," said the prefect, "my wish is to protect your youth, and so I won't punish your blasphemy; and because you are still sane, presumably, I advise you not to anger our gods with such stubborn spite."

"Don't," she said, "count on my physical youth, O vicious prefect, so far as to suppose that I want you to be kind to me. Virtuous faith doesn't consist in bodily years but in soul's knowing, and God almighty knows more than age can certify.

As for your gods, whose wrath you would not expose me to, please let them be angry whenever you wish, and let them address me in our own language and teach me how they would like to be worshiped. But they can't, so go ahead and exercise your will in me."

"Choose one," said Symphronius the prefect, "Agnes, as I declare. Either serve the goddess Vesta with other virgins, or you shall be abused with common women, and these Christian witches will be far from you, they whose craft has emboldened you to come so brazenly to this wretchedness.

"So I sentence you, and pay attention: either sacrifice to goddess Vesta for the respect and honor of your family; or if you won't—so help me my gods—to the destruction of your nobility you shall be the disgrace of a common brothel."

Then blessed Agnes, inflamed with grace and strengthened with spiritual steadfastness, standing right in front of the prefect spoke her mind: "If you knew, wretch, who my God really is, you'd judge better and not speak this way.

"But because I know the high power, the sovereign grace and works of our lord God, blessed Jesus, I certainly despise all your threats, trusting in his goodness that I shall neither sacrifice to idols nor be defiled with sinners' filth.

"For know this too, and not only you but everyone here: I have a guardian angel who protects my body and preserves and helps me in every need, and that makes me be brave and unafraid.

"Also, God's son, begotten only from his father's substance, immutable and endlessly eternal—because you don't know him you are damned—he is an impenetrable wall to me, a watchman never sleeping, a defender never failing.

"But your gods, as wise people know, are made either of brass, which is better used to make cauldrons of, or pots and pans or such things, which would at least be useful and inexpensive; or they're made of stones, which would be better laid in the slough, to keep people off a muddy road.

"As anyone can prove, immortal divinity has no habitation in stones, nor in brass or other metal, but has its supernal reign in heaven. So you and whoever else worships them will certainly come to the same pain.

"For just as these idols were composed in their present likeness in a hot fire, so shall their servants likewise be blown by hellfire and perish eternally, never to cool, because they confused others."

Hearing that, the judge nearly went mad. He commanded her to be stripped shamefully and led to the brothelhouse, with a herald in advance calling: "This Agnes, this witch, who scornfully blasphemes our gods, I legally condemn to the common brothel."

But as soon as she was stripped, the bands slid away from her hair which God gave such thickness that it cloaked her all around and so completely hid her nakedness that she seemed to be better covered with her hair than with her clothes.

When Agnes thus devoutly arrayed entered the place of uncleanness—the brothel, I mean—she found there an angel ready to cover her with light so bright that when she was fully surrounded with it, no one could touch or see her.

This glorious brightness so illuminated her entire cell that never did the sun in its heavenly compass or its greatest power shine brighter than did this house by grace divine; and whoever presumed to look at it felt a sudden twinge in his eye.

When Agnes saw this brightness sent her by God through her prayer, she lay down prostrate to him, and there appeared before her a white stole. She gladly took it and put it on, then said to God,

"Thank you, lord of all gentleness, for grace and comfort and kindness shown to me through your goodness now and always in various ways. Thank you, lord, who, numbering me among your handmaidens, have now sent me from heaven this new white vestment."

When Agnes had put on this cloth as white as snow or lily, it fitted her so perfectly that no one who saw it could doubt it was made by angels' hands.

Behold this gracious permutation! A brothel is made, through prayer, a special place of devotion in which whoever entered went out worshiping God gladly and wholeheartedly, purer through God's grace than when he entered the place.

When the prefect's son heard that Agnes was in the brothel he grew quite jolly, and with a company of young fellows he hastened there, hoping now to perform his foul fleshly lust with her.

When he arrived and saw many young men wantonly entering the place where she was and coming out quite soberly and with great respect, he loudly rebuked them and called them wretches, saying, "Vain cowards, foul befall you!"

Thus scorning them he went to the place where Agnes lay in prayer; and because he presumed to enter irreverent and impudent into the clear light that she was in, he suddenly fell down on his face and the devil strangled him there.

When his companions outside saw that he tarried so long inside, they assumed he had overcome her by some trick and was occupied in the work of sin. They ran in merrily to congratulate him on his victory.

When they entered and looked about, they found him lying dead on his face. Their eyes bugged out as if they were mad, and, ripping their clothing, they cried: "O noble Romans, kill this witch here inside, who through her witchcraft has taken the prefect's son's life!"

When rumor circulated through the city about this young man's death, everyone ran to the place to witness the unfortunate accident, and when they saw it they loudly expressed their various opinions: some called her a witch, and some innocent.

But when the prefect heard this news of his son's death, he went mad and ran to the theater in despair. He saw his son's body lying there stark dead and accused Agnes:

"O you cruelest of all women, why did you want to practice your witchcraft on my son this way, without pity? What was your reason, now tell me!" And since he asked her often, she modestly replied,

"Your son's death, sir, do not blame on me, for I am guiltless of it. But he whose will your son would have done took control of him quite rightfully. If you ask why all others who came before him escaped harmless, I answer thus:

"All those who entered before him to me—to whom God's goodness sent this great light by an angel and arrayed me in this white garment—they humbly thanked God and dared not move to touch me, and so they escaped without harm.

"But your son did not as they did. When he entered, he would shamelessly have done his fleshly foul will and did not reverence the light I was in. When he presumed to come near me, the angel of God in my defense drove him away to death, as you see."

"Agnes," said the prefect, "by one thing it shall appear to me clearly that your working is not by witchcraft: if you will pray your angel that he agree to restore my son, whom I see here dead, living to me." Agnes answered,

"Although your faith is not worthy to have what you ask," she said, "nonetheless because it is time to show the power of our lord Jesus in front of this crowd of people— go out, all of you, that I may now, as I was accustomed to do, offer him the sacrifice of prayer."

When everyone had left, Agnes fell down flat on her face, and weeping sadly with devout heart she prayed God through his special grace that he might show a token of his mercy and pity there and that the young man might be reinvigorated.

An angel appeared while she prayed, lifted her up and encouraged her and said that her request was granted. The young man immediately arose and hurried out, crying loudly,

"One God—the Christians' God—is in heaven and earth and sea, for all the temples made to gods are mere vanity and the same for the gods worshiped in them, for they can't help themselves nor anyone else in any emergency."

At this all the witches and bishops of the temples cried aloud, "Put away this witch and kill her, for she changes minds and turns them around." With these words a rebellion grew among the people, more than in a long time.

Seeing this, the prefect was astonished and also afraid to be proscribed if he did anything to defend Agnes contrary to the pagan bishops' decree. So, to quell the popular sedition, he appointed a vice-regent in his stead.

Then the prefect went home in a hurry, saddened that he could not rescue Agnes from torment as he wished, since she had raised his son from death to life.

Aspasius, the prefect's vice-regent, assenting to the seditious people, made a huge fire and put Agnes in the middle of it. Immediately the flame divided in two and burnt people on each side but didn't come near Agnes.

The furious people would not ascribe this to God's power but to a witch's working, and they loudly blasphemed and screamed. Agnes, standing amidst the fire with her hands spread wide, devoutly made her prayer to God with these words:

"O almighty God, most full of power, most worthy to be worshiped and feared, father of our lord Christ Jesus, blessed are you for through your son I have escaped wicked men's threats, and through your grace I have avoided the devil's uncleanness by an undefiled path.

"Now I see, lord, that by your spirit I am bathed in dew from heaven. The fire dies beside me and the flame is miraculously divided, so that no heat comes near me but it burns them, according to your will, who built it to torment me.

"Now blessed are you, father, most worthy to be preached and praised in every country, who through your grace have kindly made me fearless among the flames of fire, and though others would torment me, you make me come to you happily.

"What I've believed, lord, now I see; thanks to your blessed grace, what I have thirsted for I now hold; what I have coveted I now embrace and hold to my great spiritual comfort, wherefore with lips and heart, lord, entirely, I will evermore confess and desire you.

"See and behold how I come to you, living and true and almighty God, who with Jesus your son in equal degree and with the holy ghost inseparably now live and reign interminably in one substance as I well know, from world into worlds evermore, amen."

When Agnes had completed her prayer as devoutly as she could—and in much better fashion than I can write here— so suddenly quenched was the whole fire that there was no more heat or fire than if no fire had ever been before.

Aspasius, the prefect's vicar, seeing this and in order to appease the seditious people, commanded a sword to be plunged into her throat. Thus this holy maid, this innocent, cruelly martyred for Christ's sake, Christ took unto himself as his spouse.

Her father and mother were not saddened at her death, for they were Christians, but with great joy they took her body to a place of theirs outside the walls and buried it there near the highway called Nomentana because it goes to the city of Nomentum.

There, while they watched many nights at her tomb with others, a great company of maidens came near, just at midnight. The maidens wore golden garments and a great light went before them.

Among these maidens they saw their daughter, blessed Agnes, in a similar shining garment, at her right hand a pretty snow-white lamb walking beside her, and to them this was a marvelous sight.

Agnes begged her companions to stay still a moment, and she addressed her friends: "Don't lament me as dead but be glad of my exaltation, for with this blessed and glorious company I have now entered the bright seats of heaven.

"And I am perpetually joined in heaven to him whom, while living on earth, I loved past every living thing." Then in the twinkling of an eye they all vanished away and no one saw more of them ever again.

When the rumor of this revelation was spread about by the trumpet of Fame to many a castle and many a town, so that it continually grew, the whole story was told by some who knew it well to Dame Constance, daughter of Constantine the emperor.

This Constance was a glorious queen and prudent maid, as the story tells, but she had a serious disease: she was covered with sores from head to foot so that no limb was free from sores.

Since no medical lore could help or cure her, she was advised to go to Agnes's tomb, hoping and trusting to recover her health. And so she did, and when she arrived she prayed devoutly, although she was a heathen.

As Constance lay in prayer, she fell asleep and blessed Agnes appeared to her saying, "O Constance, be constant and believe Christ, God's son, to be your savior, and he shall cure and heal your disease."

Constance awoke at this voice, as healthy and healed as she could be, and when she looked at herself there was no sign of infirmity on any limb. She went home to her palace and told her father and brothers what had happened.

For joy the whole city assembled, and when they heard the news all were amazed. Heathen unfaithfulness was confounded, and the faith and high power of the faith of Christ Jesus commended.

In Rome and elsewhere this opinion became known: that whoever came to Agnes's tomb with devotion would be healed of whatever infirmity; and no wise man doubts that Christ still does it to this very day.

Meanwhile Constance begged her father and brothers that they would grant a church to be made over Agnes's body, and nearby a place where Constance might live the rest of her life in black clothing and serve Saint Agnes the pure virgin.

The emperor's daughter, blessed Constance, whom Agnes had cured of all disease, persevered in perfect virginity. Through her, many Roman maidens of high and low degree were consecrated with a holy veil to God and to blessed Agnes.

And because faith suffers no damage by death, many of the young Roman virgins—following blessed Agnes with devout courage, as if she were still living—persevere by example of Agnes's powerful working, hoping to get thereby the glorious palm of perpetual victory.

Lo! now I have briefly completed Saint Agnes's life as I promised to do in the prologue, according to the writing of Saint Ambrose whom it was my purpose to follow—not word for word, for, as Jerome states, that is impossible in any translation—

But from sentence to sentence I dare say I have followed him pretty carefully. Yet it is hard to follow him, for he writes most elaborately and most oddly among all the doctors of the church, and whoever doesn't believe me can test it by reading his books.

Thank you, Saint Ambrose, holy doctor, who had such affection for Saint Agnes that you wished to undertake the blessed labor of writing her life for the instruction of virgins. You found it secretly concealed in a corner of oblivion and thought it a pity that it should be lost by negligence.

Thank you also, blessed virgin and martyr, most gracious Agnes, who willingly inclined your ears to the opening prayer I made to you. Thank you, lady, for now I have done everything, and for my reward, lady, obtain for me that after this misery I may see you in bliss. Amen, thank you Jesus.

THE LIFE OF SAINT DOROTHY

When Christ's faith was young and new and not yet firmly rooted, many a tyrant persecuted it and attempted to destroy it utterly. Among them the cruelest in violence were Diocletian and his companion in malice, Maximian.

In their time there dwelt in Rome a worthy man called Dorotheus, descended by senators from the high and noble blood of Romulus; he had a wife suited to his rank, named Theodora.

This Dorotheus, seeing the persecution of Christ's faith grow (for he was Christian), left Rome and all his possessions, including vineyards, fields, and stately homes; he left with his wife Theodora and their two daughters Christen and Calisten.

He fled into the kingdom of Cappadocia and into the royal city of Caesaria, where he and his wife begot a daughter, whom they named Dorothy at the baptismal font; she was secretly baptized by the bishop Appolinar.

Dorothy, from her youth filled with grace of the holy ghost, grew in virtue and goodness, and her special comfort was to preserve bodily chastity and to avoid fleshly corruption. As for physical beauty, she surpassed all the maidens of that country.

But the devil, who always has enmity against chastity, pricked Fabricius—prefect of the city—with such keen love for glorious Dorothy that Fabricius sent for her, offering plenty of treasure and to endow her with property and to wed her with a ring.

When Dorothy heard his talk, she—inwardly stabilized with grace and despising these temporal delights—set at nought all worldly wealth. When brought before him she confessed openly that she was Christ's spouse.

Fabricius went mad with this answer and ordered her placed in a barrel filled with burning oil; but trusting in her spouse Jesus she was as merry and glad in it as if she'd been anointed with sweet balm.

Many a pagan, seeing this miracle, was inwardly converted to Christ. Fabricius, ascribing it to witchcraft, had her taken quickly to prison, where she went without food for nine days, by angels' ministration fed with heavenly consolation.

When she was brought before the judge and her beauty was not diminished at all but rather increased, all who saw her wondered how she, so long without food, might increase in physical beauty.

Fabricius, blinded in his madness, set no store by this great miracle and said, "Unless you worship my gods meekly and without delay, I shall have you hung on a gibbet." "I will worship God," she said, "not devils nor dolls such as your gods are."

With that she fell to earth and lifted her eyes heavenward, praying thus: "Lord, for your mercy, show your power here publicly and prove by some token from heaven now that you are God, and none but you."

Then a high marble pillar which Fabricius had set up and on which there was an ugly idol, was so violently wiped out by angels sent from heaven, that no part of either idol or pillar was left after her prayer.

And a voice was heard high in the air, crying, "Why do you bother us so often, Dorothy, tender young maiden?" Because of this many a pagan was converted from misliving and martyred there for Christ.

Up on a gibbet with her feet in the air they hung Dorothy horribly, and beat her body with rods and whips, and with iron hooks tore her flesh cruelly, and burnt her breasts with firebrands, and after taking her down half dead they shut her in prison.

The next day when she was brought before the judge, not a spot or wound appeared on her. Fabricius was amazed and said, "O noble young girl, I advise you to convert, for you are sufficiently chastised now."

He sent her two sisters, Cristen and Calisten, who had forsaken Christ for fear of torture; he imagined he would convert her through them. But the contrary occurred to what he planned, for through Dorothy her two sisters were both reconverted to Christ.

Hearing this, Fabricius went nearly insane, and in his madness he devised a new torture: he ordered the two sisters chained back to back and cast into a fire. This done, he began to menace glorious Dorothy:

"How much longer will you occupy us with your witch-craft day after day? Now both your sisters are dead and gone, but you may live if you will. Sacrifice to my gods and I will relieve you; otherwise I will cut off your head."

Dorothy answered this meekly: "I am ready to suffer whatever you wish for my lord and my spouse Jesus. I always have been, since I first knew him in whose garden I shall gather roses and apples and be merry with him in eternal joy."

At this the furious tyrant commanded his torturers straightaway to batter her lovely face with great clubs until her face was unrecognizable; and when there was no face left they shut her in a dark prison.

But early the next day, when brought before Fabricius the judge, she was as whole as if she had suffered no torture. Fabricius, utterly confounded, could do no more. He ordered that she be beheaded immediately.

As she was led outside the walls, one Theophilus—pro-tonotary of the kingdom—scornfully asked her to send him some roses from her spouse's garden. She faithfully promised she would, although it was the dead of winter.

When she was brought into the place where her sentence of decapitation would be executed, she prayed God on behalf of those who would commemorate her passion, that through his special grace he would save them from every tribulation and especially from the shame of hateful poverty and of slander.

Also that he would grant due contrition at their last hour and full remission of all their sins; and if pregnant women had mind of her that he would aid them; and that any establishment owning her passionary would never be endangered by fire or lightning.

No sooner had she made this prayer than a voice gave answer: "Come love, come spouse, for what you have asked is granted, and all the people you pray for shall be saved." With that word she bent her head to end her life.

As she humbly bowed, a child appeared clad in purple, barefoot and with nicely curled hair. In his clothes golden starbeams spread out, and he carried a basket with three roses and three apples in it. He kneeled and offered it to Dorothy.

She requested him to bear it to Theophilus the scribe and to say that it came from her as she had promised. He went; she meekly and fearlessly took the death stroke and her soul rose up to heaven.

This blessed Dorothy was martyred in the year of grace 280 if you add another eight, the sixteenth day of February under the cruel prefect Fabricius, while Diocletian and Maximian occupied the empire as stated above.

To Theophilus—who was in the palace publicly—the child appeared and politely took him by the hand, leading him aside and saying, "These roses and apples are sent by my sister from her husband's garden." This said, he vanished away.

Theophilus began to praise and glorify Christ, Dorothy's God, who in the month of February, when frost and cold conceal the earth and no leaves are seen on the trees, can send roses and apples to whomever he wishes. Blessed be his name endlessly.

Through the important credible witnessing of Theophilus and through his devout preaching, the whole city, rich and poor, were quickly converted to Christ. Fabricius, seeing all this, was so astonished that he scarcely knew where he was.

Especially when he saw Theophilus convert and preach so faithfully, he almost lost heart; but he attacked Theophilus with more torture than he did even Dorothy, for he cut his body into small pieces and threw the chunks to beasts and birds.

But first Theophilus was baptized and took communion, and then was cruelly assailed with torture. So he followed his instructor Dorothy and came to Christ who reigns in bliss. May Christ bring us there too, through Dorothy's merits.

Now, blessed virgin, O Dorothy, who are glorified in heaven above, grant John Hunt before he die to prove his friendship as he desires, and his wife Isabel, for they both love you; at their request and humble supplication I made of your life this translation. Amen, thank you Jesus.

MARY MAGDALEN'S LIFE

The Prolocutory

The year of grace one thousand four hundred and forty-five (according to the Church of Rome's computation which changes its calculation with Janus), when Phoebus (who resides nowhere stably but daily varies his shelter among the twelve signs as the First Mover himself ordained) had by circumvolution descended in his course down to the lowest part of the zodiac circle—I mean Capricorn, where he has only fifteen degrees—and had just begun his return, having gained only one degree in climbing, and drew toward Aquarius—

But why delay any longer in this matter? Quite plainly, I mean: on that holiday eve when, as Christians believe, three kings made it their business to celebrate Christ on the thirteenth day after his birth, coming from the east in royal array and guided by a clear-shining star. On that day I was with Lady Bourchier, also known as the countess of Eu. She descends from the same pedigree as the duke of York, for she is his sister. She is called Isabel after the duchess of York, her paternal grandmother who was daughter to King Pedro of Spain and who, with another sister, brought the royal title of Spain to England. Because the first sister died barren and without issue, everything depended on the other one, through whom the royal right has now come to the brother of the said Lady Isabel, that is, to Sir Richard, duke of York. May God send it to him if it is God's will.

I will speak no further of this matter but return to Dame Isabel and relate the rest of my purpose. This lady's four young sons were occupied with revel and dance, and many others were dressed up in their best clothes—for in the month of May there never was a meadow freshlier mottled with flowers white, blue, and green than were their garments. It seemed to me that Minerva herself, who has sovereignty over colorful weaving (as Ovid declares), with all her wit could never provide better clothing even if she included the whole *Metamorphoses* in one fabric.

While they walked about the chamber in their dance, it pleased my lady's gentleness to talk with me about various legends of holy women that, in my old age, my ignorance had turned from Latin into our language—such as Saint Anne the mother of blessed Mary, Margaret and Dorothy, Faith and Christine and also Agnes, and of the eleven thousand virgins. Also that holy and blessed matron Saint Elizabeth, whose life by itself could be a mirror for wives, reflecting various types of perfection. At that time I had recently begun to rhyme Elizabeth's holy legend, at the request of her whom I neither can, will, nor may deny, so much am I obligated to her goodness: I mean the countess of Oxford, Dame Elizabeth Vere (to give her proper name), whom God preserve from sin and shame and so assist in perseverance and good living here in this world that when she changes her mortal fate, she may enter the gate of eternal life to dwell therein forever.

While we were busy thus talking, my lady revealed her holy and blessed purpose to me: "I have," she said, "for a long time had a special devotion of pure affection to that holy woman who is called 'apostle to the apostles'; I mean blessed Mary Magdalen, whom Christ made pure and clean from sin, as the writers say. I desire to have her life made in English, and if you would undertake this work for my sake and for reverence of her, I would ask you to do it." I was in doubt what to say to this, for on the one hand I remembered my lack of experience in the rhyming art, my labile mind, the dullness of my wit, and my ignorance. On the other hand, I thought how hard it is to deny the request of nobility—which, next after the poet's own intention, is a mighty inducement. So I thought it better in this case that my wit were lacking than my will, and therefore assented to my lady's request according to the ability of my simple mind and on condition that she would grant a delay until I had accomplished my pilgrimage that I had promised Saint James to perform that same year.

I had promised to obtain new indulgence for my old sins through penitence at Santiago de Compostela, where, by pure confession, contrite people can have fuller remission of their sins between January 1 and December 31 during this "year of grace." This "year of grace" was granted long ago by Pope Calixtus to last during a year when Saint James's day falls on a Sunday. And when my lady heard my opinion, she kindly assented to my wish and excused me until I should return from Santiago as God would.

Now that I have performed my pilgrimage as I intended, I will apply all the courage of my wit and knowledge to perform my lady's will and commandment. But first I shall humbly follow the sage counsel of a philosopher who, as Augustine says, is prince of all philosophers: Plato, who, in his book of high philosophy called *Timaeus*, after his disciple of that name, says, "To all men it is a custom religiously observed, to begin every work whether great or small by begging the sovereign divinity to assist them in the work that they may not err or do amiss." Since even pagans observed this ritual, all the more ought we Christians to perform it and do nothing on our own but in all our works have recourse to our sovereign God with humble prayer. So that, before I proceed further in this matter, I thus pray with heart and mind to him that created me from nothing.

O sovereign and most blessed trinity, one God in substance and in persons three, father and son and holy ghost together whose might, intellect, and goodness are equal (although each of these three is appropriate to a distinct person of God, as theologians show, though all three we believe to be a single thing in their essence which has neither end nor beginning). You whose measure is nothing but eternity, who miraculously made heaven and earth out of nothing and wrought their contents: angels in the imperial heaven on high; sun, moon and stars beneath them; and sky, herbs, trees, stones, and grass; fish and fowl and all that belongs to the air; earth and water each in its proper sphere; and the fourth element called fire. After all this your goodness formed humankind to your likeness, endowing it with three natural gifts—spirit, reason, and will—that have distinct operations and yet are essentially a single soul, and this is the very image of yourself. Moreover, to conclude, you imprinted your similitude in us with those gifts which you added to the gifts of nature when at our creation you through your grace breathed a spirit of life in our face.

Thereafter, as the prophet testifies, you placed all things under humanity's rule: sheep, oxen, and every beast of the field whatever their names, birds of heaven and fishes of the sea.

But when humankind had lost this great dignity and deformed itself horribly, deceived by the envy of its enemy called "serpent," "behemoth," "leviathan," and many more names than I can now repeat, then through your great mercy and grace you reformed the human being even more marvelously than the creature was formed at first in the beginning. For this reforming, the second person of you three took on our frailty by your common assent and, here on earth in a maiden's bower, became our advocate and mediator between the father of heaven and humankind. After three and thirty winters he made sufficient reparation for humankind by suffering a terrible passion, for doubtless the least drop of blood that emerged from his blessed body—even at his circumcision—would have been adequate ransom forever for all the world's woe and for another thousand worlds. But so great was his charity to humankind that he would not redeem it with a lesser ransom than all the blood of his body and all the blood of his heart. That is why you require all humanity's love and nothing less, with meek and heartfelt praise, for you need nothing of our goods, as David says in his prophecy.

Thus, lord, I cry to you only who are well of mercy and pity, and neither to Clio nor Melpomene nor to any other of the nine muses, nor to Pallas Minerva nor Lucina nor to Apollo who, as the old books say, carries the lock and key of wisdom, colorful speech, and eloquence. All of them I utterly deny, as every Christian ought to do, and flee, lord, only to you, not desiring to have such eloquence as some courtiers have, nor such difficulty in uttering their subtle conceits in which there is often great deceit. And especially they like to make ballades and little booklets for their ladies' sake, in which they feign sorrow and weeping as if death constrained their hearts, even though they are far from death. Yet nonetheless their sentiments are so elaborate and uttered with such colorful language that I believe the month of May never embellished the soil with fresher flowers than their language is embellished with the colors of rhetoric back and forth. Never was the peacock's tail gayer, which inherited all the eyes of Argus when Mercury's flute charmed him asleep. To aspire to learn such craft of language in my old age and my condition would be foolish. So, lord, with humble will and whole heart I conclude my long prayer. May I have ability sufficient to serve the devotion of my lady as she desires, that is, to translate out of Latin into plain words of our language the life of blessed Mary Magdalen, specifically to my lady's spiritual comfort and generally to the comfort of all who shall read it. By this reading may they gain, first, remission of all their sin such as Mary Magdalen obtained; and then may they come to the bliss that she is in. Let everyone say amen, for charity. Amen, thank you Jesus.

The Prologue to Mary Magdalen's Life

Of a Mary I shall write the life, as God gives me grace. I don't mean Mary without sin, who gave birth to the solace of humankind; but I mean her who obtained pardon through repentance for her trespass when she entered Simon's house, and who is called Mary Magdalen.

Worthily this name "Mary" is hers, I believe, for as *Legenda Aurea* specifies, "Mary" has three interpretations. First it means "a bitter sea," then "illuminer," and then "made light." And these three things Mary Magdalen has aplenty.

By these three things we may understand the three best things this Mary chose: outward penance, inward contemplation, and upward bliss that shall never end. God said for certain that of these things Mary "chose the best part"; they shall never decrease but shall always endure and abide with her eternally.

The first part, penitence for sin, is the way to get bliss and shall not be stolen from her. Nor will the second, contemplation, for it is blended with heavenly joy which is stable, and so it cannot fail. Nor may the third cease, for it is from heaven and its measure is eternity.

Since this Mary chose the best part of doing penance, she may suitably be called "a bitter sea," for she felt great bitterness when, repenting, she stood modestly behind Christ and with her tears devoutly washed his feet.

Since she chose the best part of inward contemplation in this life, the second interpretation also is appropriate—"an illuminer" or "giver-of-light"—for in her contemplation she took such light as helped many another in spiritual goodness to shine full bright.

Since this Mary chose the best part of heavenly bliss in her affection, she is suitably called "illumined," for now above the celestial region she is illumined with clear cognition in her soul, and when the general resurrection is complete she shall finally be illumined in her glorious body.

This Mary is also appropriately called Magdalen according to the statement of Voragine, for this Latin word "Magdalena" is interpreted to mean three things: "guilty," "strengthened," and "worthy of elevation." These three things, correctly analyzed, can clearly show what she was before, during, and after her conversion.

Before her conversion she was guilty of the abomination of sinful living, severed from God and holy associates, and defamed in worldly reputation in Jerusalem and that entire region. For all this misbehavior, she was bound by obligation to the devil to dwell in endless fire.

But after this, in her conversion, when she forsook all her former folly and repented of her transgression and obtained mercy through her penance, then she was strengthened and made mighty, for as many various delights of sin as she had had in her body, so many sacrifices she made of herself.

How strong and mighty she grew in spiritual grace after her conversion, let whoever wishes to know this not pass hence until they have finished this story, which combines gospel and legend. The reader will find that where sin wretchedly reigned, now grace superabounds.

Now, gracious lady Mary Magdalen, who found copious grace after sin, let not Satan with his subtle tricks confound the souls of them who serve you. And especially, lady, let your grace redound to Dame Isabel, countess of Eu. Comfort her, keep her safe and sound, and all temptation help her to eschew.

Also, lady, vouchsafe to listen to the humble intent of him who occupied himself in translating your legend at this said lady's command. Obtain grace for him to amend his life before he leave this outlawry, and help them both to ascend, after their life's course, to heavenly bliss. Amen.

Here Begins the Life of Mary Magdalen

This blessed Mary Magdalen was born—to speak about worldly dignity—of the worthiest kin in the country, for she was descended from royal blood. Her father was the worthy Syrus, and her mother was Eucharia.

She had a brother who was a soldier at first: Lazarus, whom our savior raised from death to life through his grace, at the request of their hostess Martha—Mary's sister, as John testifies in his true gospel.

These three, as the story tells, divided among them the inheritance of their parents Syrus and Eucharia, so that a village called Magdalum was Mary's share. That is why she was named Magdalen, as Voragine's legend asserts.

Mary had not only an enormous fortune through inheritance but was also supreme in the country for her natural gifts, surpassing all women in excellent beauty. All men agreed that in their sight no woman might be fairer.

In her, then, were joined youth, wealth, and beauty. But for lack of proper supervision these qualities are often agents of insolence and importers of vice; and so they were in Mary Magdalen.

For she spent her youth so shamelessly in promiscuity, and was so common in sinfulness that she lost her good name. Her reputation in the city was so much for folly that they called her "Mary the sinner."

For a long time she continued in her wretchedness and pursued her desires, until at last she was goaded to remorse by our lord Jesus, who lived and taught virtue. Because of his teaching she intended to make amends for her previous way of life.

Shortly thereafter she heard that our savior was invited to meet with Simon the leper, a Pharisee. She bought a box of sweet-smelling precious ointment and went uninvited to Simon's feast.

When she arrived at the place where Jesus was, for shame of her horrid life she would not appear in front of him but stood behind him and began to weep, and fell down and began to crawl toward his feet.

When she came to his feet, she shed such plentiful tears that she could wash his feet with them, and so she devoutly did; and she dried them with her hair and then anointed them with the sweet balm.

And though she expressed no outward word with her mouth during the whole time she showed this meek obsequiousness, yet by the plenitude of her weeping she showed her strength of heart, just as though she had used this language:

"O meekest lord who know everything and are the inward knower of hearts, it seems by your teaching that you desire not the sinner's death but his conversion and long life. You know, lord, what my weeping and my sighing and sorrow mean.

"I am a sinner, horribly contaminated with the dirt of every crime, and so I've been for a long time, since I first had wit and discretion. Reform me now, lord, for your mercy, and aid me in my need, you who care about sorrow and trouble."

When Simon saw this woman thus occupied at Christ's feet, he thought, "If he is a real prophet he should know for sure who and what this woman is; for she is a sinner, and her bad reputation circulates throughout this city."

But Christ, who knows everything, both word and work and private thought, wishing to give Simon a rebuke for his presumptuous judgment, benignly turned toward him and kindly said, "Simon, I have something to say to you." "Master, say what you will!"

"Two debtors," said Christ, "of a usurer were once living in a country, Simon. Five hundred pence one debtor owed, the other only fifty; but because poverty constrained both of them, he pardoned both. I ask you, Simon, which of these two debtors was most beholden to the creditor?"

"It seems to me," said Simon, "a reasonable judgment that the one who had most pardon from his debt was the most obligated to be grateful to his creditor. That's my opinion, master." "You answer," said Christ, "correctly, Simon, but now hear what I say.

"Simon, I entered your house and you gave me no water for my feet. This woman, whom you deem vice ridden, as soon as she entered, devoutly washed my feet with tears shed plentifully from her eyes and wiped them dilgently with her hair.

"You offered me no kiss, but she kissed my feet often; you put no oil on my head, but she has anointed both my feet with sweet ointment. Because she has done this, and shown so many signs of love for me, many sins are now forgiven her."

When she was thus courteously excused to the Pharisee by Christ, she left everything and followed him wherever he went. Because she was abundantly rich, she ministered to him and his in their need, as in Luke's gospel you may plainly read.

Eventually she became so familiar with Christ that he cherished her especially and often stayed with her sister who maintained hospitality for him and his; I mean Martha, whom he cured from a hemorrhage that had lasted for twelve years.

This was in Bethany, where Martha and Mary and their brother Lazarus dwelt, and there our lord Jesus often turned for shelter, as the gospels tell, for he was hated in the city of Jerusalem and could seldom find anyone so kind as to shelter him.

O how blessed and fortunate was that house in which that gracious lord was willing to accept hospitality! Blessed too were those three chosen to be his hosts and to feed in his bodily need him who feeds angels with his godhood.

Lo, thus we may see how ever-merciful God is, how concerned to save sinners. This woman demonstrates it particularly: she was sinful at first and later craved mercy, through which she not only had remission of her great sins but also attained to high perfection.

Not only did she attain to perfection of holy life but also so specially extended her affection to Christ that wherever he was she drew near and listened devoutly to his words, so that when anyone accused her, Christ was ready to excuse her.

An example is given in Luke's gospel, which says that our gracious lord Jesus once entered a village and Martha received him into her house there. But her sister Mary was so desirous of hearing his words that she sat down right at his feet.

When Martha—who was busily serving Christ—saw her sitting there, she began to accuse her idleness and said, "O lord, don't you care how my sister lets me do everything by myself? Please ask her to get up and help me serve you."

But Christ, who as Augustine says in a sermon is called "judge," acted as Mary's advocate and found a reasonable defense against her sister's accusation. This is what he said to Martha in her busyness:

"Martha, Martha," said he, "you are busy and worried about many things. But one thing is necessary, Martha, which Mary has chosen: to listen to my teaching, which never shall fail. Know therefore that she has chosen better, and this shall never be taken from her."

In this way we see that the occupations of active life in this mortality may in no way be equated with the life of inward contemplation; which two lives we find represented in the two sisters Martha and Mary, as Saint Augustine testifies in his commentary on John's gospel.

Martha's life is mingled with great bitterness, but Mary's life is embalmed with sweetness; yet both are good, as the previous example describes, so that there ought to be no more envy between them than between a positive and a comparative degree.

Moreover, to show the singularity of love that God had for these three people beyond others, Saint John says clearly in his gospel, "God loved Martha and her sister Mary and their brother Lazarus." No testimony of love can be more plain.

Still, among these three, to speak about love in terms of comparison, Mary stood in the superlative degree both before and after the resurrection, as we shall see: before, in the miracle when Christ called the dead Lazarus up from hell, as John tells.

When Lazarus lay sick and languishing in Bethany, and Christ was absent beyond the Jordan out of Jewish territory, Mary and Martha sent him this message: "Lord, he whom you love is very sick."

Meanwhile Lazarus died and then Christ said to his disciples, "Our friend Lazarus is asleep. Let us go wake him." They said, "If he is asleep he is safe enough. What are we supposed to do there? Have you forgotten that the Jews threaten to kill you?"

Then Christ told them openly that Lazarus was dead, so he wished to return to Judea to recall him from death to life. And so he hurried along the road to Bethany.

To make a long story short: Martha met him outside the town and had a long conversation with him, while Mary was at home in contemplation until she was told of Christ's arrival and then went out to meet him a long way.

Weeping she said, "Lord, if you had been here I believe my brother would not have died." And when Christ saw her weeping he wept too, out of sympathy, and said, "Where have you laid him?"

When he went there they said, standing by the grave's brink, "Sir, four days have passed since he died and we are sure the body stinks; so we think it's useless to do any more." "Nonetheless," he said, "remove the stone from the grave."

When the stone was off he began to lament and be terribly troubled in spirit, and, lifting his eyes to heaven, cried in a loud voice, "Lazarus, come out!" Immediately he came out all wrapped up, and Christ gave him to the disciples to undo his bandages.

It was a wonderful sight to see, that a man who had lain four days dead and seemed to have been stinking should thus be raised again to life; but there is no more to say about it except that love can do such miracles: "Quia fortis ut mors est dileccio."

Later, at a supper at Simon's house, one of the guests was Lazarus and Martha was serving. Mary, inflamed with spiritual grace, went to anoint Christ's feet with a precious ointment.

When she had done so and he had sat still, she poured over his head the rest of the oil, whose odor filled the house. Judas said, "Why do you waste this ointment which could be sold for three hundred pence that could be distributed to the city's poor?"

Christ, to save Mary from blame, used his advocacy and said, "The poor you shall always have with you, sirs, but not me. This woman who devoutly took the care to anoint me has revealed a mystery of my burial.

"Know, then, that when the gospel shall be sown throughout the world by preachers, then it will be said in many a country that she did this in worship of me." Lo: What Judas said to discomfit her, Christ made redound to her praise.

Observe how this perfect creature was joined with her creator through the affection of true love, and he to her in special amour, for near the last hour of his life, only a little before his passion, he made a special commendation of her.

After this, when Christ was captured and cruelly nailed up on a tree and all his disciples had forsaken him, so fervent was her charity to him that for no fear would she leave him but attended him until he was buried in the evening.

When he was buried, with great mourning she went to buy sweet ointments, and the next day after Sabbath she hastened to the sepulchre. With her went another Mary, and her intention in going there was to anoint Christ's body.

But when they arrived and he was gone—as an angel told them—and everyone else left, only she stayed there, often searching the grave with weeping eye to see whether she might find her love anywhere.

Since she was so perseverant when others had left, she had the special grace to see our lord before anyone else. He appeared, as if to joke, in the likeness of a gardener; but when he said "Mary," she knew his expression.

When she recognized him, she fell down at his feet and would have kissed them, but he would not allow it. "Mary, do not be frightened. Go tell Peter and all my disciples that I am risen, as you see, and shall go before them into Galilee."

In this and many other ways was Mary privileged (as can be read in the gospels, much better than I can narrate). She was specially cherished by her love, Messiah, both in his living and in his ordeal, and from death to life after his resurrection.

Now I have displayed a great part of Mary's life according to the gospel. Now I will tell the rest as Voragine narrates it, if grace will guide my wit and pen and if God will vouchsafe to prolong my life till the work is done.

But before I proceed further in this material which I have promised, I beg you, Mary, with my entire heart, to get me the grace to lead a better life than I do yet and help that lady in all her works and get her bliss who is principal cause of this writing.

The fourteenth year after Christ rose from death to life, when the Jews had stoned Stephen to death, as Voragine relates, and drove Christ's disciples out of Judea, they visited many countries to sow and teach God's word.

In the time of this persecution, as Voragine tells, one of the seventy-two disciples dwelt in Jerusalem with apostles. To this man Peter committed Mary Magdalen, and his name was Maximian.

With them were also Lazarus, Martha and Marcella her handmaiden, and blessed Cedonius who, as the gospel relates, was blind from birth and Christ miraculously made him see.

All these together and many more Christians were, by the harsh decree of the Jews, set out on the sea in a ship with neither steering nor rudder, so that they would be drowned. But as God's providence guided them, they arrived safely at Marseilles.

They thanked God for their passage and went to land, but no one would grant them shelter. So they took their shelter, until better might be found, in the porch of a temple.

When blessed Magdalen saw so many people come there to sacrifice to their idols, she rose cheerfully and with calm eloquence called them away from their idolatry and preached Christ to them steadfastly.

All who heard her were astounded, partly because of her beauty, partly because of the fluency and sweetness of her eloquence which came so pleasantly from her mouth that they felt a great desire to stand still and hear her preach.

No wonder if that mouth—that so often and so devoutly had set such sweet kisses on Christ our savior's feet whenever she met him—had favorable grace more than any other to show the savor of God's word.

Shortly thereafter, the prince of that country and his wife came to that altar to sacrifice to Diana, so that she would deign to send them a child. When Mary Magdalen saw this, she made them a long sermon and counseled them to abandon their superstition.

But at that time Mary's words accomplished nothing, for as they came they went home again, standing obstinate in their error. Not long afterward, while this lady slept, Magdalen appeared to her, saying,

"Why is it that your husband and you abound in plentiful wealth, yet you permit God's dear saints to perish wrongly in hunger and cold?" Mary threatened that the princess would be sorry, unless she got her husband to relieve their suffering.

But the princess wouldn't for anything tell her husband about the vision; so the next night while she slept as usual, Mary Magdalen made an identical appearance to her; but still she would not tell her husband.

Because the princess refused to do as she was told, the third night Mary Magdalen appeared to the two of them as they slept, angrily and with as urgent an expression as if the house had been on fire. Looking at them with a terrible eye, she said to them both together,

"Are you asleep, O cruel tyrant, limb of your father Satan, with this serpent your wife who would not tell you my word as she was ordered to do, because she didn't want to burden you? Since she would not do my errand, I now appear to both of you.

"What reason is there, you cursed enemy of Christ's cross, that you should be fed delicately on various meats and afterward rest easy, while you see God's servants perish before your eyes with hunger and trouble? You'll pay for this.

"You lie here in a stately palace, wrapped in clothes of silk and gold, while they lie in straw huts, likely to die of cold. And you don't care to see it once, nor have pity on them, though you're told about it every day.

"Do you imagine you'll escape free and painless for this great trespass? No, tyrant, I plainly warn you that you stand in danger and are likely to cry 'alas' forevermore, unless you listen to my words and amend your wrongdoing."

When blessed Mary had spoken this way, she went her way. The matron suddenly started up out of her sleep and began to sigh and groan. To her husband, who made moan for the same reason, she said, quaking for dread,

"What cheer with you, sir? Did you see anything of this sight I had in my dream?" "Yes, yes, wife! and that causes me great tribulation now. I don't know what's best for us to do: to do as she says, or to maintain our old way of life."

"My opinion, sir," she said, "is that it's better to obey than to fall into the indignation of her God and wrongly die." "So be it, then," he replied. Later they went to the Christians' house and brought whatever they needed.

One day when Mary preached, the prince asked her, "Do you believe that you can defend the faith that you teach?" "Yes, that I can," Mary said, "by daily miracles and by the witness of our master Peter who is in Rome."

Then the prince and his wife said, "We are ready to obey whatever you command us to do, on one condition. If you will beg your God that a child be born to us as our heir, we ask no more."

"Without delay," Mary said. Instantly she began to pray for them with her entire heart, and she was heard, and within a short time this lady conceived and was with child, a great solace to them both.

When the prince saw his wife with child, he was fully disposed to believe and planned to visit Peter so that he might prove Mary's doctrine. Intending to take leave of his wife, the prince went to her, and she answered,

"Ah, good sir, what are you doing? Would you now forsake me in my present condition? No, no, it may not be. I'll go with you and be a partner in your adventure as long as I am alive."

"No, wife, not in your condition, for many great dangers are at sea, and many a wave rises roughly. So stay at home and rest, and I shall go for both of us to do this holy pilgrimage."

Nonetheless, as is women's way, she would not give up her plan. Often she fell humbly at his feet weeping, and wouldn't stop until he promised to let her go with him. Then she was very happy and got herself ready to go.

When their ship and all else was ready, they handed everything of theirs over to Mary Magdalen, and she marked their shoulders with the sign of Christ's cross so that the devil would not harm them.

They had sailed only one day when the wind blew hard
into their sail and a great storm blew up so that all the
men knew nothing except that they were to die, and they
screamed for fear.

While they were in this distress, pitched back and forth
by the tempest, the princess felt such great anguish that she
had her child in the midst of all that woe. The prince went
to her and found her dead, and the child lying under her
right hand.

The child began to cry, desiring some comfort from
his mother's breasts, but they were dry, for she was dead.
When the prince saw this pitiful situation, he sorrowed and
wept bitterly, crying,

"Alas, alas, wretch! What shall I do? I desired a child
but unluckily, for mother and child are both lost. Alas!
Why am I not dead too?" Thereat the shipmen began to
shout, "Throw this corpse out into the sea, or else we are
all likely to perish!

"For we all know this for certain: while it's inside, the
tempest won't end." As they took it to throw it out, the
prince pressed among them and said, "Sirs, I beg you
relent, and though you have no mercy on her or me, yet
have some pity on the young infant.

"Wait, sirs, a while for God's sake: perhaps the woman
is in a coma and may revive." While he spoke, he saw an
isle not far off, and thought, "Better to bury them both
yonder than that fishes should prey on them."

And even though he beseeched the seamen with watery
eye and also gave them gifts, they were reluctant to carry
out his plan. When he came to that isle, he labored hard
to dig it up in order to bury them as he intended. But no
tool would enter the ground.

When he saw it would not be, he laid down his wife's
dead body wrapped in her cloak, under a tree, and on her
breast placed the crying child; and before he took his way
thence, he knelt down and prayed as devoutly as he could:

"O Mary Magdalen, why did you come to Marseilles to my perdition and to increase my misery and put me in such distress? Did you ask your God's goodness for my wife to have a child only so that both should die?

"I don't know, but I do know this: that she is dead and so will the child be soon, for he has nothing to be fed with. Nonetheless, since I had him because of you, I commit him to your and your God's keeping, as I have done all my other things.

"If he is mighty, as you teach, may he have the mother's soul in remembrance; and through your prayers, I humbly beseech that the child not perish; may God show mercy." He wrapped them both in the cloak and for sorrow was unable to say another word, but returned to the ship.

Later, when he landed, he continued his journey to seek Saint Peter in Rome. When Peter saw him, he asked his intention, and what the mark meant and whence he came and why, and the prince told Peter all about it.

When Peter had heard everything, "Peace be with you," he said, "and patience. You are welcome, for you have given credence to wholesome counsel. Do not regret your wife's absence, though she and her child sleep a while, for God is strong enough to take care of them."

Then, to confirm his holy intent and to establish the prince in his new grace, Saint Peter went with him to Jerusalem where, to increase the prince's spiritual comfort, Peter showed him every place where Christ preached and suffered and rose again, and where he was last seen by his disciples.

When the prince had been away two years in pilgrimage and prayer and in diligent learning of the faith, he devoutly took his homeward journey again. It happened that he neared the isle where he had left his wife when she died on the outward voyage.

He begged the shipmen, and gave them gifts too, to ride at anchor for a time nearby, while he might go to the isle to see what had happened to his wife and child. They agreed, and launched him in a boat toward the isle.

As he went toward it, he perceived a little child running naked to and fro on a cliff, busily playing as children do and throwing little stones into the sea. He seemed as merry and as jolly as if he had more company.

This same child was the prince's son, whom blessed Magdalen had miraculously fostered in that place. When the child saw his father's face, he ran away quickly for fear, having never seen a man.

He ran straight to where his mother lay, as he usually did, covered himself with her cloak, took her breast in his mouth and busily began to suck. The prince, astonished, followed him.

When he came to where the child lay and sucked, he picked it up in his arms and knelt down, thanking Mary Magdalen with all his heart as devoutly as he could:

"O blessed Mary Magdalen, honor, praise, and worship to you whose kindness has kept and fostered this baby of mine these last two years. You have convincingly shown, lady, that grace far surpasses nature's power.

"Moreover, blessed lady, I could have no further felicity than if my wife, who lies here dead, were to be recovered to life and return with me to my country. I have full confidence in your capacity, by experience of my child's survival."

And as he made this prayer, his wife rose up as if waking from sleep. Devoutly as she could she said to Mary Magdalen, "Great is thy merit in God's sight, O blessed lady, and so is thy might.

"Thanks, lady, who through thy grace and charity helped me in the pressures of childbirth and were willing to be my midwife; and through thy kindness were as ready to help me as any handmaid to her lady."

When the prince heard these words, he cried, "Are you alive, my own dear wife?" "Yes, sir, that I am," she said, "indeed, and now I have returned and have finished the voyage you have made, and the same pilgrimage.

"For just as Saint Peter led you to Jerusalem and showed you every place where Christ preached to our frailty, where he died and rose and passed hence, so blessed Magdalen led me with you and showed me everything, and I've learned it well."

She began to repeat her husband's journey, what they saw, and where and when, and missed nothing. Then, thanking God heartily, they went to ship and soon arrived at Marseilles.

When they had landed and were entering the city, they found Mary with her disciples preaching to the people, as was her habit. The prince and his wife fell weeping at her feet and told her all their journey.

Thereafter they were baptized by blessed Maximian. Forthwith they destroyed all the idols' temples in the country, founded churches, and chose blessed Lazarus as bishop of the city.

This done, blessed Magdalen and her company left Marseilles and went to Aix which, through many miracles, was readily converted to Christ. Maximian was made bishop of that city, and Magdalen was glad,

For her heart was determined to give herself only to contemplation and to give up anything that might interfere; so, by heavenly inspiration, she made her habitation in a wilderness as ordained by angels in a barren place, where she stayed thirty winters unknown.

No tree grew in that place, nor herb nor water nor any solace to her bodily comfort at all. This was to show that our savior's grace did so embrace her that he would feed with heavenly food her every need.

For every day in that desolate place seven times high in the air she was lifted with angels' hands, and with her bodily ears heard heavenly harmony there, with which melody she was fed so well in body and soul that she needed no bodily food at all.

Meanwhile it happened that a priest, wishing to live solitary, made a cell only twelve furlongs from the place where Mary dwelt. There he occupied himself holily in the study of devout contemplation, and God showed him this revelation:

He thought he saw with his bodily eye angels come down in great brightness and bear up a body above the sky with great sweetness to melodious song. When they had been singing an hour or more, they brought it down to the same place again.

When the priest had seen this sight, fervently desiring to know what it was, if he might, he planned to go nearer the place. First he prayed God devoutly to speed him in his journey and lead him the right way there.

When he set out and had come within a stone's throw of the place, his legs began suddenly to falter and he could go no further; but his legs were strong enough to go back home again!

When he had tried several times forth and back and couldn't get there, he realized it was not to be done to force his way. He understood he was unworthy to know, wherefore in the name of our savior he cried,

"I entreat you by the pure virtue of God, you who dwell in that cave, if you are a reasonable creature, let me have some knowledge of who you are, with no deceit!" This said thrice, Mary answered him in plain words:

"Come nearer, and you shall have sufficient confirmation of everything your soul wishes to be verified, as far as you need to know." Fearfully he went forth, but scarcely had he gone halfway when Mary said to him,

"Are you aware of Mary in the gospel, the most famous sinner who, as Luke tells, washed Christ's feet with many a tear and wiped them with her own hair and so by God's grace obtained full indulgence for her sins?"

"I am well aware of this," said the priest. "Thirty winters and more have passed, as we find written in holy church, since she left human company." "I am she," said Mary, "and in this place I have dwelt solitary all this time unknown. "As you were permitted to see yesterday, angels lift me up seven times a day and have done since I first came here. For now it pleases our lord's mercy to take me up to continual bliss. Go tell blessed Maximian all this.

"Also tell him that on next Easter day, when he arises in the grey dawn for matins, as he is accustomed to do, let him go immediately to his oratory, where he shall find me ready, brought by the ministry of holy angels."

When the priest had heard this voice, like an angel's clear voice, though he saw nothing, still he was glad to be the messenger of so holy and blessed a matter. He went speedily to Maximian and did his errand properly.

When Maximian heard all this from the priest, he thanked, praised, and honored our savior with all his heart. At the assigned day and hour he found Mary standing in his oratory among the angels' hands that had brought her there.

She stood there like this: fully two cubits' space off the ground with angels' hands supporting her, and with such great brightness in her face that it was easier to behold the sun's circle on the clearest day, than the brightness of her beauty.

Maximian was abashed to behold the brightness of her complexion. She turned her face to him and said, "Father, be not in doubt, but boldly come near. I am your daughter, why do you flee? Come fearlessly, father, to me."

When all the clergy was gathered, including the aforesaid priest, she received Christ's body from the bishop, shedding many a tear. And forthwith without fear she lay her head down at the altar and painlessly died.

When the soul of this most holy and blessed woman passed on, a redolent odor suddenly grew and lasted seven days. With it many were cured of sickness, through the merit of her goodness.

Then blessed Maximian buried the body of the apostle Mary Magdalen, anointing it with sweet-smelling ointment. And when he was to die, he commanded his body to be buried by hers, and so it was, with great solemnity.

Long afterward, when the year of grace ran to seven hundred and forty-nine, this holy apostle Mary Magdalen was translated to Vézelay and there laid in a shrine by a Burgundian lord named Girard; she still lies there, as we know.

Now, glorious apostle, who above the sky are crowned in bliss in the heavenly region, govern and guide your servants on earth, keep them always under your protection, and purchase remission of their sins for them; and when their mortal fate sends them hence, bring them to the joy that never ends. Amen.

SAINT KATHERINE'S LIFE

Prologue

"Katherine" is derived from "kata," meaning "all," and "ruina," which signifies "a fall." To put it plainly, we may see that into her there fell everything that might instruct the devil: as pride is instructed by meekness, lust by chastity, and covetise by contempt of worldly goods.

Or else the word "katerina"—as Voragine says in *The Golden Legend*—is the equivalent of "catenula," a "chain"; which means that she by a copious affluence of good works made herself a chain by which she might attain heaven.

This chain, according to the said writer, had four links or a fourfold nature. The first is innocence in deeds; purity of heart he places second; the third is contempt for vanity; the fourth is avoidance of deceit in speech. These four the Prophet teaches us:

"Who shall climb up the hill," says he, "of our lord, or stand in this holy place? Whoever has innocence of hand and purity of heart, nor accepts vanity in his soul, nor swears treacherously to his neighbor." How these four things existed in blessed Katherine, the story of her legend can show.

Before I proceed to narrate it, I beseech you, O glorious virgin, vouchsafe to lead me in truth of word and work so

125

that I never decline from it, and when I end my temporal life, help me ascend to that bliss where you reign forever.

And whoever shall read or hear this treatise, I beg as humbly as I can to not expect me to tell how she first became a Christian, or how she was converted and christened by one called Adrian in her youth, for all that material is unknown to me.

But whoever wants to know and wishes to be informed in the matter, must acquire the book by my spiritual father, Master John Capgrave, and there the reader will see, in skillfully rhymed ballade stanzas, everything that my ignorance omits.

But since that book is rare and hard to acquire, I will compendiously narrate only the passion, for the spiritual consolation of Katherine Howard and also to the comfort of Katherine Denston, if grace will illumine my wit.

O blissful Jesus, let some beam of heavenly influence shine on me that I may terminate this legend now begun, to the praise and reverence of that holy virgin who, after your mother, has the excellence of virginity by many a prerogative, as the story of her life shows.

Here Begins the Life of Saint Katherine

Once while Maxence was emperor and a cruel tormentor of Christian people, in the city of Alexandria there dwelt a young and beautiful maiden, daughter of King Constance. Her name was Katherine, whom Dame Nature had given many fair features. It seemed that in forming Katherine, Nature had forgotten everything else, and so busy was she in pouring out all her treasure on the girl that she seemed impoverished when she had done. To the gifts of Nature, Dame Grace added so much of her treasure that soon, by solicitude and diligence, Katherine was well informed in every one of the seven liberal arts—so well that she could communicate with any scholar in the entire country. Her fortune was great too, for she was a king's daughter; and when her father died he left her a great abundance of worldly wealth, for he loved her dearly. But God so advanced her in grace that she set little store by transitory things, for she intended to obtain goods that cannot pass away, or end, or fail: such as virtue in this life, and joy in the next. So she occupied herself in prayer and alms while living in her father's palace.

When she was eighteen years old, Maxence in his fierce rage made a proclamation requiring everyone, rich and poor, to assemble in Alexandria on a specified day to sacrifice to his gods with him. If anyone rebelled against his will, Maxence ordained that the rebel should be killed as a transgressor of the law and as a Christian. When the day and hour came for the sacrifice, great crowds of people came. Some brought beasts to sacrifice, some brought birds, and some came who in secret intended to do no sacrifice at all, for they were Christians in their commitment. As everyone assembled, ready to make offering at the king's command, the trumpets began to blow loudly as a signal to begin the offering. The king went first, as was their custom; and then one saw many a spear and lance and sword drawn to slay the beasts that were to be offered in sacrifice according to the law. While they were busy sacrificing to the honor and pleasure of their gods, the noise of beasts' and peoples' cry, with the voice of organs and various musical instruments, impelled the air so rapidly that the sound came quickly to Katherine's ears. She sent a messenger to find out what it was. When she learned what was the cause of this great noise, she took a few of her servants and went to the place of sacrifice. There she noticed many people weeping. They were secret Christians and sacrificed only for fear of death. When she saw this she was saddened. Forthwith she marked her face and breast with Christ's cross and drew near to the emperor as he sacrificed.

To him she said, "The dignity of your rank should compel us to salute you, sir emperor, who are lord and governor here. Reason would say the same, if these sacrifices that you make to false gods were made instead to one God above, creator and sole governor of heaven and earth and all therein. But these things that human error feigns to be gods are actually devils, or devils' dens, so that you sacrifice to them wrongfully." She then began, standing before the temple gate, to expand her thesis with diverse illustrations, and with syllogisms and arguments she eloquently made her point. After doing so, she turned her words to the emperor himself and said, "Sir emperor, I have spoken to you as one speaks to the highly educated; but now I shall return to common speech. Tell me, why have you gathered this multitude of ignorant people to worship the foolishness of your gods? Tell me clearly why you wonder at this high temple built by masons' hands, with its ornaments that, however fresh and gay, will decay and blow away like dust before the face of the wind. Wonder rather why heaven is up and earth is down, each with its contents such as fish and fowl; marvel too at the heavens' circular revolution from east to west, ceaselessly; marvel why sun and moon and five other stars drive a contrary course against the rest of heaven and have done since the world's beginning and shall to its end, performing their office to that intent for which they were set in the firmament. And when you have considered all this, understand that one is mightier than all of them, the creator of all, unmovable mover of all. And if you glimpse him through grace, then praise, worship, and glorify him for he is God and none but he."

When she had spoken long on this theme and more (including the incarnation of Christ), the emperor was astonished and said to her, "Woman, let us carry out and complete our sacrifice as we have begun it, and you will be answered later." He had her led to the palace to be taken care of there, for he marveled at her prudence in speech and at her great beauty, more than any he had seen before. So he planned to reconvert her if he could, and when the sacrifice was done and he returned to the palace, he called for her and said, "Damsel, you know that earlier, when we were devoutly occupied in our service, you approached us publicly and by way of exhortation you made a long peroration in which we perceived great eloquence and were impressed with your prudence. But because our mind was fully occupied at that moment with performing the sacrifice to our gods according to our laws, we could not fully grasp your purpose nor clearly understand what you meant. Therefore we sent you home here to our palace until we might have more time and leisure to talk. So first, before we go any further, I would like to know your family, and when that is clear, then I will speak of other things."

With serious expression Katherine replied, "Sir, as I find written by a poet, no one should beget himself, nor extol himself by pompous fame, nor blame himself extravagantly either: for fools do so who are pricked with vainglory. So I will neither hide my birth nor exaggerate it. I was a king's daughter. He died long ago and left no children but me, so that I am his heir, and I am named Katherine. But although I was born in royal purple and instructed in the seven liberal arts, I set no store by my knowledge or my honorable birth. In fact, I now forsake them with all my heart for Christ's sake; he is my spouse, my lord, my love, for whose sake I am now ready to suffer reproof and always shall be, for there is no other God but he. He is mighty, knowing, full of goodness, and ready to help in all distress. He cannot deny his grace to the needy who cry to him. But all the gods you yelp about are so feeble that they can help neither themselves nor anyone else. Only fools put their trust in godhead that can't help them in need, nor send aid in tribulation, nor defend from danger."

"Then it follows," said the emperor, "that the whole world errs at the present time, in the mistake of false belief, and can achieve no truth—except for you. But this isn't correct, for all evidence depends on several witnesses, as the wise teach, and not on one alone, as you say. So even if you were an angel or a heavenly power and told us the contrary of what we believe, we would have no obligation to believe you. And all the more since you are no angel nor have any part of heavenly power but are only a woman, by nature a frail creature, variable and unstable, fickle, false, and deceitful, as we well know by experience. So we should give no credence to your words or your speech."

"Sir emperor," she said, "I beg you: don't allow yourself to be overcome by credulity or insanity, for in a wise man's soul no troublesome passion can remain. Therefore be ruled by equity if you wish to rejoice in liberty. For as you may find in the poet, whoever is ruled by reason and not by sensuality deserves the name of king. And on the other hand whoever will not be ruled by reason but follows the desires of sensuality, for all his lineage he may not avoid the title of serfdom. By my advice, sir, abound in virtuous liberty that will conserve your honor always." "I see," said the emperor, "that you aim to ensnarl us in your treacherous subtlety, and by philosophical examples to bring us all to folly. I have guessed your intention." Forthwith he sent her to prison, there to await his leisure.

Then he sent a messenger with letters to all the scholars within his rule, commanding that all the masters of grammar and rhetoric should come to the palace in Alexandria to debate with a maiden who pretended to be wise. If they could win the victory, they would be rewarded worthily. From various provinces fifty rhetoricians were brought to Alexandria; their knowledge excelled that of all other men, and that was their reputation, blown by the trumpet of Fame from town to town. When they came before the emperor, they asked why they had been sent for so urgently. "Sirs, because you are wise, and I have a great need for wisdom. I have in my court here a maiden who pretends to surpass all men in intelligence, and she despises our gods, calling them 'devils' or 'devils dens.' To enforce her thesis she multiplies many an argument, and whatever she says she proves quite effectively with poetry or rhetoric or philosophy. If you can win over her, I shall reward you well for your labor and send you home again with great honor."

With great disdain one of the scholars replied, "Sir emperor, saving your reverence, I am surprised at the carelessness of your advice and that you would call us all from so far away, particularly for so trivial a matter, to which I dare say the least scholar among us would have sufficed." The emperor answered, "I know full well that I might compel her to sacrifice by force, and also I could restrain her elaborate language by violence, and silence her by torture. But it seems better to me that she should be refuted by the wisdom and subtlety of your arguments, so obviously and publicly that she can't deny she is wrong. When you have done, then I will persuade her gently to accept our belief, or else force her by torture. Now, sirs, you know my will. Do your duty as you can and must."

Meanwhile Katherine was kept in a dark prison. When she heard about the debate, she knelt down and commended her cause in this matter to God on high. Immediately there appeared a bright angel, who told her to be of good comfort, for she would not only win the next day over all the scholars but would convert them all, and they, converted through special grace, would pass by martyrdom to heaven's bliss. Next day the emperor was ready early and sat on his tribunal throne. He called Katherine, placing her on one side and, opposite her, the fifty scholars full of pride. When Katherine saw this, she said, "Why do you do this, pray, that against one tender young maiden you bring forth fifty great scholars? If they win against me, you have promised them great reward, great respect, and honor; but you put me to this effort with no help from you even if I should win: no thanks or respect or status. But nonetheless, O wise old men, I ask you for time to speak my mind plainly, without rhetoric, in words bare of formal argumentative disputation. For I confess that since I am instructed in Christ's sacraments, I forsake all arguments of secular knowledge and of philosophy, and I refuse to know anything other than him who is the well of all virtue and knowledge, my lord Christ Jesus, the giver of whom and father of heaven made everything from nothing, both heaven and earth and all that is contained therein. Later, because of humanity's sin, he took on the frailty of our nature in a pure virgin and became human for love of humanity, that humanity might experience his charity. Willingly he died for humankind, rose the third day, and ascended to heaven the fourth day after he had suffered his ordeal. There he reigns still, equal with his father in bliss, and evermore will until it please him to return again and judge living and dead as they deserve, punishing them who die in sin with interminable hell pain, but rewarding those who are stable in virtue with everlasting bliss. Lo, sirs, this is my philosophy, my wit, my art, and all my knowledge. Beside this I admit no other knowledge. This knowledge surpasses treasure and coffers."

All the philosophers were so astonished by her speech that none could bring forth a word, but they all stood as still as new-shorn sheep. When the emperor saw how dumb they were, in his fierce rage he uttered this tirade: "O you ignorant knaves, what's the matter with you? Where is your formal philosophy now? Where is your boast and bragging that you made when you first arrived? Why stand you still? Are you tongueless?" With that, the one who was considered the worthiest of the group spoke up and said, "We want you to know that ever since we became scholars we never found anyone who could stand up to us, but we always won—except for this maid over there. She is so filled with the influence of God's spirit, she utters her language with such high prudence, that she enfeebles our wits so badly that we neither can nor may contradict her. Finally, please know that unless you can bring forth a more persuasive and more probable statement about your gods— whom we have worshiped until this moment—we utterly forsake them and commit ourselves to Christ's faith."

When Maxence heard this answer he ordered a great fire to be built in the center of the city and all of them to be thrown in to it with hands and feet bound. Katherine comforted them with her sweet words and exhorted them to steadfast patience and instructed them in the faith of Christ Jesus. One of the scholars said, "Our greatest regret is that we have not been baptized before we die." Katherine said, "Don't worry about that, for the red stream of your blood shall be sufficient baptism and will bring you to heaven's bliss." They were then thrown into the flames; but in order to confound the false belief of the heathens, God through his grace showed this miracle: that as soon as they fell into the fire, they yielded their souls to God's mercy with no hurt to their bodies, neither hair of head nor thread of cloth. And despite the emperor's wrath, Christians brought their bodies to burial.

The emperor commanded Katherine to his presence and spoke in a friendly way: "O gentle maid, whose beautiful face is worthy of the imperial purple, listen to me. Be advised: Humbly sacrifice to our gods, and I promise that you shall be second in my palace after the queen. I shall also have a glorious marble statue of you made, with scepter in hand; it shall stand in the middle of the city and everyone will offer it frankincense as long as the city stands." Said Katherine, "Stop saying such things to me and cease that language, for it is sin to think of them. I don't need such vain favor, for I am secure in much greater honor than you may give, for my lord Jesus Christ has chosen me to be his spouse. He is my joy, he is my health, my love, my comfort, and all my wealth. From his love neither fair words nor torture shall separate me as long as I live." The tyrant commanded that she should be stripped of her clothing and scourged until her body sweated red blood. He then sent her to a dark prison and ordered that for the next twelve days she should be brought no food or drink, intending to starve her into submission.

Meanwhile, the emperor was forced to visit the borders
of his kingdom. When he was gone, the queen desired
to see Katherine. She confided her wish to Porphyry, the
emperor's prince of chivalry and highest officer, much in
favor. She asked him to bribe the jailer so that she might
do as she wished. And so he did and arranged it with all
the prison officials. How pleased the queen was! Secretly,
in the first watch of the night, the queen and Porphyry
went to the prison. When they approached Katherine's cell,
through God's grace they perceived a light so bright they
could hardly endure it, so that they fell to the ground. And
suddenly an odor so sweet and comforting rose to their
nostrils that they revived. Katherine bid them arise and have
no fear, for God had heard their heart's desire and called
them to his chivalry. As they arose, they saw Katherine
sitting ceremoniously in a glorious seat, attended by angels
occupied in healing her wounds with sweet ointments more
redolent than balm.

Katherine asked the queen to approach and addressed
her seriously. "Be strong in heart, lady, for know that you
will go to God in heaven by his special grace, for by the
providence of predestination you are ordained to eternal
salvation. So be of good cheer and fear no pains, for though
they are sharp they are momentary and transitory, and
their result is the heavenly glory that will never cease but
always endure. This exchange is a good and secure one,
producing great profit. To pay earth and receive gold: that
is what they do who by martyrdom receive the kingdom
of heaven." Porphyry said, "Teach us about that kingdom.
Is it a place of such happiness?" "Indeed," said Katherine,
"it is a place of such brightness and clarity that it may be
compared to nothing more fittingly than the sun, and it is
still incomparably fairer and brighter. As for comfort, there
is no trouble or adversity, no anger, rancor, sadness, no
worry, tiredness nor sickness, no hunger or thirst to distress
you. All sorrow and pain is absent. In fact, there is love
and charity, concord and peace, mirth, joy, and everlasting

gladness more than I can express. For as the apostle John teaches us, neither tongue could tell with speech nor heart think, no, nor ears hear the joys that God has ordained to his well-beloved in the bliss of heaven. So we ought to love such a lord."

When she had talked until midnight, the queen and Porphyry were comforted and happy. They returned home cheerfully, thanking God he had given them grace to obtain his mercy and had made them so strong that they would rather die for his sake than offend him. Porphyry also converted two hundred knights in his retinue and taught them the faith, so that they were at all times ready to live and die with him. But Katherine remained in her dungeon, and since she was without food for twelve days, as the tyrant had ordered, Christ himself fed her from heaven, to compensate nature's need, by means of a white dove. When the twelve days were done, Christ appeared to her with a large company of angels and spoke to her benignly: "Behold your creator, daughter, for whose name you have begun a great struggle. Be steadfast, for I will not fail to be with you in every need." And he returned to heaven.

The next day the emperor came home. He sent for Katherine, hoping she would be endangered or dead, but he beheld her brighter and fresher of color than before she went to prison. In his frenzy he blamed the jailers and beat them, assuming they had given her food or permitted someone to bring her food. Katherine intervened to excuse them: "Sir, you beat your men without their guilt, for truly (believe it if you wish) during all these twelve days that I have been imprisoned in a dark dungeon, I have had no food from any earthly man; but my lord Jesus has fed me delicacies from angels' hands every day." "Katherine, listen to me," he said, "and let my words sink into your heart. Abandon this dubious and perverse answer, for I don't wish to treat you like a servant with awe and fear, but I would rather you were honored in my court like a queen and everyone obey you as they do me." "Sir," said Katherine, "heed my words and listen to me. Decide now with a just judgment whether I ought prudently to choose him who is mighty, stable, and reigning eternally, gracious, glorious, beautiful; or him who is the contrary, weak, and unstable, whose reign is short and temporary, graceless, unglorious, deformed. That's how it is between my lord and you, so I will forsake you for him."

"All right," said he, "then I will negotiate no more delays with you as I have done. Choose: Will you sacrifice and live, or die with cruel torment?" Katherine answered, "Know, tyrant, that I wish to live so that Christ, my love, may be my life. I don't dread to die for him, for I fully expect to obtain eternal reward in heaven that way. So delay no longer whatever you have decided to torment me with, for I am called by my lord Jesus. For his sake I am ready to sacrifice my flesh and blood wholeheartedly, just as he for my sake once offered up his flesh and blood to the father of heaven, with hard pains and without complaint."

The emperor was like a madman when he heard these words; he considered how to destroy her. A limb of Satan called Cursates, the prefect of the city, came to him, saying, "O mighty emperor, Katherine has not yet seen a torture device that will make her tremble for fear of it and consent to sacrifice to our gods. Sir, I come to invent one for you. Command that within three days four huge wheels be built, whose moving circles will be thickly studded with iron spikes. Each spoke should also be fitted with iron saws, ground as sharp as possible, so that when the wheels turn each one will catch in her flesh, and what one leaves the other will get when she is set in the middle of them all." This advice was followed, and on the third day everything was set out in the middle of the courtyard, and everyone who saw it was afraid. No wonder it terrified people, for the wheels were arranged so that two would rip on the way up, and two on the way down.

When Katherine was placed between these wheels that would either kill her or force her to sacrifice for fear, she prayed to God to send his grace for the worship of his name, and that the people who stood there to watch would be converted, and the device be destroyed. At that very moment, an angel gave the machine such a blow, like a thunderclap, that it fell to the ground in a thousand pieces. In falling it killed a thousand heathen standing by and neither hurt nor touched any Christian. The Christians made great joy and gladness, thanking God, but there was sorrow and shame among the heathens. And when the emperor had seen this accident, he stood as if in a trance.

The queen came to him: she was Christian, but had kept her decision secret until she saw this miraculous event. To the emperor she said, "O you cursed, miserable villain, what is wrong with you that you struggle with God? What madness compels you now to rebel against your creator? At least you might learn from this the power of the Christians' God and the feebleness of your gods, who in this disaster, for all the strength they pretend to have, could not protect their servants from death. Who wants to worship such gods!" The emperor was astonished to hear this, and shouted as if he had fallen into a frenzy, "What! How, O queen! What are you saying? Are you now deceived with witchcraft? Who has deceived you? Have you forsaken the religion that we have observed together for so many years? I swear by the great empire of our mighty and immortal gods that unless you fall meekly to the ground and worship them with a pure will, I shall have the breasts ripped from your chest and your head cut off and your body thrown into a place where beasts and birds will destroy it."

Because she would not perform his will, he commanded his tormentors to do exactly as he said. When she went to her sentencing, she humbly asked Katherine to pray to God for her, and Katherine answered, "O queen, dread not, but steadfastly stand firm in your faith, for today you shall make a noble exchange in taking an eternal kingdom instead of a temporal reign, and an immortal spouse for a mortal husband." Made strong with these words, the queen asked the torturers not to take too long, but to do as they were commanded quickly; and so they did. When they brought her into the field where she was to be slain, they spared not, but with iron forks cruelly ripped the breasts from her body, and then struck off her head and left her dead body lying in the field to be devoured by beasts and birds.

But Porphyry took the body out of the field that same night and prepared it with sweet ointments and buried it worthily. Early the next day an inquiry was made as to who had buried the queen's body against the law. The emperor put many to death on suspicion. Then Porphyry came forth publicly and said, "O tyrant, I am the man who buried the body of this blessed woman who was martyred as a servant to Christ in heaven. I am vulnerable to the same treatment, for I believe in the Christian faith and completely reject all false gods with all my heart." At this the tyrant leaped up as if he had been wounded with a spear, and shouted, "Alas the moment when I was born!" So horribly he began to roar that the whole palace could hear: "Alas, Porphyry, my companion, my soul's keeper, my special comfort, to whom I always resorted for advice. He is now deceived, it seems, alas! For he praises the Christians' God and utterly despises our gods." He called out Porphyry's knights, inquiring of them if they knew anything about how this had happened. And with one voice they all cried, "We are ready to die with our lord Porphyry, and we reject false gods as he does, and we fully believe in the Christian faith. For this opinion we will flee no torment." When the tyrant saw their steadfastness, he gave sentence in his madness that Porphyry and all his knights should be beheaded together and their bodies left as the queen's was, to be devoured by beasts and birds.

Next day he dressed in his best array and sat on his imperial throne and called Katherine to him. In order to persuade her he said, "O Katherine, with your witchcraft and your misbelief you have bereft me of my knight Porphyry and my queen. Yet it is my will that you shall be second in my palace and, after me, rule. No one in the palace, on pain of death, will be so bold as to contradict you—on this condition: that you humbly and devoutly sacrifice to my gods with frankincense. If you will not consent, I will grant no further delay but will behead you today. Take this for my final word." "Tyrant," said Katherine, "I desire no further delay at all. So whatever you wish be done to me from the passion of your ire, I am ready for it." At this word he gave his decree that she should be immediately beheaded. When this decree was publicly known, and the tormentors led her toward the place where she would receive the sentence, many a matron and widow and young maiden followed after her, weeping for sorrow that she should die thus.

To them Katherine kindly said, "O noble wives and widows and young maidens, leave your sadness and your weeping and make no plans to delay my ordeal. Instead, rejoice and be glad that my lord, my love, will permit me to stay here no longer but to his house will lead me home as his own spouse." Then she lifted her eyes upward to heaven and said, "O hope and help of all who trust in you, O worship and glory of all virgins, O gracious Jesus, to you I call with all my heart, thanking you that you grant from your goodness to count me among your handmaidens. I beseech you with all meekness, lord, to show your handmaiden this grace: that whatever man or woman in whatever place remembers my ordeal in worship of your name, or prays to me for help in the hour of their death or in any anguish or necessity, you will hear their request readily. Moreover, Jesus, since I am ready to take the sword of death for your sake, vouchsafe to receive what the tyrant cannot keep, I mean my spirit, which I commend into your hands."

Scarcely had she ended this prayer when a voice answered, "Come, love! Come, spouse! Come here to me! For the gate of heaven is open to you, and through it a great many saints are coming to meet you, my sweet spouse, bringing with them a triumphal crown of everlasting bliss to please you, and you shall wear it forever. Come forth, and be concerned with your requests no longer, for they are accepted in my court and enforced to last forever: that whoever with pure heart remembers your passion or calls to you in any anguish or tribulation, for your sake the petition shall be quickly heard."

Her fair white neck she stretched out and bid him strike, and with one stroke the soul went to heaven and the body to ground. This done, God showed two miracles for her sake. The first was that instead of blood, there ran from her neck such a flood of milk that all the ground around it was wet and as white as any lake. The second was that angels took up her body and quickly carried it many miles away, to Mount Sinai (where Moses received the commandments from God), twenty days journey from Alexandria. They made a royal burial for her there, and out of her tomb flows oil, continuously and plentifully, which through her merits heals and cures all illness or accident, if it is received with devotion.

Now, blessed Katherine, be intermediary for me to God's mercy in heaven, so that the wretchedness of my forelife may be amended through his grace before I pass hence. Also, lady, I pray for your two Katherines, Howard and Denston, for whose spiritual comfort and consolation I made of your legend this short translation into English in five days. Grant them, lady, to be so practiced in virtue in this life—and me also—that when we have completed the mortal course of this wretched outlawry, we may, through your guidance and special grace, enter that glorious place where you live and reign, as everyone knows. Let everyone who hears this legend say "Amen." Thank you Jesus.

SAINT CECELIA'S LIFE

Prologue

"Cecelia" is the equivalent of "lily of heaven" or "a way to the blind"; or else this word "Cecelia" is put together from "celum" and "Leah"; or else "Cecelia" signifies "lacking blindness," according to its etymology; or it denotes "celo" and "leos," which means "people." To each of these interpretations a suitable development is given in her legend, according to Voragine, the author of the story. First he calls her "the lily of heaven" because of the heavenly gem of virginity that she had in great excellence. Or else people may call her "a lily" (according to Voragine) for three reasons: she first of all had the whiteness of chastity, then the greenness of conscience, and the redolence of good name far and wide. She was both way and guide to the blind by offering fuller knowledge. She was heavenly by her love of contemplation, and, as this author says, "Leah" in her steadfast good works. She can also be called "heaven" another way, as he says, for, as Isidore teaches, the philosophers say that heaven is mobile and always revolving; it is round, and ardently aflame. Cecelia was habitually turning through her care for good works; round by perseverance; and ardently burning with charity. Voragine says she is also "lacking blindness" by the great brightness of wisdom that she had outstandingly, as people can see who read

141

her legend earnestly. Last of all he calls her "the people's heaven," proving this with a similitude: for just as the people physically see the sun and moon and the seven stars in heaven, so in Cecelia they may spiritually perceive the distinct brightness of distinct virtues, as this author says: the sun representing wisdom, the moon faith, and the stars the distinct variation of different and separate virtues.

Now, blessed Cecelia, since you are lily of heaven in chaste purity and way to the blind by perfectness of good works; since you were endowed with both active and contemplative life; since the great brightness of wisdom made you devoid of inward spiritual blindness and an exemplary heaven of all virtues—therefore help them that call to you in need and worship you with special affection; get them protection against their enemies, obtain cleanness of living for them, be their leader that they never fall into the darkness of sin. Turn their hearts to heavenly conversation so that when they pass from this outlawry they may attain to that high glory where, according to the holy Prophet's doctrine, the rightful shall shine like stars in perpetual eternity. Everyone say "amen" for charity. Amen.

Here Begins the Life of Saint Cecelia

Cecelia was born of noble Roman blood which at that time was most highly respected socially. From the cradle she was fostered in Christ's faith and carried Christ's gospel secretly within her breast. She never ceased day or night from prayer or holy talk, commending her virginity to God. She was engaged to a young man named Valerian, also born of high lineage. When the day set for their marriage arrived, Cecelia put on a hair shirt next to her skin, and over that a fair white smock, covering them both with clothes of gold beautifully worked, to blind the world with her external appearance. But covertly in her inward mind, while the organs sang melodiously, Cecelia sang to God: "Lord God, I meekly beg you to preserve my heart and my body undefiled, in cleanness of chastity, so that I should not be ruined." For two or three days she fasted and prayed humbly, commending to God what she dreaded.

To continue with the story: On the marriage day, darkness had put the day to flight and everyone had returned to his house. Valerian and Cecelia went then to their bedchamber where, in their silent privacy, Cecelia spoke her mind: "O sweetest young man, O dear spouse whom I love best with all my heart, I have an extremely intimate secret that I would confess to you on condition that you swear you will not betray it but will always respect it firmly." Valerian agreed, swearing that he would never disclose it to anyone as long as he lived. Cecelia then said soberly, "I have a lover, an angel of God, who preserves my body jealously. If he finds that you have touched me even slightly with unclean love, intending to defoul me physically, he will be angry with you and take cruel vengeance, so that, for a little fleshly lust, you will lose the flower of your youthful beauty. If he sees that you love me in perfect chastity and do not oppress me nor pluck the flower of my virginity, then he will love you as well as he does me, and show you his grace plentifully."

Valerian answered seriously, like one restrained by mercy, "If you want me to believe you, show me that angel you speak of. When I have proved him to be an angel, then I will perform what you suggest. But if I find that you love another man than me, your spouse Valerian, I vow to strike off your head instantly, and his." Cecelia replied, "I agree. If you take my advice and purify yourself in the well of life and believe there is only one God in heaven, then you will see my angel." "And where might there be any such man," said he, "that might and can purify me so that I can see an angel?" "I know one, but he is old; he has the knowledge and power to purify people and make everything so clear that they may behold an angel." "And where might I find that man? If I knew, I would seek him out," said Valerian. Cecelia said, "I will show you. First go three miles from here down the Appian Way, and you will find poor people sitting in the street. Greet them on my behalf, for I have always been fond of them, and they know me and my teaching quite well. Say I send them my blessing, asking them to tell you where to find Pope Urban, for you have a secret errand from me to him. They will know where he is. When you come to him, tell him everything word for word as I've told you. He will gladly purify you and dress you in new white clothes, and when you are dressed and return here, you shall have grace to see the angel who will love you as well as me and grant what you ask."

Valerian arose and began his journey. When he was a mile outside the gates, as Cecelia had instructed him, he found Urban lurking among the caves and graves, and he did his errand as Cecelia had said to do. When the pope heard it he rejoiced, lifting his hands and eyes to heaven. Kneeling and weeping he said, "Lord Jesus Christ who knows everything and who sows the seed of chaste counsel, take up to yourself the fruit of the seed that Cecelia has sown for your sake. Take heed and behold, O lord Jesus, how Cecelia your virtuous servant is as industrious in serving you as ever any bee was to gather flowers and make honey. For here is her husband, first as fierce as a mad lion, whom she has made as obedient to you as a lamb and has sent him here to test the truth. He would not have agreed to come, I believe, had he not given credence to Cecelia's words. Therefore, lord, I pray for him here and now. Vouchsafe to open the gate of his heart and to widen it for learning. Illumine him with grace that he may know his creator, his lord, his God, his redeemer, and renounce all the devil's black works and forsake all idols which he previously worshiped and never serve them again."

While he was thus occupied in prayer, suddenly there appeared before them an aged man dressed in clean white clothing. In his hand he held a text written with letters of gold. When Valerian beheld him, he was so astonished that for fear he fell down as if dead. The old man lifted him up and said, "Fear not, young man, but read this written text and believe it, so that you may be pure and clean enough to see the angel which your wife Cecelia has promised you." Valerian arose, looked at the writing, and silently read. The statement was this: "One lord and one faith and one baptism there is, and one God who is father of all things and is over us, near us, and in us all." When Valerian had thoroughly taken it in, the old man said, "Do you believe this or not? Or do you stand in doubt? Say honestly." Valerian loudly cried, "There is nothing under heaven, it seems to me, that may be more truly believed than this." With that the old man vanished away, they knew not where. Then Urban baptized him and instructed him in the faith of Christian ways and sent him home again to Cecelia.

When he arrived, he went to the bedroom and found Cecelia in prayer. Beside her stood an angel with wings glittering brighter than gold. The angel held two garlands of red roses and white lilies, like royal diadems, of such sweet odor that neither balm nor frankincense smelled so sweet. The angel distributed these garlands, setting one on Cecelia's head and the other on Valerian's, saying, "These two crowns, which I have brought from paradise, are to be kept with cleanness of heart and body, as a sign of which they will always keep their color and odor and never fade. No one will see them except those whom chastity has pleased, as it has you. And, Valerian, since you have assented to chastity, God has sent me to you so that whatever you like to ask of him, ask and you shall have it. Go ahead, ask: I await your answer."

"Indeed," Valerian now said, "there is no creature on earth so dear to me, after my wife, as my brother Tiburtius. Out of compassion and pity I would like him to know, as I do, the truth about his errors and his misbelief. For it would be cruel and against the rule of brotherly charity for me to be saved and him lost. Since God has granted me my request, I make my full petition: that just as God has saved me from perdition through my wife Cecelia, so let him guarantee to recall my brother from death to life through me, and let us both be perfect in his love. This is the entirety of my wish." The angel said cheerfully, "Since you have so charitably asked what God is highly pleased to grant, I promise that your petition is heard. Moreover, God has granted through his special grace that you shall both on the same day come through martyrdom to heaven's bliss, to abide there with him in joy forever."

The angel glided away, they knew not how, and at that moment Tiburtius came and called at the door. When he entered, he courteously kissed Cecelia's head, as was the custom in those days, and said, "I wonder why I smell such a sweet odor of lilies and roses at this time of year, as if it were midsummer eve. Truly, brother, it couldn't be a sweeter smell if I held lilies and roses in my fist. I feel it has refreshed me more marvelously than I can say." "Tiburtius, brother," said Valerian, "through my prayer, thank God, you have had the odor of lilies and roses, but through his grace and your own belief you may see them. Both your sister Cecelia and I have beautifully made garlands sent us by God from paradise. They can't be seen by anyone blinded with despair, so they are still invisible to you and will be until you give credence to a better doctrine and are subject to Christ's faith."

"Do I hear this in a dream or awake?" replied Tiburtius. "Is all this true, brother?" "We have lived in sleep up to now, brother, and that's a shame; but now we are in truth and there is no falseness in us, I am confident. For those dolls, which up to now we have served with godly honor, are in reality only devils." Then Tiburtius said, "How do you know this, Valerian, brother, I ask you?" "An angel of God taught me, whom you will not be able to see until you are purified from the filth of false idolatry." "Then why should I not hurry to be purified, if it will help me to see an angel? Help me to do it quickly." With that word, Cecelia went to him and kissed his breast and said, "Cousin, now I acknowledge you to be truly mine. For just as God's love has proved your brother to be my husband today, so contempt of idols shall show you truly to be my cousin. Go with your brother to purify yourself, and hurry, so that you may get the grace to see an angel's glorious face."

As they were leaving, Tiburtius said, "Kind and faithful brother, before we go, I ask where I will be purified, and by whom." "We are going," Valerian answered, "to the holy Pope Urban, who has power to purify and liberate people so that they can see angels." Said Tiburtius, "Isn't this Urban the one who is so hated in this city that he dare not live in a house, but skulks among tombs and hides in caves? Hasn't he been condemned to death or burning by a public decree? If we are found with him, I dare say we will be burnt with him and then our intentions will be frustrated. Where we seek immortal life, we shall find a cruel fall, and therefore it's better to avoid such things."

Cecelia said, "Tiburtius, listen to me a little and I will kindle a better opinion in you with God's grace. It would be good to fear and avoid losing this life if there were no better one elsewhere. But whoever thinks that is wrong. For there is another life incomparably better than this one and worthier. Whoever has grace to grasp it can never be taken from it by death, nor can hunger, thirst, or sickness ever distress him. To teach about this life, the son of heaven's father came down with mild voice, born temporally of a maid in our frailty, but born eternally before all time from his father, to whom he is, was, and ever shall be equal. In and by him everything was wrought, and without him nothing was ever made. To him and the father the holy ghost is consubstantial and coeternal, and though they are personally distinct, yet in substance the three of them are one, undivided externally in their operation."

Tiburtius said, "This way of talking seems completely irrational to me, for you posit first one god and then three, and I can't understand it." "No wonder," Cecelia said, "for unless God illumine you with the special influence of his grace, you shall never attain to comprehension of this matter. Nonetheless I will offer you one or two examples so that you may empirically prove a thing to be single in substance yet rationally distinct in three even without another substance. First I'll demonstrate this with the soul, which has three distinct powers—mind, reason, and understanding—and yet substantially they are only one soul. Another example I can adduce is fire, which has threefold variation in formally distinct properties and yet in substance they are one fire. Similarly, snow, hail, and ice are distinct in name and form, as wise philosophers note, but substantially they are only water. The same may theoretically be conceived of the trinity: trinity in persons, unity in substance. However, none of these similitudes can fully prove the truth as it really is, for logic fails here and only faith prevails. That is why Scripture says that unless you have faith and belief, you cannot achieve understanding.

So abandon rational evidence and believe in scriptural doctrine, which teaches us that in the sovereign deity, three distinct persons are one substance. The second of these, as I said before, was born from a maiden without a man and as a mediator to his father in heaven undertook to make reparation for our forefather's transgression, which infected all his descendants with original sin. So he suffered cruel torment: he was taken and tied, scorned and scourged, crowned with a crown of thorns and nailed to a wooden cross hand and foot, hung up between two thieves as their master and the worst of them, and given vinegar to drink in his great thirst. After all this, when he pleased to do so he commended his spirit into his father's hands and willingly sent it forth. When he was dead he was cruelly cut to the heart with a sharp spear through the right side so that water and blood poured out: blood as ransom to buy back mankind, water to purify humanity from sin by the sacrament of holy baptism (if it is received with a good will). To this give faith and full credence, receive baptism with reverence, and you shall be cleansed and purified and made able to see angels."

Then Tiburtius said to his brother, "Have mercy on me and lead me to the man who can purify me with that sacrament, which I intend to receive according to the counsel of my sister Cecelia." So Tiburtius, led by his brother, was baptized by Pope Urban and made a Christian, and shortly he grew so perfect that he could see angels when he pleased and speak with them face to face. Such was his grace that whatever he asked of God, he had. He and his brother abandoned everything else to devote themselves to holy alms deeds, and because they loved and feared God they worked hard to bring bodies to burial that had been slain by Almachius, prefect of the city, because they were Christian.

When Almachius heard about this, he had them arrested. He asked why they were so concerned to bury people whom he had condemned for wickedness. Said Tiburtius, "Would God that we were able to be the servants of those whom you wrongfully called condemned. With all their hearts they wisely despised that which seems to be something in appearance but which is nothing in real existence. Against such appearance they have found, and with death they have purchased, what most truly is and yet seems like nothing." "What may that be?" asked Almachius. "Listen and I will tell you. What seems to be and is not, is everything here in the world, which deceives us and ruins everyone who trusts in it when they die. But the thing that most perfectly is and seems not to be, is the eternal bliss ordained to them who dwell in heaven above—or in hell whose inhabitants shall never cease being tormented." "I believe," said Almachius, "that you are mindless, for you speak like a man without intelligence." To Valerian he said, "Since your brother Tiburtius is witless, I assume that you

who are better in your mind will find a wiser answer. It
seems to me that they err greatly who forsake peace and
choose war, and love sorrow more heartily than joy."

Valerian answered him: "Often in winter, as I hear tell,
many people joke and play in frost and snow, scorning
those who labor to till the ground. But in summer when
the fruit of their labor has come, they are well fed, and
have abundance of wealth, while the others weep and are
distressed in misery and need. This is how you and we are:
for we suffer wrong, pain, and torment here and now in this
present life, and they will soon end; but when we go forth
we receive joy that never ends. You do the contrary, for you
have transitory and momentary joy here, but when you go
forth you go to a place of endless woe." "Then you conclude," Almachius said, "that we who are princes of temporal felicity shall go to the place of endless sorrow, and you
treacherous criminals to endless bliss?" Said Valerian, "You
are wrong, for you are manikins and no princes, born in
your time, little durable, and accountable to God when you
pass away—even more so than others." Almachius replied,
"Why do we circle about in verbal battle? Take this for
my sentence and conclusion: Offer sacrifice to our gods
here, and you shall leave without harm; otherwise you
will die."

With one voice they said, "Every day as soon as we get
up, we offer a sacrifice to our God." "What is your god's
name?" asked Almachius. "If you had wings and could
fly a thousand miles above the spheres, you still wouldn't
come where he dwells." "Ah," said Almachius, "then I
suspect his name is Jupiter." "Fie, for shame!" said Valerian.
"Never dishonor our God by likening him to a homicide
and braggart like Jupiter." "*Ergo*," said Almachius, "all the
world errs except your brother and you, and only you two
have the true belief?" "No, for sure, tyrant, whether you
like it or not there are many hundreds who believe the
same as we do." When Almachius saw that he could not
move them to sacrifice, neither by stern nor by pleasant

treatment, he delivered them to Maximus his adjutant, with the command that until they had humbly sacrificed they were to be confined.

When Maximus had them at home in his house, he addressed them: "O purple flowers of delightful youth, O brotherly affection indissolubly knit as one, how may it be that you go to death as gladly as to a feast?" Valerian replied, "If you will promise to believe, you shall see our souls go up after death to that joyful bliss which never ends." Then Maximus said, "Great God in heaven make me die with thunder and lightning if I don't believe in him when I see the reality of your words!" Forthwith he was converted and also the torturers and all his retinue, and they took baptism from Pope Urban, who came there secretly at night. So did Cecelia, who was glad that they had converted such a multitude. And so they spent the night in holy talk until Aurora began to rise, whose brightness drove away the night's darkness. Then Cecelia said, "Be happy, Christ's knights, and throw away the works of darkness, for you have begun a good chivalry. Persevere in it while you die, and never forsake your belief and the way of life you have chosen. If you do so, you shall certainly receive the crown of bliss from Jesus Christ, most rightful judge who will judge everyone according to their merit at the great meeting on the last day."

After sunrise, they were led four miles out of the city to be beheaded unless they would humbly sacrifice to the statue of Jupiter. Because they wouldn't, they were both beheaded. Then Maximus swore that at that moment he saw bright angels bear up their souls to heaven, brighter than the sun or than any maid who ever came out of her chamber freshly dressed to bring in her spouse. When Almachius heard this, he ordered Maximus beaten to death with lead rods. Cecelia buried his body with Tiburtius and Valerian, and then Almachius made an investigation of her property. He was told about her, that she was Valerian's wife, and sent officers to her house to arrest her.

On her arrival, he gave her a choice: either sacrifice or be shamefully slain. When the officers led her away to compel her to the deed, they considered the high nobility of her birth and the seemliness and great beauty of her person, and they began to weep for pity, saying, "Alas! Why is this maid willing to lose her youth?" To them she said, "Don't weep for me, young men, but listen to what I will say. That I now choose to die rather than to sacrifice is not to lose my youth but a wise substitution, as if a man made a contract to give earth and take gold, or to exchange a rotten old house for a royal palace of precious stones. But now I ask you: If for each penny you could receive a whole shilling at a market or fair, as many as you brought, wouldn't you hurry there? I believe you would! Now, sirs, truly God has set up an even better market in his court above, for to everything that is sold to him the set price is a hundredfold and, on top of that, eternal life. A hundred for one, with this added benefit? What do you think? Tell the truth." They all said, "We truly believe that Christ your lord is the only God, and none but he, who has called you—so prudent and wise—to his service." Then Pope Urban was sought and secretly brought at night to christen forty and more of these newly converted, with joy and gladness.

When Almachius discovered this, in his insanity he sent new officers for Cecelia. When she presented herself before his bench, "Of what status are you?" he asked. "A gentlewoman born, and noble," she said. "I am asking about your religion and your belief." "Then your asking is ignorant if it can produce two answers to one question." "Where do you get this bold presumption in answering me?" asked Almachius. "From pure conscience and unfeigned faith the answer came to me," said Cecelia. "Don't you know my power?" "Yes, yes!" said she, "I can tell very well what your power is. It seems to me that all your power can be likened to a bladder blown full of wind until it is firm, but anyone can deflate it, for with a needle's point anyone can let out the wind and slacken the firmness. That's what your power is like." "You started with insults and you continue the same way," said Almachius. She replied, "Something is not an insult unless uttered with words of deceit. So first prove that I spoke falsely, and, if you can't, you are to blame for defaming me with false calumny."

"Don't you know our princes' decree? They have ordained that whoever denies and forsakes Christ shall be entitled to freedom and respect, and those who won't deny Christ shall be tormented to death." "Your princes err as much as you do if they can shame us innocents in no other way than to accuse us of Christ's name. But we want you to know that we who know this holy name neither can nor will deny it. We think it better to die blessedly than to live cursedly." Almachius said, "Come, now! Choose either to sacrifice to our gods, or quit being a Christian; either way you can escape harmless."

Then Cecelia said, as if joking, "Look, everyone, to what extremity this judge is brought, that he would make me quit being an innocent in order to make me nocent!" Said Almachius, "Don't you know, wretch, how far my power may stretch by our prince's commission, to revive or to kill? Then why do you answer me so proudly now?" "As for pride," said Cecelia, "I dare say it has nothing to do with me, but my answer is founded and grounded in constancy. But if you don't fear to hear the truth, I'll show how you have lied. You just said to me that your prince had committed to you the power to revive or to kill, but there you lied, for you can perform only one of these: you can kill but not revive. So if you don't want to lie, say this: that your princes have made you minister of death and no more; for if you claim more, your veracity is gone." "Leave this boldness," said Almachius, "and prepare to sacrifice to our gods, for by philosophy I have learned to endure my personal misfortunes and suffer them patiently, but I can't tolerate patiently any irreverence toward our gods." "Indeed," she said, "since you first opened your mouth, no word showed you to be a fool as much as this, for not only your inward reason is blind but even your bodily eyes. You call a god a thing we all see is a stone. So for your own benefit, do this: reach out your hand and prove it a stone by touching the thing you foolishly imagine, by seeing, to be a god. Let your hand teach your eye the truth, and then you'll no longer be laughed to scorn as you have been before, by many people who know for certain that God dwells only in heaven, and that these figures of stone, brass, or wood are not true gods but false idols who can neither help nor rescue themselves or others, as both reason and experience can prove."

When Almachius saw from this statement that he could not persuade Cecelia, it disturbed him. He sent her home, ordering that she should be scalded in a hot bath there. When she had been in it an entire day and night with no physical harm anywhere, she was as cheerful as if she were in a cool green arbor; there wasn't a drop of sweat on her. Informed of the case, Almachius thought, "Alas! What can I do to win the victory over this wicked woman? For while she lives I will never have peace of mind." So, to please himself, he decreed that she should be beheaded on the spot. He sent a tormentor to do it, who gave her one stroke of the sword, and then two more; but in spite of three strokes her head could not be cut off. Since the law said that people being beheaded could have no more than three strokes, the lictor went away and left her half dead.

Many Christians came and gathered up her blood in clean handkerchiefs. For the three days she lived this way, she never ceased her holy teaching, exhorting the people she had won to Christianity to be steadfast to the faith. She shared out her possessions in alms, and when this was done, she commended the people to the tuition of Pope Urban, to whom she meekly said, "Holy father, I have asked for three days' respite to commend to you these people that I have won over by God's grace, and to ask that my role in serving God be commemorated in a church." Her soul then went where God would have it go, but through a special grace Pope Urban buried her body in the same place where popes were buried. He then went to her house to bless and consecrate it, as was her wish, into a church, where numerous miracles have been shown in honor of God and his dear martyr.

Whoever wishes to know when she was martyred, I say that Cecelia the holy virgin was martyred in the year of grace 223 (as *Legenda Aurea* teaches), and the tenth calend of December, when Alexander reigned as Roman emperor. Now, blessed Cecelia, flower of maidenhood, gem of steadfastness, rose of martyrdom and lily of virginity in your holy purpose, benignly hear the simple prayer of him who translated your legend and who long ago took you, Faith, and Barbara as his valentines and never will forsake you while he lives. Purchase for him the grace to make satisfaction before he dies for the wretchedness of his earlier way of life, so that when body and soul are parted and he passes away from this outlawry, he may be joyful with you in heaven. Amen and thank you Jesus.

SAINT AGATHA'S LIFE

Prologue

As I find written in *Legenda Aurea*, the word "Agatha" may be expounded in five ways. First from "hagios" which signifies "holy," and "theos" which means "God"; so that "Agatha" is equivalent to "God's holy." This is fitting for her, for three things belong to God's holy, as says John Chrysostom, and these were well known to Agatha: chastity of heart, presence of the holy ghost, and abundance of good works. Another way of interpretation, as Voragine suggests, is that "Agatha" comes from "a-geos": "a" is "without" and "geos" is "earth," meaning this: that Agatha in her inward will was devoid of all earthly desires. Or, third, "Agatha" comes from "aga," "speaking," and "thau," "ending," because she was first and last perfect in her speaking, as her responses show. Fourth to our purpose, "agad" connotes "servage" with "theos" added, which means "sovereign," implying that she taught the best service to be the service of Christ. The fifth and last derivation of this well-known name "Agatha," according to the authorities, is from "aga," interpreted as "solemn," and "thav," meaning "consummation"; this is fitting for Agatha because she was perfected by the burial of holy angels. Now, blessed Agatha, take care that they who love and worship you, God's holy, may be endowed with chastity of heart, abundance of good works pure from earthly desires, and to have such perfection of speech that all their words may bespeak virtue. Grant them to be practiced in the service of Christ Jesus so that when their bodies are laid in bier, their souls may be led by angels to that place of heavenly felicity where you dwell. And especially attend to Agnes Flegge, O blessed lady, and help her to purchase such grace before she passes out of this world that she may have due contrition of all her wrongs, and plenary confession, and time and leisure to make satisfaction and to take the holy sacrament of Christ's body with such holy will that the devil cannot keep her with any interference from that sovereign bliss where joy and mirth are endless. May our lord Jesus bring both her and us there through thy merits.

Here Begins the Life of Saint Agatha

Agatha, of whom I have spoken above, was born on the island of Sicily, in the royal city of Catania. She descended lineally from the noblest blood of that country, according to *The Golden Legend*, but I find no source that can declare her genealogy, nor her progenitors' pedigree, nor her father's nor mother's name. I do find that she was most excellently endowed with the gifts of grace and nature. She had not only great beauty of body and soul but also served God in all holiness, day and night. Privately she despised wealth and all fleshly lusts, and worldly considerations could neither encourage her nor divert her from God's love.

A man named Quintian was sent from Rome to rule the country and to occupy the office of consul. Low of birth he was, by Fortune set high on her wheel that is always unstable, changing, and mutable, never standing still but always turning—as Quintian's end shows, which at the end of this legend they shall hear who care to attend. This

Quintian was not only ignoble but also a thoroughly vicious man, and especially he was libidinous because of fleshly lust. As well, he was greedy, false in belief, and an idolator who paid godly honor to statues and denied true God in heaven. When this Quintian observed Agatha's intention, he sent his officers for her and handed her over to one Aphrodisia, a woman who lived sinfully, offering her body to the uncleanness of whoever came. She had nine girls with her of similar wickedness. Quintian charged them to do their best, whether by threats or promises, within thirty days to remove Agatha from God's grace and turn her heart to idolatry.

He urged them to that end, but it would not be. "Know this," Agatha said, "that my heart is grounded on such a rock, and so steadfastly founded in Christ Jesus, and built up so well, that all your windy words, your flood of threats, and your promises like rain are vain and frustrated in me. For however hard you attack my foundation, you can't prevail against it, nor can you make the building fall down beneath you." Thus she often said, weeping, and prayed God with devout heart to let her take death for his love and so to enter into that bliss where joy and mirth are endless. When Aphrodisia saw the constancy of blessed Agatha, and the goodness from which she would not be moved, she said to Quintian: "Sir, as far as I can see, it is easier to mollify stones and make them as soft as bread, or make iron as malleable as lead, than it is to convert this tender maiden's heart from Christian faith: all are impossible."

Quintian commanded Agatha into his presence and spoke to her thus: "Damsel, tell me of what kindred you are born." Said Agatha, "I say without arrogance that I am a gentlewoman, as all my kin can bear witness." "If you are a gentlewoman," he said, "why do you present yourself as a menial in behavior and status?" "Because I am Christ's handmaid, and for Christ's sake I am not afraid to present myself as a servant." "Then satisfy this question: since you are noble and freeborn, how can you be a handmaid? For

I assume nobility and servitude are contrary and cannot be combined." "Indeed," said Agatha, "if you were illumined with the influence of heavenly grace, you would change this declaration and in your ideas would observe that Christ's servitude is the greatest gentry, and the supremest freedom and liberty are in his service. To serve him is a kingly duty."

"Do leave off this talking, silly woman! Choose one of two things: whether you will lose your life with violence and pain, or humbly offer frankincense, kneeling to our gods who are immortal and who wield everything in their subjection." "Since such high renown," she said, "is in your gods as you say, I wish your wife were like Venus your goddess and you like Jove your god, whom you pretend sits above all other gods and whom you call on for help and beg for aid in every trouble." He ordered her slapped in the face, saying, "Be not presumptuous to open your mouth to the injury of your judge but hold your tongue as is wise and don't joke with me, I advise you." "Certainly," said Agatha, "I marvel that you who consider yourself so wise have grown so foolish and silly and erroneous that you honor and solemnly worship such gods as you don't deign to be compared with. You won't have yourself or your wife assimilated to these gods in your living, but you consider it an injury and a wrong that I wish you to live as long as your gods do. If they are such perfect gods, then I am wishing you nothing but good. On the other hand, if you separate yourself from their life, deliberately disdaining their images, then you agree with me and value them as little as I do."

"Why are you so concerned," said Quintian, "to trick me with vain and wily speeches and to kill time cleverly? Briefly I say that unless you humbly and wholeheartedly sacrifice to our gods, I shall torture you so that you will die of pain and lose all worldly solace." To which Agatha soberly replied, "Little I care how you threaten me, for though you promise to send me to wild beasts, they would grow tame on once hearing Christ's name. Though you try to intimidate me with fear of fire, I won't change my behavior, for angels will bring me the dew of healthful salvation down from heaven. And though you threaten torment and wounds and beating with rods and whips, I hope to have comfort from the holy ghost that will save me and make me so strong that whatever you can devise in pain and cruel torture, through his grace I despise it all with my whole heart." Quintian had her led to prison, for she had completely defeated him publicly in front of everyone.

She went as gladly as to a royal feast, and, both on her way and in the prison (as Voragine tells us in his *Golden Legend*), she humbly commended her cause to God in devout prayer. Early next morning, Quintian called for her and said, "Agatha, I advise you for your own good to forsake Christ your God here, publicly, and to offer to my gods reverently on your knees." But Agatha would not forsake Christ or sacrifice to Quintian's gods, so he commanded her to be hung on a gibbet and beaten cruelly. She said to him quietly, "I welcome these pains like someone hearing good news, or like someone receiving a visit from a person he has long desired to see, or like someone who has just found a buried treasure. For good wheat isn't stored in the lord's granary until it is threshed and beaten and separated from the chaff and made clean; similarly my soul can't enter the place of glorious paradise by the palm of martyrdom until you destroy my body with your torturers and purify my soul from vice. Spare not, for I am ready to suffer whatever you wish to do."

"Go ahead, you tormentors," said Quintian, "and show this young lady some of your skills. Touch her near the heart, on her breasts, and hurt her, and let her know what pain is." They began to force her; some with blunt, dull pincers began to pull violently at her breasts; some brought firebrands and burnt her breasts; some tore out the flesh with iron forks so that it was atrocious to see how the blood ran out everywhere plenteously. Then he bade the torturers to cut her breasts off and throw them away, alas! When the skin and flesh were cut away, Agatha said, "O criminal, cruel, cursed tyrant, have you no shame, to cut away what on your mother you sucked for nourishment when you were small and before you had wit or discretion? It should be any man's perdition to disfigure a woman as you have done to me in your rage. But despite your cruelty and your furious violence, through heaven's help I have in my soul complete breasts that you can never take from me with any pain. With them I nurse and sustain my wits diligently; I have consecrated them to God from the beginning of my adolescence."

Quintian had her led to prison immediately and forbade any doctor to come to her. He also ordered no one to be so bold as to bring her meat or drink, intending, in his melancholy and ire, to starve her out. But God, lord and ruler of heaven, who commands everything at will, would not permit Quintian to kill his servant with such a cruel judgment. And so about midnight he sent an old man to her in the prison, led by a child with a light. This old man seemed to be a doctor, and he brought with him various medicines that could cure her wounds. When he came to her, he said, "O maid Agatha, although this madman, this consul Quintian has tortured you badly, yet you have tormented him with your answer more than he has you. He is confused in his conscience and at his wit's end. But because I was present when he tore the breasts off your chest cruelly, with neither pity nor mercy, I know that through my skill they can be restored and made whole again if you wish. That is why I have come and have brought with me many effective ointments to cure your every sore; otherwise I would not have come here now."

Steadily Agatha replied, "Sir, I wish you to know that never since I was born have I used medicine on my body and it would be shameful to begin now." "Daughter, I am a Christian," said he, "and you needn't be embarrassed in front of me." "No, no, I am not at all embarrassed in front of you, nor afraid, for you seem by your face to be far along in age, and I on the other hand am so badly wounded and torn from torture that no man would be tempted in lust to me. I thank you gratefully for your charitable offer to cure me, but it can't be, so go away." "I ask why," he said, "you will not permit me to cure you." "Indeed, sir, because I have a lord called Christ Jesus, who is so powerful and mighty that with one word he can cure all my grief and every sore, and restore me to perfect health. If he wishes, it shall be done." "And this same lord sent me to you," said the old man, smiling, "and I am his apostle, in whose name you are delivered from all distress and your wounds cured." This said, he suddenly vanished and was seen no more in that place. Voragine says it was Saint Peter. Then Agatha fell down on her knees, thanking God meekly for all his grace and goodness, for all her wounds were cured and her breasts restored to her chest at the very moment of Peter's departure.

The jailers were so astonished and fearful at the brightness that shone in the prison when Agatha was cured by Saint Peter, that they left all the prison doors open and fled. Someone said to her then, "O high-born young woman, since all your jailers have fled, go where you like, for every door stands wide open. Why stay here any longer?" Agatha said, "Do you want me to run away and lose the fruit of perfect patience? God forbid, because not only would that happen, but my cowardice would make trouble for my jailers if they lose me. I won't flee, but I will await in this prison whatever is to happen as long as it pleases my lord and love Christ Jesus, who lives and reigns in heaven above most powerfully with his father and the holy ghost, and always has and always will."

Four days later, Quintian sent for Agatha and spoke his mind: "Choose one or the other: either sacrifice humbly to our gods in front of everyone, or you will be tormented to death with even crueler torture than you have already suffered." "Your words are full of folly," said Agatha, "wicked, perverse and vain. They defile the air. Tell me now, you wretch in your feelings and even more wretched in your understanding, do you wish me to sacrifice to stones, and forsake God who is in his heaven and who has delivered me from all distress through his goodness and cured my every wound?" "Who is it—tell me instantly—that has healed you?" "Christ, God and man, son of her who through special privilege was maiden, mother, and wife, and son of God who sits in high heaven." "How dare you so impudently name in my presence him whom it offends me to hear of?" "However much it angers or troubles you," said Agatha, "I will believe in Christ my lord while my life lasts, and love him with a chaste and pure heart, and with my lips call him in every need, whatever happens; this, if he wills it, can save me."

"Now we will see if your Christ has power to save and heal you from the pains you'll feel very soon!"

He had broken shards spread, and under them hot coals strewn, and Agatha was laid naked thereon. While they were busy raking the hot coals under her, suddenly the earth began to quake. It shook the city so hard that a good part of the city fell down, killing two counselors who sat with the judge, and many others as well. The woeful people cried loudly, "Sir judge, we are suffering this because of the unjust tormentry you have done to Agatha, so we counsel you to cease, whatever happens." When they called on him this way, he desperately cast about for a way to end the matter, for he was afraid when he saw the earthquake, with houses, castles, towers, and walls falling down. As well, he dreaded a rebellion of the people which was likely to develop in the city. He ordered Agatha released and the fire quenched. She was taken to prison, where she prayed thus:

"Lord Jesus Christ, who made me from nothing through your grace, and from my youth have preserved me from sin's servitude and kept my body from pollution of fleshly corruption and removed worldly love from me, you who have vouchsafed me victory over all torment, and endowed me with the virtue of patience without resistance—take up my spirit now, I pray heartily, and command me to come to your mercy." When she had quietly prayed, she yielded up her spirit to the father of heaven with a cry, as Voragine says about the year of grace 253, when Decius was emperor. While the faithful hurried to prepare her blessed body for burial, a young man dressed in silk stood unnoticed by Agatha's grave, and with him a hundred children clad in white. He held a marble tablet with this epitaph engraved in Latin: "Mentem sanctam spontaneam honorem deo & patrie liberacionem." Which writing Voragine explains as follows: "This Agatha had a holy soul and offered herself freely to her passion; she gave honor and worship to God and obtained freedom for her country." When the inscribed tablet was set up on the grave, the youth with all his company vanished suddenly, never to be seen again in all the counties of Sicily.

When this miracle was known and recounted by pagans and Jews young and old, many of them came to her sepulchre to revere this holy martyr and blessed virgin. Soon after she ended her life, as Quintian rode with pomp and pride to investigate her patrimony, two of his horses went savage and began to neigh in their fierce rage. One of them bit him and the other kicked him and threw him off into a river. His body was never found nor shall be until, at the last judgment, it shall go to hell, rejoined to the soul, where it shall remain with devils in endless pain. You see, thus does God throw down justly those whose conceit elevates them above the sky for a time. This is always the conclusion of pride and of them who put their creator out of their mind, who are unresponsive to his goodness, who hate and argue with his servants and do not wish to know their God until they are plunged into pain. We have infinite examples of this, but for the moment this Quintian is sufficient to our purpose: he whom Fortune took up from servile condition with the rotation of her wheel, whom she placed in high degree and advanced to great respect, to whom she gave the rule and governance of that worthy and commodious island long called Sicily and also the dignity of consul.

When he had climbed so high, he was overthrown for his bad character as you heard, and laid low. I will say no more of this matter, but turn again to blessed Agatha and make an ending of her legend.

First I will tell one miracle, as Voragine tells, which occurred in the city of Catania about the time Agatha suffered her passion. At dawn the day after she died, a fearful thing happened by way of vengeance. A mountain near that city burst open, and out of it came copious fire that burnt fervently and ran toward the city as swiftly as a brook of rainwater; and whatever it took in its course, whether stick or stone or earth, was ablaze in fire and immediately consumed. When the multitude of pagans saw everything burning around them, they ran down from the hill to Agatha's grave, out of their wits for fear. They took the veil that covered the grave, ran to the fire, and set the veil between the city and the fire, trusting thereby to prevent the fire's progress and its furious rage and violence. And so it did, for the veil made such resistance that when the fire came to it, it ceased and did no more harm. This was doubtless done to show the merit of blessed Agatha and how plentifully she abounded in grace; and also to destroy the wickedness of pagans, who never will believe how mighty God is until they experience it through some miracle shown empirically.

Now, blessed Agnes, who in high heaven, crowned like a queen with joy and bliss, live and reign as is right, and always will: get us grace before we go, to live and behave in this outlawry in such a way that at our departure, fully purged from all our sin, we may come to the glorious place that you are in, there to abide forever with God and thee. Let everyone say "Amen" for charity. Amen and thank you Jesus.

SAINT LUCY

Prologue

Lucy takes her name by derivation from "light," as Voragine states, for, as Ambrose says, the nature of light is to offer gracious consolation in being seen, to distribute itself without contamination, to proceed straight ahead without crookedness, and to go a long distance with no delay because of its great speed.

Through this *exemplum* Voragine expresses that Lucy had the beauty of virginity with no taint of filth or uncleanness, and that she shed her charity wide about; that she had a straight intention to God without obliquity; and finally, that with perseverance she completed the line of good works. This is the meaning of Voragine's text.

Now, blessed Lucy, called light or light's way, to whom the holy ghost gave such great strength by a unique property of special grace that a thousand men could not drag you to the brothel, even with many a pair of oxen: grant us to be so strong in virtue that no vice can damage us.

Here Begins the Life of Saint Lucy

This noble virgin, this blessed Lucy—whose life I intend to narrate briefly in English if God grant me grace, time, and place to do it—was born in a commodious island that the histories call Sicily, in the city of Syracuse. She was lineally descended from the worthiest family that dwelled in the city. Her father died in her childhood; her mother, wise and good, was called Eutice. It happened that the terrible disease called dysentery afflicted the mother for four years, so badly that no doctor could help her. Whoever wishes to understand what dysentery is should try to acquaint himself with some of these men: Hippocrates, Constantinus Africanus, or Galen. They are the princes of medical theory and are called sovereign because of it: they can declare clause by clause for every disease the root and cause, and how it should be cured.

But I have no skill in that faculty, so let no one expect me to say more about it here than that in our language dysentery is commonly called the "red flux," which with corrosion of the guts exudes bloody emissions. But how this disease has three types caused by three humors—namely red choler, salt phlegm, and dry brown choler (the worst of the three)—nor why it is incurable, especially when the color of the flux is black; since I am barren of that capability I will not presume to say anything here. It suffices to know that this sickness is extremely troublesome, as they can best testify who have experienced it, especially Eutice, who had a great expense because of it for four years.

When the glorious fame of the blessed virgin Saint Agatha was spread among the people up and down the province of Sicily (she was newly martyred with great violence in the city of Catania), then on her feast day many people went to seek her from every region of Sicily and specially from Syracuse, which is only forty-five miles away. At that time, Eutice, encouraged by her daughter Lucy, planned to do the pilgrimage and, notwithstanding her illness, she and Lucy went. When they had done their pilgrimage and offered as was the custom, the procession was completed by the annual reading of the gospel that tells how a woman could not be cured of the red flux until she had touched with faithful will the lower hem of Jesus's garment. When this gospel reading was finished, Lucy said to her mother, "Mother, if you believe the meaning of this gospel, believe that Agatha always has present here him for whose name she suffered torment. I advise you to touch her grave with full faith, and you shall soon have remedy for your sickness." Later, when everyone went home to his inn to refresh himself with bodily food and other diversion, they remained and together went to Agatha's tomb to offer their devout prayer.

Soon, before she was aware of it, Lucy fell asleep. While she slept she thought she saw blessed Agatha standing amid a great company of angels, royally arrayed with bright, clear gems and saying, "Lucy, sister and devout maid, why do you come out to ask me a boon for your mother that you yourself could grant? For through your faith and goodness your mother is cured of her sickness. Moreover, know that just as this city of Catania is honored because of me, so Syracuse will be worshiped because of you, for you have made it a joyful dwelling place for God and your maidenhead." With this word Lucy started up from her sleep and said to her mother, "Mother, be glad! For now you have relief from your compulsion and are healed of your sickness. For the goodness of her by means of whose prayer you are made sound, I beg that you will never, neither in earnest nor in game, choose a mortal husband for me nor desire from my body the fruit of offspring through fleshly corruption. But all the things you would give me if my virginity went to a mortal corrupter, give me because I am uniting with the conserver and guardian of my virginity, Christ Jesus, may he ever be blessed!"

Eutice said, "O daughter Lucy, these nine years since your father died I have carefully preserved your patrimony which he left you and haven't spent any of it; and the same for whatever is mine in my own right that will also be your inheritance. So, daughter, bury me first and then you shall have full power to do whatever you like with all of it."

"Mother," said Lucy, "to tell the truth, this doesn't seem best to me; for it's more pleasing to God that a person should refuse for God's sake what he can still use. So I advise you, if you wish your gifts to be accepted by God, give him everything while you still have the choice to take it or leave it. The gifts you give when you're dying you give because you can't take it away with you; and such gifts seem little thankworthy in my opinion." Said Eutice, "As you wish, daughter, I agree." And after this they went home and from then on they distributed generous alms every day, so that there was great loss of their temporal possession, and it dwindled every day.

This was seriously considered by the man who had agreed to be Lucy's husband. In order to find out the truth of their financial affairs, he privately approached Lucy's maid to make inquiries. "Yes," said the maid, "I know quite well why she is dispersing her movable goods. It's because she has found something she wants to buy very soon, to both your profit." He was very glad of this, and assented—imagining, the fool, that the maid meant some temporal merchandise. But when he saw what was really happening, and that her fortune was nearly all consumed in alms, and nothing bought with it, he looked for a way to accuse Lucy. Against her he raised a complaint before Paschasius, the consul, to this effect: that she was Christian and lived against imperial laws.

When Paschasius was incited against Lucy, he had her arrested and thus disclosed his intent: "Lucy, you are accused here of being a Christian and of living contrary to the laws of our emperors, in damage to your ancestry. If it is true, you are to blame, so if you will avoid shame and harm, be a wise woman and sacrifice to our gods, meekly offering them frankincense." To him Lucy thus spoke her mind: "A true and immaculate sacrifice is made this way to God, the father of heaven: when a person takes pleasure in visiting fatherless children and comforting the troubled. Since I now have nothing else but myself to take as a humble sacrifice to the father of heaven, I offer myself to his sacrifice, ready to die for his sake."

"You can say such things to a Christian fool like yourself. But as for me, who am and always will be keeper of the emperor's decree, your words are in vain. So cease, Lucy, I ask you." "Yea, Paschasius," she said, "listen to what I say! You dread your mortal princes, and I dread the eternal God. You hold your prince's decrees in awe; I try to keep my God's law. You fear to offend your princes; I, to offend my God. You desire to do your prince's pleasure; and I, to please God. So now you do as you wish, and I will do as I think best." Said Paschasius, "You have wasted your patrimony on corrupters and lechers, and you speak like a strumpet." "My patrimony," replied Lucy, "I have bestowed in a secure place; but I never had corrupters neither of soul nor of body."

"Of body and soul, foolish Lucy, tell us, what are the corrupters?" "Corrupters of soul," she said, "and spiritual adulterers are all of you who try to make souls forsake their creator. For as Saint Paul says, cursed talking corrupts good manners and good living. But corrupters of the body are those who prefer here and now the pleasure of their flesh, which is mortal, to the delights that shall always last." "Indeed," said Paschasius, "these words will stop as soon as torture touches you." "That's a lie," said Lucy, "for God's word shall never cease." "*Ergo* you are a god?" he said. "Your argument is meaningless," she said; "I am no god, but I am the handmaid of him who said in the gospel: When you stand before kings and mayors who try to separate me from you, don't think at all about the form or result of whatever words you say there; for I wish you to know that it is not you who speak but it is the spirit of your almighty father on high in heaven's bliss."

"*Ergo*," said Paschasius, "the holy ghost is within you and teaches you this manner of speech you use here." "This I know for sure," replied Lucy, "that those who live always chaste here in this world are, through grace, the holy spirit's temple and its dwelling place." "Then I shall prescribe a remedy to drive the holy ghost from you. You shall be led to the bordello where, whether you want to or not, you will have to accept the lust of every comer according to the laws of nature. And when you are thus befouled with corruption, I guarantee the holy ghost will desert you." To which Lucy responded, "I know perfectly well that the body is never fouled without the soul's assent, as you may see in this example. Suppose that you force frankincense into my hand and compel me to shed it with shaking hand on red coals before your gods: do you imagine this would please your gods as a sacrifice? I believe not. But in no way can any act of that type offend the high reverence of my lord God, who cares more about the intention than the deed. So even if you in your cruelty violate the integrity of my body, I will never assent to it in my soul. I am ready to endure whatever torment you care to inflict on me. Why delay? Begin now, you devil's son, and don't hesitate to use on me any device of pain that you can invent, because I'm not afraid."

When Paschasius heard this answer, he called into his presence the ruffians of the city: men who sinfully buy and sell women and profit from their work at the bordello. They make women ply their vice-ridden trade to earn a living for their masters and themselves, under threat of punishment if they don't do so. When the ruffians came to Paschasius, he spoke his mind: "Sirs, I order that when you advertise this woman, whom I consider a prostitute, you are to proclaim throughout the city that anyone who wants to can come to the bordello to fulfill the lust of his flesh with her as he pleases; and let them know that she is young, healthy, and nice looking so that men will approach her more eagerly. Let her be used this way until she is dead of fatigue."

They prepared to lead her forth, as Paschasius commanded, but the holy ghost had weighted her down so heavily that with all their might they could not budge her. Paschasius ordered all his men to run and help pull, but nothing helped. He ordered that her hands and feet be bound, and many a team of mighty oxen be harnessed, but neither men nor beasts could do anything. She stood there as firmly rooted and as still as an island. When he saw this, he called forth the witches and priests out of the temples, asking them to help move Lucy with their incantations and invocations to their gods. But for all their skill and praying and anything else they could devise, they could not budge her. Then he supposed that she had become so heavy through witchcraft, and threw oil on her head, hoping to disperse the power of the enchantment or magic spell (as was the common superstition); but nothing helped.

When Paschasius saw everything fail, "Lucy," he said, "I beg you, tell us what is your witchcraft." "Know that there is no witchcraft in me, but whatever is done is done by the power of my lord Jesus." "How is it then," he asked, "explain, how a young and delicate girl cannot be moved by a thousand men?" "Because the holy ghost gives me such weight that even if you put another ten thousand men to it, they can neither stir nor move me. For I believe in that Scripture that says of them who call to God in need: 'A thousand shall fall on your left side, and on your right side ten thousand shall be overthrown, and be they never so determined, none of them shall approach you.' "

Paschasius was disturbed with this answer and set all his wits to figuring how he could most cruelly kill her. When Lucy saw him sunk in thought this way, she cried, "O wretched Paschasius, why are you so troubled now? It's your own malice that oppresses your heart. Why are you so pale? Since you have had proof that I am the temple and dwelling place of the holy ghost, made so through his virtue and special grace, leave your error and believe. If you won't, then leave. Why should you stay here any longer?" When he heard this, he screamed in anguish of heart. He ordered a fire built around her and had it fed with wax, pitch, and grease: the tormentors were glad to perform whatever Paschasius bade. Then he had boiling oil thrown over Lucy, who, standing amidst the flames, steadfastly said,

"I have asked my lord Jesus that this fire may have no power to touch me, for two reasons. One is so that I can make you feel more anguished; the other is to take the fear of death away from Christians and strengthen their endurance of ordeal." When Paschasius's men heard this they were angry and behaved like madmen. They thrust a sword into her throat, wanting to destroy her. But notwithstanding this terrible wound, she kept her power of speech and spoke to the faithful who stood nearby: "Sirs, be glad, for I tell you, peace is given now to Christ's church. For Maximian is dead this day, and Diocletian thrown down from his reign. Moreover, just as Agatha is for Catania, likewise I am ordained through God's grace to be a mediator for this city. Thank God for his goodness, who takes such good care of you and after great sorrow sends good news."

While she stood talking this way, Paschasius was seized by Roman officers sent to arrest him and bring him back to Rome, for they had heard of the depopulation he had caused in the province of Catania. At Rome he was quickly accused, convicted, and sentenced by the Senate to beheading. And so he hastened home to hell. But blessed Lucy neither died nor moved from the spot where she had taken her mortal wound, until priests came and administered the sacrament of Christ's body, and until everyone there had answered "Amen." Only then did she commend her soul to God and send it forth to heaven's bliss through God's grace. Her body was buried in the same place and a church built over it, in which it is reverently enshrined, awaiting the great judgment day. On that day, O Lucy, I humbly beg that the translator of your legend may for his labors (by mediation of you who are called "light" according to your name) have a glimpse of him who is the sun of righteousness and who illumines everyone with his grace. To see him once is joy. Amen and thank you Jesus.

SAINT ELIZABETH'S LIFE

Prologue

In the year of grace 1231 (as Voragine says in his *Golden Legend*), on November 19th, which is the thirteenth calend of December, by the twisting course of fate-dealing death there passed out of this world Saint Elizabeth, daughter to the king of Hungary and wife to Landgrave, prince of Thuringia. Her life it is my wish to declare in English, however barren my speech.

"Elizabeth"—my author says—means "my God knows" or "my God's seventh" or "my God's fulsomeness." In this threefold interpretation, if it is clearly explained, people may know the particular praise and commendation of this blessed Elizabeth.

First, as I said, "Elizabeth" represents "my God knows." That fits her, for she was so plentifully enbalmed with the sweet breath of grace in her youth that God approved her works and made her known and caused her fame to be spread worldwide.

Moreover, in this threefold cognition of God may be understood the three divine virtues, in my opinion. That is, faith, hope, and charity, which Elizabeth had in excellent degree, as every intelligent person may ponder who diligently reads her legend.

What made her despise the world in her youth, and conquer it in so many ways, if not perfect faith? Moses grew so great and high through faith that he refused to be Pharoah's daughter's son. And so did Elizabeth refuse this world's vanity.

What made her have such great patience in suffering trouble and adversity, and never want to make resistance, if not the hope of God's reward? The gospel says: "They shall be blessed who for righteousness meekly suffer tribulation and distress."

That she had charity is easy to know, since charity includes love and pity for God and for our neighbors rich and poor. I believe no one had more than she did, and whoever patiently reads her life will hear plenty of proof of that. So we see she had these three virtues in outstanding quality.

The second meaning of "Elizabeth" is "God's seventh day," which, as my author shows, can well be applied to Elizabeth because she always occupied herself in the seven works of piety, or because she is now in the seventh day of soul's rest, awaiting the octave of body and soul in bliss.

Or by this number seven may be understood the seven states she was in: namely virginity, marriage, and widowhood; active and contemplative and conventual; the seventh is the heavenly region where she now dwells. And so the word said to Daniel may be affirmed of her: that seven times have passed over you.

The third interpretation, as I said before, of this name "Elizabeth" is "God's abundance," and it signifies the joy that forevermore Elizabeth has entered through God's goodness. Of this joy King David explicitly said, "I shall be satiated with your abundance, Lord, when your joy shall appear to me."

Now, blessed Elizabeth, in your charity help us all to arrive at that blissful place where you are in joy that will never decrease and where you behold God's glorious face. And especially help, through your special grace, I beg you, to dwell with you there, after this outlawry, Dame Elizabeth Vere.

The Life of Saint Elizabeth

This blessed Elizabeth was daughter to the king of Hungary, noble by birth but in religious learning more noble, for she enhanced her family tree with her examples of perfection and embellished it with miracles brighter than the sky, through the grace of her holiness.

And no wonder, for the sovereign author of nature extolled her high above nature when she—flower of beauty, nurtured with royal care with others of her family—despised all infantile things or else turned them to the service of God.

In this kind of behavior we can see with what simplicity her childhood began and with what devotion she occupied herself in the daily practices of goodness. Frivolous games she hated so as to avoid the favor of Fortune's fickleness, but she loved to perfect herself in reverence for God.

When she was five years old or less, as the *Legend* tells, her heart was so devoted to God that she would often go to church to pray, and when she was there she so desired to serve God that her playmates and servants could scarcely get her away without great difficulty.

When she was brought to play with her playmates and the children chased each other as children do, she fled to the church, looking for a way in, and when she entered she fell down on her knees, or on the tiled floor on her face, worshiping God.

And though she was unable to read, she would hold a psalter spread open before her and would pretend to read it, unwilling to give it up and making up an excuse not to be taken away from it too quickly.

Often in her playing she would fall down on the ground on her face, prostrate, as the game required; but her real intention in doing so was to have an occasion, under cover of the game, to worship God whom she loved above all.

She also had a noble habit that if she won something in a game, she would give it away to other little girls, poor ones, exhorting them to say their pater noster often and their Hail Mary, and thus she persuaded them to learn to pray.

So as she grew up her devotion also grew. Because she wished not to be overthrown by the devil's sleight or suggestion, she put herself under Our Lady's protection, beseeching her to be her advocate; and she chose Saint John the Evangelist as keeper of her virginity.

Therefore, on Saint Valentine's day, when, according to the custom of that country, the names of various apostles were written at random on altar candles and each girl took whichever one fell to her, three times Elizabeth got the candle inscribed to Saint John.

Thereafter her affection was so strongly set on this blessed apostle that she could deny no petition made her in his name. And so that no parade of worldly prosperity should make a fool of her, she made a point of throwing out some rich item every day.

In playing, when she saw wantonness follow mirth, as is the way with children, she would stop, saying seriously to her playmates: "One song is enough, so for God's sake let's restrain ourselves from another song." And with similar wise words she used to restrain her servants from vanity.

As for her outward manner, what more can I say than that in her dress she loved honesty and scorned fancy clothing? She also would say certain prayers every day, and if they were omitted because of other occupations, even though she were made to go to bed by those responsible for her, she wouldn't sleep until she had done her stint.

Solemn holy days this girl observed with such devotion that she would not permit anyone to lace up her sleeves until after mass. On Sundays she would not wear gloves until noon, no matter how cold it might be: this was in devoted reverence for the dominical solemnity.

And so that she should not be prevented from performing any of the special practices she was committed to, she often knelt down and vowed that she would never—despite the persuasion of man or woman, rich or poor—be deterred from these rituals until death prevented her.

She also heard divine service with such reverence that when the gospel was read or when Christ's body was present in the sacraments, she would stand up with sleeves unlaced and put aside her brooches, and anything else belonging to her head she would place on her shoulder instead.

When this innocent body had thus prudently governed the time of her virginity, and in the course of years attained the age of womanhood, she was compelled by her father to enter the state belonging to married people—matrimony, which in the faith of the trinity stands alongside the keeping of God's ten commandments.

Although she was reluctant to enter the state of matrimony, she did agree to it: not because of lust or physical attraction but to do her father's will and, also, if God should send her fruit, to educate them in his service. These considerations moved her to accept this conclusion.

But before she was bound to the law of marriage and still in her liberty, to show that no fleshly lust was to be found in her she had a vow written down: that if her husband should happen to die before her, she would observe perpetual chastity.

So Elizabeth, mirror of continence, was wedded to Landgrave, prince of Thuringia, as ceremoniously as her royal magnificence required and as God's providence had ordained so that through her prudence she might bring many to love God and teach them to serve him.

So that although this blessed Elizabeth changed her condition, by her father's decree, to one quite strange to her—I mean from virginity to matrimony—yet in her secret heart her unchangeable desire would have preferred to remain a maid than to be a princess, queen, or empress.

About her great devotion and reverence and meekness toward God; about her abstinence toward herself; about her generosity and piety toward the poor, and her tender care for the sick, and how she cheered and comforted the needy: all this the following account will declare.

To speak first of prayer: she was so fervent that she often

preceded her servants to church by several hours. She spent the time there so devoutly that it seemed she intended to obtain with her private prayers some new grace from him who sends all goodness from heaven.

And she prayed this way not only in church, but also she would often arise at night to do the same, remaining an hour or two in such prayer as she thought best. Her husband often asked her to spare her body and give it some rest.

But because she wished to maintain this ritual and not be kept from it by chancing to oversleep, she commanded her favorite handmaiden to grasp her by the bare foot and shake her by the foot until she awoke.

One night it happened that this damsel came toward the bed without a light, and accidentally shook the prince's foot so that he suddenly awoke. But when he understood the reason, he forgave the intrusion and pretended it had never happened.

So by the tolerance of this good man the blessed Elizabeth arose every night. And that the sacrifice of her prayers to God might be ever more acceptable, she often used to water them with plentiful weeping.

Despite this copious weeping, the tears produced no disfiguration in her face, but rather gladness, and whoever saw her might truly guess that joy and sorrow had such balance in her that though she showed outward sadness, she had abundance of inward joy.

To speak of her meekness, there was never a meeker creature anywhere than she; I am sure there couldn't possibly be, for the more despised and contemptible a thing was, the more charitable she was toward it and the gladder to do it.

This was demonstrated when one of her servants became so terribly ill that people were terrified to look at him and would not touch him—except for her only; for she had such tender regard for him that she allowed him to lay his head in her lap.

And notwithstanding his horribleness, her grace in meekness was such that, when no handmaiden would come near him, she did not hesitate to open his sores with a pin or needle to let out the filth, and she clipped his ragged hair and with her own hands washed his head.

During rogations she always wore linen clothes and followed the procession barefoot, so grounded in humility was she. At stations where sermons were preached, she would not take her place among the upper ranks but would always sit among the poorest women.

In her purifications she would not cover herself with precious gems nor with brooches nor cloth of gold as is the custom of high-ranking ladies, but, following Mary's example and despising worldly pomp, she held her children in her own arms and dedicated them with a lamb and a candle.

And when she returned home from church, she quickly went to her chamber, took off all the clothes she had worn to church and, before she would sit down to dinner, gave every single one to some poor woman dwelling nearby.

It was also a token of great meekness in one who stood in such liberty as Elizabeth did, that she subjected herself to one Master Conrad, especially considering his poverty; but he was outstanding in erudition and doctrine, and perfect in his living.

To him, with her husband's permission, this meek and humble creature made a solemn vow to obey him in everything without fail while she lived; she did this to obtain the merit of pure obedience and to follow Christ's example in dying obedient.

Not long afterward, when Conrad had summoned her to his preaching, and the marquise of Miseno had kept her away so that she could not do his bidding, he took Elizabeth's absence so badly that he would not forgive her until, stripped to her smock, she was beaten with other guilty women.

O true meekness! O blessed obedience! What woman could now obey such a commandment without offense as did this mirror of patience: Behold! Scarcely any nun would do it meekly; and, to tell the whole truth, I believe that neither priest nor monk, canon nor friar would hear it without murmur and grudging too.

For these days the clay of both men and women is so badly alloyed with stubborn will that if they were assayed with such obediences, they would complain and be ill pleased. And this is one important reason, I dare say, why religious discipline is so deeply disturbed, for due corrections are all put away.

But I will walk no further in this matter nor make of it any longer clamor; for no doubt if I were to speak the whole truth some people would be highly indignant that I needlessly digressed from my material. Therefore I promise to cease and hasten back to Elizabeth.

I say this mirror of true obedience, this blessed Elizabeth, practiced great rigor of strict abstinence, and with vigils and disciplines pained her body. She also often kept from her husband's bed and secretly lay sleepless all night in her prayer.

And if, after long waking, she wished to grant her body some rest, forced by the common necessity of sleep as human frailty requires, she would not return to her lord's bed but would lie down to sleep on the floor, all dressed, on a rug.

She also used to make her maidservants beat her violently with large, thick rods. She did this to make recompense for the bitter pain of Christ's scourging, and also to control her flesh from wantonness.

Moreover, if we wish to know her abstinence in eating and drinking, and her temperance in all such things, I say that she often used to excuse herself from the table in order to refuse refined foods and be content with simple bread.

For Master Conrad had strictly ordered her to eat no household food except what was bought by her servants.

Because she would not forget this order, she and her maidens often devoured the grossest possible foods, even when delicacies were available in plenty.

But despite the great strictness with which she treated herself, nonetheless she would serve and prepare food and distribute it plentifully throughout the hall. This was so that there would be no comments about overscrupulous or irrational religiosity in her, and so she courteously entertained all guests.

It happened once, after a long journey when she was faint and weary, that she and her lord sat down to dinner and were served with food that she believed was certainly not rightfully obtained; so she ate with her handmaidens and was content with hard black bread moistened in hot water.

For this reason her husband assigned a portion of his budget to support her and her maidens, who had agreed to live as their lady did; but nonetheless she often left court food and ate the food of some good poor person.

When Landgrave heard about his wife's discipline, he patiently tolerated it, never begrudging it in word or behavior but, rather, approving it in his private thoughts. In fact, he often said sincerely that had it not been for the world's shame and the trouble of his household, he would gladly have done the same.

Notwithstanding her high dignity, Elizabeth desired the state of voluntary poverty. She did so for two reasons: first, to sympathize with Christ's poverty, and then that the world with its pompous array should find nothing of its own in her.

Therefore this blessed matron, when she was alone with her maidens in her chambers, would dress herself in poor people's ugly clothes, and put a foul kerchief on her head, saying, "Look, this is how I'll go when I come to the state of poverty."

And though she governed herself with the bridle of abstinence, as you have heard, yet she practiced such generosity of alms to the poor that she could not bear to see anyone fall into misery or trouble; so that throughout the country people called her "mother of the poor."

She attended diligently to the seven works of mercy and fulfilled them devoutly, so that she might achieve the friendly blessing that Christ shall send to his chosen children, when he shall specially commend them for these works and say, "Come, take the eternal kingdom!"

To give a short summary of them, I say she would gladly clothe the naked poor, nor fail to bury poor pilgrims properly. She made christenings for poor children when they were baptized and was willing to be godmother the better to help them.

Often with her maidens she would spin and prepare cloth with her own hands, for three reasons: first, to exclude idleness by her labor; also to give the example of meekness; third, with the labor of her own hands to do alms for the poor who asked, and this was in honor of Christ.

Moreover, she used to feed the hungry, distributing victuals generously to the needy but most plentifully in times of famine. Once when her husband was with Emperor Frederick at Cremona, she completely emptied his warehouses to distribute grain where any needed it.

She gave drink to the thirsty, and in this connection a great miracle occurred, as you shall hear. Once she served beer to a large group with her own hands because of her meekness. When they had all drunk enough, there was no less beer in the cup.

To speak of her hospitality, she loved it so much that she harbored pilgrims and all poor people. She even built a hospital down in the valley below the castle, so that people who could not climb up could be received there and take their alms.

Notwithstanding the difficulty of going up and down, she would visit this hospital at least once a day and administer to the sick, giving them what they needed and exhorting them to patience.

And although she could barely stand the stinking exhalation of the air there, yet for God's love she did not abhor sick people's putridity but endured it, and diligently tried to help them and cure them even when her maidens could scarcely endure the patients' breath.

Poor women's children she sponsored at the hospital, showing them as much charity as if she had been their mother. When she came, some ran to her as children to a mother, and some crawled; but when she left, they all wept as if she had been their mother.

She once bought little glass pots and fragile trinkets for the children to play with, as was the custom in that country; and, as she brought them down from the hilltop in her skirt, they fell, but not one was broken, though they fell on great stones.

Her special pleasure was to visit bedridden women, young and old. She would peer into their rooms to learn their need and hasten to comfort them charitably with word and deed.

In these deeds she obtained God's eternal reward by a fivefold consideration: first by personal visitation; and by work in going back and forth; third is compassion and pity; fourth is spiritual consolation; fifth is abundance of temporal support.

She also loved to bury the poor, so that when she heard of one who needed it, she hurried to the place, carrying with her cloth of her own making in which she could lay the dead body; and until it were buried she would not go home again.

Once it happened that she could not find anything suitable to wrap a man's body in, for what she had asked for had been left behind in haste. She thought of her veil and tore it to wind the body in, and buried it.

So this blessed woman was accustomed to practice the seven works of bodily pity, in more ways than I can tell now. Her husband, too, may be commended for this, for he was very devoted to God; but because he couldn't himself perform this kind of work, he gave his wife permission and authority to do as she wished for both their benefit.

Thus these two lived long and virtuously together, Elizabeth and Landgrave. One day she said to him, "Dear spouse, whom I love best after God and always have done, I advise you to leave these worldly occupations and visit the promised land,

"I mean Jerusalem, and all that country where Jesus made his bodily pilgrimage and died for our sake on a tree, betrayed by the Jews' cruel violence. That country heathens now hold in slavery. If you wished to exercise your courage in the effort to liberate it, I can't see where that courage could be better spent.

"Better? No, nowhere else in this world so well spent, I dare boldly say! For he who by the turn of fate's wheel happens to die on that holy journey, if he is confessed, is assured of going to heaven. So, husband, I advise and request that for your soul's salvation you do not abandon this work."

With these words and many more from Elizabeth, Landgrave was moved to go on pilgrimage to Jerusalem and manly to fight the heathen. When he was all prepared and ready to leave on his pilgrimage, he came to take proper leave of Elizabeth, standing on the shore.

Many a tearful face of lords and ladies might be seen there, and the commoners tore their clothes and wept too. Some cried loudly, "Alas, alas, why do you forsake us, lord Landgrave?" But Elizabeth kept her eyes dry from tears and womanly spoke to him:

"With what affection and how entirely I love you, dear spouse, and always have, no one knows but God and you and me. He has joined us not only physically by the knot of marriage, but through his charity has united us spiritually so that the knot is impossible to undo.

"But I see no reasonable cause to weep now, since I see you going to serve him whom I love best. In the past I have sorrowed when you went away from me, but now I may neither sorrow nor weep, as long as Christ through his kindness grant you grace to serve him to his liking."

So Landgrave, leave taken of everyone, as Christ's own knight, armed in virtue and in charity, took up his journey to Jerusalem. When he had been there a certain time and manly acquit himself in God's cause, he received the fruit of his labor there and died and went to God's mercy.

Thus Elizabeth entered the state of widowhood, in which she virtuously exerted herself, and was assailed with much adversity and her patience tested in many ways. But she was so rooted in steadfastness that she could not be hurt, for she endured everything with gladness.

As soon as Landgrave's death was blown throughout Thuringia by the trumpet of Fame, Elizabeth's distress began to grow, for suddenly Landgrave's brother tyrannically expelled her from her dowry and from all her property, as if she had been a waster and destroyer.

When she was reduced to such poverty that she had no place to lay her head, she lay in the pigsty in a taverner's house until midnight. Then she went to an establishment of Minors and asked them to sing Te Deum Laudamus, that he might make her worthy, before she died, to suffer spite and persecution.

The next day she was forced to stay, with her young children and her maids, in the place of one of her enemies, where she was assigned cramped quarters. Her host and hostess did her all the malice they could. When she saw this, she bade the walls farewell, saying,

"If I had found any kindness in the men and women here, I would gladly have taken from them with gratitude, but since I find none, I'll leave." So she went back to her first lodging; but first she sent her children to other places to be cared for.

Once she happened to walk in a very dirty road, deep and difficult, in which was laid many a stone and block and horse's bone on which one could walk securely: otherwise one couldn't get through with dry clothes.

As she entered the street, she met an old woman to whom she had often shown her mercy. But the old woman would not make way for her, so she fell in the mud. As soon as she could she rose, not angry but laughing, and wiped her clothes.

After this a powerful abbess, Elizabeth's grandmother, taking compassion on her poverty, brought her to her uncle, the bishop of Bamberg. He received her properly, proposing to remarry her.

Her maidens were sorry to hear this, for they had vowed chastity along with her and dreaded utterly that they might be made to marry. They wept piteously, and when they told Elizabeth about it, she was at first astonished at the news and then comforted them, saying,

"I trust only in my God, for love of whom I have vowed perpetual continence, that he will approve my purpose and destroy every contrary violence and make resistance against everyone's counsel. And if I can't be sure of it any other way, I will cut off my nose in their presence. Then, so deformed, no man will take me."

At the bishop's commandment, the humble and blessed Elizabeth was sent willy-nilly to a castle to await her friends' decision about her marriage to some worthy man. But she committed herself to God in her thoughts. Meanwhile, by God's grace, her husband's bones were brought from beyond the sea.

She was sent for to welcome the bones, and she and the bishop with a great assembly went in procession to receive them. When they were received, Elizabeth turned her eyes heavenward to God, saying with devout heart:

"Everlasting honor, lord, to you who, in sending my husband's bones home again have benignly granted to give your wretched handmaid comfort and joy. You know well, lord, that though while he lived I loved him second only to you, nonetheless for your honor, lord, I gladly did without him and without weeping I sent him to Jerusalem to rescue it.

"And although I would dearly love to have lived with him always in poverty and been beggars together and sought our physical needs all over the world, yet I wouldn't, lord (you are my witness), give one hair of my head for his ransom if it were against your will. Therefore I humbly commend him and me to your grace alone."

When she had in this way received her husband's bones from beyond the sea, she rejoiced inwardly. Then she buried them with due ceremony and addressed the bishop plainly: "Sir, since my lord has now come home to me, I will never have any other husband."

And so as not to lose the hundredfold fruit that accrues to them who steadfastly choose the perfection of Christ's gospel and that passes from the left hand of wretchedness to the right hand of heavenly bliss, she entered the state of poor religion, keeping voluntary poverty, the cleanness of chastity, and the subjection of obedience.

Her worthless, contemptible habit was russet, the worst that could be found, which was often lengthened with cloth of another color so that it would reach the ground; and because she wished to destroy all foolish pride, she pieced out her sleeves the same way when they were torn. Because she abounded in meekness, she had no shame to spin and card.

When her father, the king of Hungary, heard all this, how she was reduced to misery and poverty, he sent a trusted earl to comfort and cheer her, and to persuade her to return to him again. When the earl saw her, he was astonished and said,

"No king's daughter, I am sure, was ever seen so horribly dressed or sitting like a rustic and performing menial labor!" Kneeling down to her, he said, "Leave all this, lady, and return with me home to your father with no more delay." But he saw it was for nothing, for her heart was set to live and die this way.

So that her heart might pass up to God directly and nothing impede her devotion, she prayed God that by his special grace he would grant her contempt for all temporal possession, and remove from her heart every trace of pleasure in her children, and make her constant and patient against all spite and desolation.

When she had prayed this way, she said to her maidens, "God has heard my prayer so well that I now despise all temporal things as dung. My children here are no dearer to me than other people's, and I care nothing about contempt and reproof. So it seems to me that I love nothing with my whole heart except for God."

Master Conrad, to test her, often enjoined her to things she disliked. Two maidens who had been with her since her youth, and whom she had loved the longest, he banned from her company. He did this only so that they should not remind her of her former dignities and glory.

But to all his precepts she gave ready obedience, without resistance or murmur or grudging, and was always patient. Through this she was able to rule her soul and, by meek obedience without violence, have victory and heaven as reward.

Often she said, "If on account of God I fear any earthly man, I ought much more to fear the heavenly judge; and so I choose to be subject and obedient to this poor man, who is only a beggar, rather than to a richer man, so as to avoid any occasion for temporal comfort."

Once it happened that she entered a nunnery without his permission, having been piously invited by the nuns. This angered him so much that he not only reproved her with words but beat her so violently that three weeks later one might still see the bruises.

To her maidens she said, for her and their consolation, "Just as grass goes under when a flood rises high, and when the flood falls back the grass rises again, so, when affliction comes to us, we ought meekly to submit, and when it ends we may rise up to God with spiritual joy."

So well was she grounded in humility that she would never permit her maidens to call her "lady" or "mistress," nor to rise at her arrival as is the custom among the high-born, nor to address her in the plural number but only in the singular as sovereigns are accustomed to address their subjects.

She would often wash and dry dishes in the kitchen, sending her maids to do other things at such moments so that they could not hinder her. She often said cheerfully that if she could have found a life in any way more miserable, she would have chosen it willingly.

Later, so that she might share a portion of the best with Mary Magdalen, she diligently applied herself to the practice of contemplation. In this she had such great consolation that after copious tears she had many a heavenly visitation and industriously persuaded people to love God.

But her distinctive grace was that when she seemed happiest, then she shed copious tears of devotion, so that often she appeared to be weeping and rejoicing at once, for when she wept there was no contortion of her face, or even a wrinkle.

"People who inordinately contort their faces in weeping," she said, "seem to scorn God in such uncomely behavior. It's to everyone's advantage that what one gives to God is given gladly, for God loves a glad giver."

In the state of contemplation that she practiced like Mary, many a holy revelation was showed her, and many a vision of high emprise. I will tell one now, as Voragine relates in his *Golden Legend*.

Once, at the time when every Christian does his duty with all diligence to clear his conscience of sin—I mean in Lent—inflamed with the fire of perfect charity, she was visited as she lay in a church praying.

As she cast her eyes up toward the altar, they were as firmly fixed as if she had been in God's presence, and this lasted a very long time. She was refreshed with heavenly influence and spiritual comfort.

When she came home and weakly lay in her maiden's lap, she again turned her eyes heavenward out the window, and immediately there appeared in her such gladness and joy that she laughed aloud heartily.

When she had been comforted for some time in this vision of gladness, she suddenly grew downcast and shed a great many tears. Then she laughed as at first and then wept again plentifully, and until compline she alternated this way.

At last with cheerful face she began to speak, as if in dialogue with another: "Yea, lord, will you be with me? I should like to be with you and never part from you." Afterward, when her maidens begged her to tell them the content of her revelation and its meaning, she spoke to their importunate request:

"I saw," she said, "heaven on high; it seemed to open before me, and I saw Jesus my love kindly bowing to me. When I beheld his bright, shining face, I was so full of joy that I thought I could no better express it than with laughter.

"And then, when he pleased to withdraw himself from me, I was as oppressed with sadness and sorrow as you saw; and because I couldn't keep him with me as I wanted, when he left I could only sorrow and weep.

"But when it pleased his mercy to pity me and show me once again the brightness of his face, he said, 'If you want to be with me, I will be with you, don't be afraid.' And I answered him as you heard."

Then her maidens begged to be told the vision she had had in church at the altar. But she answered them thus: "You don't need to hear that, but I can tell you this: I was in complete joy and I saw many a prince of God."

Not only did this blessed woman have the honor that her contemplation was inspired with heavenly revelation, but her prayer had such favor, it was so strong and vigorous, that some who were physically and spiritually cold were warmed by it, as you may learn from this story:

Once she saw a young man dressed, as she thought, in too worldly a fashion. She told him, "Young man, you live too dissolutely and you are not serving our sovereign lord on high. Do you desire any help from my prayers?" "Indeed I do," he replied, "and ask it of you wholeheartedly."

And she, desiring to win over this young man, gladly began to pray, and urged him to pray also because of his sins. Immediately he grew very hot in his whole body and asked her gently to stop praying.

But she prayed on with devout heart and pure will, and would not cease, and his heat continued to increase so that he thought he could no longer stand it. He cried, "O blissful creature, stop praying, I beg you; for I am burning so that my body is consumed and dried out, but I don't know how."

And in truth he was so hot that he sweated and reeked amazingly, and he flung his arms and body about as if he were mad. Every bystander could see this, though they could neither control nor direct him. And so he continued while Elizabeth continued her prayer.

When she ceased her prayer, his heat also ceased, and, kneeling meekly, he thanked her for it. Then, conscience stricken and seeing how strong her prayer was, he forsook the world utterly and joined the Minors.

Whoever wishes to know further examples of the holy conversation of this woman, blessed Elizabeth, may have them in Voragine's well-known *Legend*. Two or three come after this last one that I related, but I think it best now to eschew prolixity and make an end.

For even if I were able to rhyme and compose as copiously as Gower or Chaucer did in their time, or as John Lydgate the monk of Bury does now, yet I could not sufficiently commend this blessed woman Elizabeth according to her merits. Therefore I now intend to cease.

When God in his goodness wished to deliver this holy Elizabeth from the foul ordure of this woeful world's wretchedness and bring her to the happiness of heaven's bliss, he sent her a fever and she received it with gladness.

As she lay in this sickness, she turned suddenly to the wall and began to sing a melody of great sweetness. Her maidens went to her and asked if she would reveal to them the cause of this melodious song.

Steadily she answered, "I want you to know that here, between me and the wall, a beautiful bird came flying such as I never saw in my life. It began to sing so sweetly that I couldn't help myself but sang with her, as you heard."

And in this sickness she was always cheerful and never ceased to pray. But when her time drew near to die, the day before she said to her maidens, "What would you do if the devil, who is always trying to betray people, came now to you?"

So saying, she began to cry in a loud voice, as if speaking to the devil, "Flee, get away"—and three times she spoke this word "flee"—"for I despise you!" After which she spoke to her maidens:

"Look, now midnight approaches when Jesus Christ was born, and in that same hour he has called me to his heavenly home. Now farewell, all!" With that she yielded up her spirit into her creator's hands, and he led it in at the gates of his heavenly tower.

And though her body was kept unburied for four days after her death, no evil odor came from it but, rather, an odor of solace that marvelously comforted all who entered the place to visit the body.

Moreover, a great flock of birds, such as no one had ever seen before, sitting on the church roof outside, began to sing wondrously and made such melody in their song that everyone was amazed who heard it; for it seemed they were chanting a dirge in their joyful way.

Now, blessed Elizabeth, with whole heart and humble will I beg you to accept the intent of my prayer: be mediator to the heavenly doctor for my sins, and teach me the means how without punishment I may escape cruel revenge on the day of the last judgment.

Finally, lady, attend to the true intent of her who particularly commanded me to compose your legend and who loves you affectionately in her heart. I mean Dame Elizabeth Vere. Purchase her a charter of pardon, and when she shall pass from this outlawry, bring her to the contemplation of God. Amen and thank you Jesus.

In this book are written the saints' lives of, first, Saint Margaret; then the lives of Saint Anne, Saint Christine, the 11,000 virgins, and Saint Faith. The lives of Saints Agnes, Dorothy, Mary Magdalen, Katherine and Cecelia, Agatha and Lucy, and Elizabeth.

Translated into English by a doctor of divinity named Osbern Bokenham, Austin friar of the convent of Stoke Clare. It was transcribed in Cambridge by his son Friar Thomas Burgh, the year of our lord 1447. He spent thirty shillings on it and gave it to this holy place of nuns, so that they should remember him and his sister Dame Beatrice Burgh, on whose souls Jesus have mercy. Amen.

NOTES

mentions "bones of saynt Margarete." The Fingall cartulary (B.L. Egerton 3031, 12th century) specifies "De sancta Margareta" only "Item de reliquiis eius in tribus locis."

6   *vigil*: the eve preceding a holy day (in this case the Virgin Mary's birthday), an occasion for devotional watching or other special observance.

6   *Thomas*: Thomas de Burgh is the Augustinian friar living in Cambridge who, according to a note at the end of the ms., had the work copied out. "Son" and "father" are honorifics to a friend and fellow priest. The town is probably Burgh le Marsh in Lincolnshire, in a district anciently called Ageland (cf. EETS note to line 216).

7   *Atropos, Lachesis*: two of the three Fates who, in Greek religious myth, controlled human life (represented as thread). The other is Clotho, who spun life's fabric, measured and cut by the others. Bokenham errs in making Lachesis (measurer) the spinner.

8   *Golden Legend*: *Legenda Aurea* of Jacob da Voragine (1230–1298) was among the most widely circulated texts of the later Middle Ages; over one thousand mss. survive in Latin alone. Its author, born in Varaggio near Genoa, was a Dominican preacher and eventually archbishop of Genoa. The work was intended as a source of material for preachers.

8   *cherubim*: Isaiah 6:2, though the text has seraphim.

9   *Antioch*: in Syria or southern Turkey, a rich commercial city and during the third century an important Christian administrative and missionary center. The life of Margaret has no historical foundation, though her persecution is said to have occurred in the late third century. The extravagantly romantic material comes from the East and occurs in other legends. Margaret is first heard of in the West in the ninth century.

10 *Gower, Chaucer, Lydgate*: the three most famous English poets of the late fourteenth–early fifteenth centuries. John Gower (1330–1408), author of *Confessio Amantis* and other works; Geoffrey Chaucer (1342–1400), who apostrophizes his friend "moral Gower" at the end of *Troilus;* John Lydgate (1370–1450), Benedictine monk

at Bury St. Edmonds, known for his prolixity and "au-
reate diction."

16   *Jannes and Jambres*: in 2 Timothy 3:8, opposers of
      Moses and of truth generally, usually identified as the
      magicians of Egypt in Exodus 7:11 [EETS]. There seems
      to have been an early Jewish tradition about them: there
      are scattered references, and a short fragment, in Latin
      and Anglo-Saxon, in which the spirit of Jamnes describes
      the tortures of hell. See M. Foerster, "Das lateinisch-
      altenglische Fragment der Apokryphe von Jamnes and
      Mambres," *Archiv für das Studium der neueren Sprachen*
      108 (1902): 15–28.

16   *Solomon*: the story of "the bottle imp" is a widespread
      folklore motif, attached to Solomon in eastern texts
      such as the *Thousand and One Nights* (third night).
      In the Arabic tradition, Solomon appears as a magi-
      cian and sage with special power over demons; cf. J.-
      P. Migne, *Dictionnaire des Apocryphes*, 2 vols. (1858);
      reprint (Turnhout, Belgium: Brepols, 1989), s.v. "Sa-
      lomon."

17   *Malchus*: in John 18:10, a slave of the Jewish high priest
      Caiaphas who bribed Judas to betray Jesus. Presumably
      a generic name for servant/traitor, here the executioner.

18   *beak*: to heat unseasoned wood by fire to straighten it:
      hence to stretch out in a warm place. For other oc-
      currences, see *Catholicon Anglicum: An English–Latin
      Wordbook Dated 1483*, ed. Sidney Herrtage, EETS o.s.
      75 (1881), p. xxix (additional notes).

19   *Michaelmas*: 29 September, in honor of the archangel
      Michael.

19   *Sergius, Berengar*: Pope Sergius III (ruled 908–921);
      Berengar, king of Italy (898–924). The events narrated
      here have no historical validity, nor have the next three
      characters named: Eusebius, Andronicus, and Siniardus.

19   *indiction*: fiscal period of fifteen years, a method of
      reckoning introduced by Emperor Constantine in 313.
      "Twelfth" means the twelfth year of a particular indic-
      tion.

20   *Euprepia*: one of three handmaidens to St. Afro or Afra,
      a converted and reformed prostitute of Augsburg said

to have been martyred about 304 in the Diocletian persecution. The three—Digna, Eunomia, Euprepia—were
martyred after burying their mistress.

20   *Cyrus*: an Alexandrian physician, said to have been martyred about 303. His relics were translated within Egypt
during the fifth century.

22   *black monks*: Benedictines. Cf. note to page 5.

23   *calend*: in the Julian calendrical method (adopted in 45
B.C.E. by Julius Caesar), first day of the month. Days
were computed before, not after, calends, so that the
16th (of the) calends of November would be the 16th
day preceding 1 November, i.e., 17 October (counting
inclusively, as the Romans did).

23   *Dirige*: opening words of a service for the dead are
"Dirige dominus deus meus in conspectu tuo vitam
meam" ("Lord God, direct my life into your presence").
The material is taken from Psalms and Job.

23   *Blaise*: though there is no evidence for his cult earlier
than the 8th century, Blaise was said to be a third-
or fourth-century healer-hermit, bishop and martyr in
Cappadocia, Asia Minor. He has been especially popular
in France.

23   *Calixtus*: or Callistus, leader of the Christian community
in Rome (217–222) and target of denunciation by those
(including Tertullian) who considered his rulings lax.

23   *Matthew*: author of the influential rhetorical treatise *Ars
versificatoria* (c. 1175). The sentiment about delay is
from *De Tobia* 4: 335–36 [EETS].

24   *Clement*: leader of the Christian congregation in Rome
(c. 88–97), author of a letter to the Corinthians. *Felicity*:
a noble Roman widow said to have been martyred with
her seven sons.

24   *1405, Urban II*: the names and dates are wrong here.
Urban II was pope 1088–1099; Henry III was holy
roman emperor 1046–1056; the relics of Margaret were
taken to Montefiascone in 1145, at which time no Urban
was pope. The error may come from the manuscript
Bokenham used at Montefiascone.

24   *Flavian's*: church dedicated to the fifth-century martyr
and patriarch of Constantinople. This Flavian was much

involved in political turmoil. There was, however, another Flavian, a third-century martyr in North Africa, who was believed to have written a prison diary while awaiting death.

26   *Cosmas, Damian*: twin brothers, healers, supposedly martyred in Cilicia, Asia Minor, in the fourth century.

27   *Hugh*: (1140–1200); Frenchborn ecclesiastical administrator educated by Austin canons; made his career in England under Henry II as bishop of Lincoln (where he rebuilt the cathedral and established a school) and as a royal ambassador. He was the first Carthusian to be canonized.

30   *Parnassus*, etc.: classical images for rhetorical skill and creative inspiration. Parnassus is the mountain in central Greece anciently sacred to Apollo and the muses; the Delphic oracle was at its foot. *Aetna*: Sicilian volcano on whose slopes Proserpina was abducted while gathering flowers with her mother Ceres; the story was told by Claudian in *De raptu Proserpinae*. *Helicon*: Greek mountain also inhabited by Apollo and the muses; its fountains were said to inspire artistic creativity. *Orpheus*: mythic musician whose artistry on the lyre persuaded Pluto to release Orpheus's wife from Hades.

30   *Katherine Denston*: married to John Denston, a coroner, justice of the peace, and businessman. Her brother, John Clopton, was sheriff of Norfolk and Suffolk in 1452.

31   *empress of hell*: in the Greek *Apocalypse of the Virgin* and other eastern texts, Mary descends into the underworld to witness the punishment of sinners. She intercedes with Jesus to gain a period of respite for the damned. Lydgate also uses the phrase in several poems about Mary, among them *Life of Our Lady* 5:338.

31   *David, Bathsheba*: 2 Samuel 11–12.

31   *Jerome*: Saint Jerome (347–420), scholar and papal official. His translations of the Bible into Latin became the basis for the Vulgate version known to the Middle Ages. Reference is to his commentary on Matthew 1:18. *Damascene*: Saint John of Damascus (675–749), scholar-theologian; cf. *De othodoxa fide* 4:14–15 [EETS]. The story of Anne is not scriptural; it appears in the

apocryphal *Protevangelium of James*, whence it is elaborated by later authors.

31 *old law*: Judaism, as opposed to Christian "new law."

32 *the law*: cf. Deuteronomy 25:5–10.

32 *Augustine*: (354–430) North African Christian scholar, bishop, and saint; author of *Confessions*, *The City of God*, and many other doctrinal, interpretive, and polemical works.

32 *Jacob supplanted*: Genesis 27.

33 *Sirach*: Jesus ben Sirach composed the "wisdom" book *Ecclesiasticus* in Hebrew about 200 B.C.E. The text is not to be confused with *Ecclesiastes*, also an example of wisdom literature from about the same period. The latter is considered canonical to the Hebrew Bible, while the former is generally deemed apocryphal.

33 *poet*: Horace, *Epistles* I.2. 69–70: "Quo semel est imbuta recens servabit odorem, testa diu" [EETS]. ("The jar will long keep the fragrance of what it was once steeped in when new": H. R. Fairclough, Loeb Library translation.) The lines are quoted by Augustine in *City of God* 1.3.

34 *barrenness*: cf. Deuteronomy 7:14, 23:1; Leviticus 21:16–23, 22:24. These passages could be interpreted to mean what Issachar says, but there is no explicit ban or curse on a childless person.

40 *Lydgate's book*: *Life of Our Lady*. The ten-volume Latin collection "Of the Wedding Songs" has not been identified.

41 *ballade-rhyme*: the work is apparently lost.

41 *Denston*: see note to p. 30.

43 *Tyre*: Lake Bolsena is in Tuscany, but there is no Italian city named Tyre, Tyrus, or Tyro. There is a popular eastern legend about the martyred Saint Christina of Tyre in Phoenicia (now Sur in Lebanon). This highly extravagant material has long been associated with a western saint of the same name of whom nothing is known.

43 *Diocletian*: Roman emperor (284–305); launched a severe persecution of Christians in 302 after a long period of toleration. Though Diocletian abdicated in 305, the persecution continued until 313. His successor was Galerius, whose assistant, Maximinus Daia, was especially

fanatical; the latter's surname may stand behind Bokenham's "Zyon." Diocletian is also said to be emperor
during the ordeals of Faith, Dorothy, and Lucy, for
whom there is also no historical corroboration. See also
notes to pp. 71 and 174.

48   *ten months*: a month is counted as four weeks, yielding
here a total of forty weeks or 280 days.

48   *my name*: both "Christ" and "Christine" come from the
Greek and Latin *chrism* (a scented consecrated oil). Both
names translate the Hebrew "messiah," or "anointed."

51   *Moses, Pharoah, Peter*: Exodus 14; Matthew 8:24, Mark
4:37, Luke 8:23, or John 6:18 (though Peter is not
singled out).

54   *fiery furnace*: Daniel 3.

54   *Apollo*: Greek sun god; also associated with music,
prophecy, and mathematics. Cf. p. 105.

57   *horned serpent*: cerastes or horned viper, a venomous
snake with a projecting scale above each eye; native to
northern Africa.

63   *eleven thousand*: the number is sometimes explained by
scholars as a misreading, whether of the proper name
"Undecemilla" (eleventh daughter, a common Roman
way of naming children), or of the abbreviation "XI.m."
(eleven martyrs). There is no mention of the story before
the ninth century, though Geoffrey of Monmouth in the
twelfth century relates a secular tale of a British king who
sends his daughter Ursula with eleven thousand noble-
women and sixty thousand others to colonize Brittany;
they are captured by Huns (*Historia* 5:12–16).

65   *Gerasina*: a fictional saint. After the conversion and
death of her husband Quintian she returned to Great
Britain, whence she came, and accompanied her niece
Ursula to Cologne. Her relics were brought from
Cologne to Treves.

65   *Tiel*: a town east of Dordrecht on the river Waal, which
joins the Rhine, which in turn flows past Cologne
(Köln). Tiel is in the Netherlands, territory controlled
in Bokenham's time by the French dukes of Burgundy.

66   *nineteenth pope*: this was actually St. Fabianus (236–
250). There is no record of a Ciriacus, an absence

accounted for in the story by the cardinals' action in expunging his name from the official list.

66   *Huns*: a nomadic and pastoral Asian people who invaded Europe in the fourth century, helping to precipitate the migration of Germanic tribes that contributed to the fall of the Roman Empire. Their king was Attila (d. 453).

69   *matins*: one of the canonical hours of the breviary, recited at midnight but sometimes at dawn.

69   *pater noster*: our father (who art in heaven, etc.)

71   *Diocletian*: see notes to pp. 43 and 174. *Maximian*: Augustus Maximianus, coruler with Diocletian from 285–305.

71   *Agen*: Agennum; on the Garonne River in southern France (not Spain).

73   *Diana*: Roman goddess of chastity.

78   *black monks*: see note p. 5.

81   *Agnes sacra*, etc.: the lines, underlined in red in the ms., mean: "May holy Agnes hear the quill [pen] of her writer and grant that the work begun may be completed."

81   *Saint Ambrose*: (340–397) bishop of Milan, preacher who assisted in the conversion of St. Augustine, prolific writer. Ambrose mentions Agnes in a sermon, *De virginibus*, and composed a hymn to her, but the details of her legend attributed to him date from the fifth century.

81   *Pallas*: Athena, Greek goddess of war, peace, and the arts of cloth-making. *Tully*: see note p. 4. *Atropos*: see note p. 7. *Gower*, etc.: see note p. 10.

82   *Augustine*: see note p. 32.

85   *Vesta*: Roman hearth goddess, whose virgin priestesses tended the perpetual fire in her temple. Roman girls of good family were selected for this office.

89   *theater*: an open public space for meetings, combat, or performance.

92   *Constance*: Constantia, daughter of Emperor Constantius I. In 354, Constantia erected a basilica in Agnes's honor.

93   *Jerome*: see note p. 31.

95   *Romulus*: legendary founder of Rome, with his twin brother Remus whom he afterward killed. The two were said to have been suckled by a wolf.

95   *Cappadocia*: in east-central Turkey, annexed as a province of the Roman empire in 17. The torturers of Asia Minor and Egypt were considered particularly sadistic.

98   *passionary*: a book relating the life and suffering (*passio*) of a martyr.

99   *John and Isabel Hunt*: no clear identification is available.

101   *Janus*: two-faced Roman god of doorways and the new year; one face looks forward, the other back. Bokenham means to specify here that the Church's year begins in January, not March as was the more ancient pagan custom. *Phoebus*: another name for Apollo as sun god. *Signs*: the zodiac. *First Mover*: Aristotle's ultimate cause, the unmoved mover, later adapted to Christian doctrine.

101   *holiday*: Twelfth Night, the eve of Epiphany (6 January) commemorating three revelations supposed to have occurred on that date in different years: the visit of the three magi, Jesus's baptism, and the miracle at Cana.

101   *Lady Bourchier*: (b. about 1409), daughter to Richard, earl of Cambridge (d. 1415); wife to Henry, viscount Bourchier, who was later earl of Essex and treasurer of England. Bourchier descended from King Edward III; his brother Thomas was archbishop of Canterbury and a cardinal.

101   *pedigree*: through her mother Anne Mortimer, Isabel descended from Edward III by the line of Prince Lionel, duke of Clarence, Edward's second son. Through her father, Richard, earl of Cambridge, she descended from Edward III via the king's fourth son, Edmund of Langley, first duke of York (1342–1402). Her brother Richard was born in 1411.

101   *Pedro*: Peter the Cruel (d. 1369), king of Castile. His daughter Costanza (d. 1394) was John of Gaunt's second wife. Another daughter, Isabel of Castile (1355–1392), married Edmund of Langley, Richard's grandfather; it is through this line that the claim to Castile would presumably have come to Richard of York, except for two circumstances. First, John of Gaunt abandoned his claim to Castile in a treaty of 1390. Second, Costanza was not barren. In 1445, however, her grandson Enrique IV of Castile was believed impotent, so that it seemed

Costanza's line would die out and her claim revert to her sister Isabel's descendants. This is the hope apparently expressed here.

102   *Minerva*: Roman equivalent to Athena. The story of her victory over Arachne in a weaving contest is told in Ovid's *Metamorphoses* 6.

102   *Elizabeth Vere*: countess of Oxford, daughter of John and Katherine Howard, wife to John Vere, twelfth earl of Oxford. Since the marriage took place without the king's permission (required because Vere was still in his minority) and because the king's councillors opposed the match, Vere was fined £2000. Over ten years later, in 1435, he was still requesting release from part of this debt. Elizabeth accompanied her husband to Rouen in 1441, along with the Bourchiers, in the retinue of Richard of York.

103   *Saint James's day*: the James meant here is one of the twelve disciples, the brother of St. John. His name in Spanish is Iago, and his shrine at Compostela in Spain was and is one of the most famous in Europe. His feast day, 15 July, fell on a Sunday in 1445. *Calixtus* probably refers to the second pope of that name (1119–1124) rather than the first (see note p. 24).

104   *prophet*: Psalm 8:6–8 [EETS]. David, formerly considered the author of the psalms, is the "Prophet" here. Some of the poems do originate in his time or even earlier.

105   *Clio*: muse of history; *Melpomene*, muse of tragedy; *Lucina*, deity presiding over childbirth; *Apollo*, god of music, prophecy, and the sun.

105   *Argus*: herdsman in Greek myth, with eyes all over his body. Hera set him to guard the beautiful Io, turned into a heifer, but Hermes, inventor of the lyre, enchanted Argus and he was killed. His eyes were placed in the peacock's tail.

106   *chose*: Luke 10:42.

108   *Lazarus*: John 11.

108   *Simon*: Matthew 26:6–13. The Pharisees were a Jewish religious and political party committed to the strict interpretation of the Torah. Unlike their more conservative opponents, the Sadducees, they accepted oral tradition

and the allegorical interpretation of Scripture. St. Paul was educated as a Pharisee.

110   *Martha*: Luke 10:38–42.

113   *Quia*: because love is as strong as death. Song of Songs 8:6.

113   *supper*: John 12:1–8.

115   *gospel*: John 9, though the name of the man is not mentioned there. Mycoff (170) notes that "no exegete . . . supports this identification," which also appears in Caxton's *Golden Legend*.

125   *"Who. . . ."*: Psalm 24:3–4.

126   *Capgrave*: Bokenham's university contemporary and colleague in the Augustinian order. Capgrave's *Life of St. Katherine* is very fully narrated in five books of rhyme royale; he also produced a *Life* of St. Norbert and a *Chronicle* of England.

126   *Howard, Denston*: For K. Denston, see note p. 31. Katherine Howard (d. 1465) was the daughter of William, lord Moleyns. She married John Howard, a fervent Yorkist with estates near Clare, who became duke of Norfolk in 1483.

126   *Alexandria*: Egyptian capital and international cultural center; became an important center of Christian education and missionary activity in the third century. Both Clement and Origen were Alexandrian. There is no evidence for the existence of Katherine, whose cult began in the West only in the eleventh century.

127   *liberal arts*: grammar, rhetoric, dialectic (the trivium); arithmetic, music, geometry, astronomy (the quadrivium). They formed the basis of medieval education, the mark of a free (*liber*) man.

129   *poet*: *Disticha Catonis*, stanza 71, lines 494–500 in the verse paraphrase made by Benedict Burgh for a son of Lady Isabel Bourchier between 1433 and 1440. See the edition by Max Förster, "Die Bürgsche Cato-Paraphrase," *Archiv für das Studium der neueren Sprachen* 115 (1905): 298–323. This collection of proverbial advice was composed in the third or fourth century but incorrectly assigned in the Middle Ages to the much earlier Cato the Elder.

130   *poet*: the idea is not uncommon in medieval literature; cf. *Roman de la Rose* 4396–98, Chaucer's *Wife of Bath's Tale* III 1158 or his moral ballade "Gentilesse."

141   *Isidore*: of Seville (560–636), Spanish theologian, encyclopedist, historian, bishop, and saint. His most famous work is the *Etymologies*; the reference is to *De natura rerum* 12:4 [EETS].

144   *Urban*: Pope Urban I, leader (222–230) of the Roman Christian community.

148   *spear*: John 19:34.

155   *Alexander*: Alexander Severus, Roman emperor (222–235).

157   *Chrysostom*: St. John Chrysostom (347–407), scholar and preacher born in Antioch; the name is Greek for "golden-mouth."

158   *Agnes Flegge*: the wife of John Flegge, knight, administrator, and business associate of some of Bokenham's other patrons. John Flegge served with Richard, duke of York, in France during the early 1440s.

163   *high-born*: the word Bokenham uses is "free," which may mean high-born, spiritually enlightened, generous, legally free (of serfdom), or at liberty. It is by no means the only place in the text where he engages in instructive wordplay.

165   *Decius*: Caius Messius Quintus Decius, Roman emperor (249–251). During the Decian persecution, everyone had to obtain a certificate of willingness to sacrifice to pagan deities.

166   *mountain*: Mount Aetna or Etna, a volcano in eastern Sicily. Catania is located at its foot.

168   *Hippocrates*: (460 B.C.E.–370 B.C.E.), Greek physician and teacher. *Galen* (130–200), Greek physician who lived in Rome as court physician to Marcus Aurelius. *Constantinus Africanus* (1010–1087), Benedictine monk at Montecassino, born in Carthage, translated Hippocrates and Galen and produced medical texts of his own.

168   *humors*: bodily fluids believed, in medieval medical lore, to regulate health and temperament.

168   *gospel*: Matthew 9:20–22.

170   *still*: I have (following the suggestion of Horstmann) dropped the negative from line 9112 in order to make good sense of the passage.

171   *St. Paul*: the sentiment is repeated in several Pauline epistles, e.g., Titus 1:10 or 3:9; 1 Timothy 6:4–5; 2 Timothy 2:16 or 23; Ephesians 4:29 or 5:6; 1 Corinthians 15:33.

171   *gospel*: Matthew 10:17–20, Mark 13:9–11; Luke 21:12–15. Also used in Augustine's *De doctrina christiana* 4.15.

173   *Scripture*: Psalm 91:7.

174   *Maximian, Diocletian*: the emperor Diocletian and his augustus Maximian abdicated at the same time, in 305, as had been agreed on their accession. Maximian was executed in 310 at the order of his son-in-law Constantine. Diocletian died in 313.

175   *Landgrave*: a title, here improperly used as a personal name.

176   *Moses*: Exodus 2.

176   *gospel*: Matthew 5:5, 6, 10, 11.

176   *octave*: eighth. Calendrically, the eighth day begins a new week. Musically, the octave is a perfect interval having the ratio 2:1 and sounding first in the harmonic series of intervals, discussed since Pythagorus. Both metaphors produce an appropriate spiritual meaning.

176   *Daniel*: Daniel 4:16 [EETS]. The phrase is said of Nebuchadnezzar.

176   *David*: Psalm 63.5 [EETS].

176   *Elizabeth Vere*: see note p. 102.

178   *St. Valentine's day*: probably a survival of the ancient Roman fertility festival of Lupercalia (15 February), which was finally suppressed only in 494. Pagan customs were often absorbed into Christian lore, in this case the 14 February feast of Valentine, a Roman priest martyred about 270.

179   *wedded*: Elizabeth was betrothed at the age of four and brought to the Thuringian court at Wartburg Castle, to be raised with her future husband Ludwig (seven years her senior). The wedding took place in 1221, when Elizabeth was fourteen, despite the opposition of many

to this alliance with Hungary. The marriage appears to
have been an unusually happy one.

181   *rogations*: four days set apart for solemn procession to
invoke God's mercy. One of them is 25 April, St. Mark's
Day; the others are the three days preceding Holy Thursday or Ascension, the fortieth day after Easter, commemorating the period when Jesus appeared to the apostles
after he died (see Acts 1:3).

181   *purifications*: after childbirth.

181   *Master Conrad*: Conrad of Marburg (d. 1233), Elizabeth's confessor, administrator of her husband's estates
in Ludwig's absence, and a harsh inquisitor of heretics
in Germany. He was murdered (as were numerous other
inquisitors in other countries).

182   *eat no food*: at Conrad's instigation, Elizabeth refuses to
use goods tainted by abuse of the poor. Food bought
and sold in the market is a commodity exchanged for a
fair price, while food produced by serfs as part of their
feudal obligation (and thus not paid for by the lord) is
the sign of exploited labor. It is an interesting example
of the uneasy coexistence of two competing economic
systems: feudalism (based in use-value) and the newer
urban bourgeois economy (based in exchange-value).

184   *Emperor Frederick at Cremona*: Frederick II (1194–
1250), Holy Roman emperor (1220–1250), German
king (1212–1220) and king of Sicily—which included
much of southern Italy—(1197–1250) and Jerusalem
(1229–1250). He was much at odds with the papacy
over territorial jurisdiction, and at the Diet of Cremona
(1226) reasserted his claim to Lombardy.

184   *emptied*: this occurred in 1225 and provoked much criti-
cism. Landgrave Ludwig's response upon his return was,
"Her charity will bring us blessing."

184   *difficulty*: the path to Wartburg Castle was called "the
kneesmasher."

186   *pilgrimage*: in June 1227, Ludwig joined a crusade led
by Frederick, who was gathering his army in southern
Italy. Frederick fell ill, abandoned the crusade, and was
excommunicated. He finally embarked in 1228 and won
diplomatic concessions in the Holy Land.

187   *died*: in September 1227, Landgrave Ludwig died of plague at Otranto in southern Italy, a port of embarcation for the Holy Land.

187   *brother*: Henry, Ludwig's brother and regent for Elizabeth's young son, drove Elizabeth with her children and attendants from Wartburg castle in winter 1227.

187   *Minors*: Franciscans.

187   *children*: Elizabeth and Ludwig had three children: Herman (1222–1241); Sophia, who became duchess of Brabant; and Blessed Gertrude of Aldenburg. Herman and Gertrude were cared for at the castle of Pottenstein, owned by Elizabeth's uncle Eckembert, bishop of Bamberg. Sophia went to the nuns at Kitzingen.

188   *cut*: self-mutilation was sometimes used by nuns as a defense against violation.

189   *buried*: early in 1228 Ludwig's body was brought home and buried in Reinhardsbrunn church. He is venerated in Germany as St. Ludwig.

192   *compline*: last service of the day.

SELECT BIBLIOGRAPHY

Editions of Bokenham's Known or Possible Works

Aspland, Alfred, ed. *The Golden Legend. A Reproduction from a Copy in the Manchester Free Library.* London: Wyman, 1878.

Barnardiston, Katherine W., ed. "Dialogue at the Grave . . . ," *Clare Priory: Seven Centuries of a Suffolk House.* Cambridge: Heffer, 1962.

Flügel, Ewald, ed. "Eine mittelenglische Claudian-Setzung (1445)," *Anglia: Zeitschrift für englische Philologie* 28 (1905): 255–99 and 421–38.

Horstmann, Carl, ed. "*Mappula Angliae,*" *Englische Studien* 10 (1887): 1–34.

———, *Osbern Bokenams Legenden.* Heilbronn: Altenglische Bibliothek, 1883.

Roxburghe Club. *The Lyvys of Seyntys.* London: W. Nicol, 1835.

Serjeantson, Mary, ed. *Legendys of Hooly Wummen.* EETS o.s. 206, 1938.

Background, Context, Genre

Aers, David. *Community, Gender, and Individual Identity: English Writing 1360–1430.* London: Routledge, 1988.

Atkinson, Clarissa. *Mystic and Pilgrim: The Book and the World of Margery Kempe.* Ithaca: Cornell University, 1983.

Bethell, Denis. "The Making of a Twelfth-Century Relic Collection." In *Popular Belief and Practise*, ed. O. J. Cuming and Derek Baker. Cambridge: Cambridge University, 1972.

Brown, Peter. *The Cult of the Saints*. Chicago: University of Chicago, 1981.

Bugge, John. *Virginitas: An Essay in the History of a Medieval Ideal*. The Hague: Nijhoff, 1975.

Butler, Pierce. *Legenda Aurea–Légende Dorée–Golden Legend*. Baltimore: Murphy, 1899.

Bynum, Carolyn W. *Holy Feast and Holy Fast: The Religious Significance of Food to Medieval Women*. Berkeley: University of California, 1987.

Capgrave, John. *The Life of St. Katherine of Alexandria*. Ed. Carl Horstmann. EETS o.s. 100, 1893.

Chrimes, S. B. *Lancastrians, Yorkists, and Henry VII*. 2nd ed. New York: St. Martins, 1966.

Colledge, Edmund, ed. *A Book of Showings to the Anchoress Julian of Norwich*. 2 vols. Toronto: PIMS, 1978.

Dunn-Cardeau, Brenda, ed. *Legenda Aurea: Sept siècles de diffusion*. Montreal: Bellarmin, 1986.

Edwards, A. S. G. "The Transmission and Audience of Osbern Bokenham's *Legendys of Holy Wummen*." In *The Transmission of Religious Texts in Late Medieval England*, ed. A. J. Minnis. Woodbridge, Suffolk: Boydell and Brewer, forthcoming.

Fortescue, John. *The Works of Sir John Fortescue, Knight*. Ed. Thomas F. Lord Clermont. 2 vols. London: Chiswick, 1869.

Fowler, Kenneth. *The Age of Plantagenet and Valois*. New York: Putnam's Sons, 1967.

Fredeman, Jane. "The Life of John Capgrave, OESA (1393–1464)," *Augustiniana* 29 (1979): 197–237.

Frend, W. C. H. *Martyrdom and Persecution in the Early Church*. Oxford: Blackwell, 1965.

Geary, Patrick J. *Furta Sacra: Thefts of Relics in the Central Middle Ages*. Princeton: Princeton University, 1978.

Gill, Paul E. "Politics and Propaganda in Fifteenth-Century England: The Polemical Writings of Sir John Fortescue," *Speculum* 46 (1971): 333–47.

Görlach, Manfred. *The South English Legendary, Gilte Legende, and Golden Legend*. Braunschweig: Universität Carolo-Wilhelmina, 1972.

Griffiths, Ralph A. *The Reign of King Henry VI . . . 1422–1461.* London: Benn, 1981.

———. "The Sense of Dynasty in the Reign of Henry VI." In *Patronage, Pedigree, and Power in Later Medieval England,* ed. Charles Ross. Gloucester: Sutton, 1979.

Guth, DeLloyd J. *Late-Medieval England, 1377–1485: Bibliographical Handbook.* Cambridge: Cambridge University, 1976.

Gwynn, Aubrey. *The English Austin Friars in the Time of Wyclif.* London: Oxford University, 1940.

Heffernan, Thomas J. *Sacred Biography: Saints and Their Biographers in the Middle Ages.* New York: Oxford University, 1988.

Hudson, Anne. *The Premature Reformation: Wycliffite Texts and Lollard History.* Oxford: Clarendon, 1988.

Hurry, Jamieson B. *Reading Abbey.* London: Elliot Stock, 1901.

Jacob, E. F. *Essays in the Conciliar Epoch.* Notre Dame: University of Notre Dame, 1943; reprint, 1963.

Jeremy, Mary. "The English Prose Translation of *Legenda Aurea,*" *Modern Language Notes* 59 (1944): 181–83.

Johnson, P. A. *Duke Richard of York, 1411–1460.* Oxford: Clarendon, 1988.

Jones, Charles W. *Saints' Lives and Chronicles in Early England.* Ithaca: Cornell University, 1947.

Kingsford, Charles Lethbridge. *English Historical Literature in the Fifteenth Century.* Oxford: Clarendon, 1913.

Lasko, Peter, and N. J. Morgan, eds. *Medieval Art in East Anglia, 1300–1520.* London: Thames and Hudson, 1974.

Lauritis, Joseph A., Ralph A. Kleinfelter, and Vernon F. Gallagher. *A Critical Edition of John Lydgate's Life of Our Lady.* Pittsburgh: Duquesne University, 1961.

McFarlane, K. B. *England in the Fifteenth Century: Collected Essays.* London: Hambledon, 1981.

Miller, Townsend. *Henry IV of Castile, 1425–1474.* Philadelphia: Lippincott, 1972.

Moore, Samuel. "Patrons of Letters in Norfolk and Suffolk c. 1450," *PMLA* 27 (1912): 188–207 and 28 (1913): 79–105.

Musurillo, Herbert. *The Acts of the Christian Martyrs.* Oxford: Clarendon, 1972.

Mycoff, David. *A Critical Edition of the Legend of Mary Magdalena from Caxton's Golden Legende of 1483.* Salzburg: University of Salzburg, 1985.

Obermann, Heiko. *The Harvest of Medieval Theology*. Cambridge: Harvard University, 1963. Reprint. Durham: Labyrinth, 1983.

Olsen, Alexandra Hennessy. " 'De Historiis Sanctorum': A Generic Study of Hagiography," *Genre* 13 (1980): 407–29.

O'Malley, John. *Praise and Blame in Renaissance Rome . . . 1450–1521*. Durham: Duke University, 1979.

Parks, George B. *The English Traveler to Italy*. Stanford: Stanford University, 1954.

Pearsall, Derek. *John Lydgate*. Charlottesville: University of Virginia, 1970.

Perroy, Edouard. *The Hundred Years War*. Bloomington: Indiana University, 1962.

Pugh, T. B. "Richard Plantagenet (1411–1460), Duke of York, as the King's Lieutenant in France and Ireland." In *Aspects of Late Medieval Government and Society: Essays Presented to J. R. Lander*, ed. J. G. Rowe. Toronto: University of Toronto, 1986.

———. "The Southampton Plot of 1415." In *Kings and Nobles in the Later Middle Ages*, ed. Ralph A. Griffiths and James Sherborne. Gloucester: Sutton, 1986.

Reames, Sherry L. *The Legenda Aurea: A Reexamination of Its Paradoxical History*. Madison: University of Wisconsin, 1985.

Renoir, Alain. *The Poetry of John Lydgate*. London: Routledge, 1967.

Ross, Charles. "Rumour, Propaganda, and Popular Opinion during the Wars of the Roses." In *Patronage: The Crown and the Provinces*, ed. Ralph A. Griffiths. Gloucester: Sutton, 1981.

Roth, Francis. *The English Austin Friars 1249–1538*. 2 vols. New York: Augustinian Historical Institute, 1966.

Saxer, Victor. *Le culte de Marie Magdalène en Occident*. Paris: Clavreuil, 1959. Scattergood, V. J. *Politics and Poetry in the Fifteenth Century*. London: Blandford, 1971.

Schirmer, Walter. *John Lydgate: A Study in the Culture of the XVth Century*. Berkeley: University of California, 1961.

Schmitt, Jean-Claude. *The Holy Greyhound: Guinefort, Healer of Children since the Thirteenth Century*. Trans. Martin Thom. Cambridge: Cambridge University, 1983.

Schulenberg, Jane Tibbets. "The Heroics of Virginity, Brides of Christ, and Sacrificial Mutilation." In *Women in the Middle*

Ages and the Renaissance, ed. Mary Beth Rose. Syracuse: Syracuse University, 1986.

Steinberg, Leo. *The Sexuality of Christ in Renaissance Art and in Modern Oblivion.* New York: Pantheon, 1983.

Storey, R. I. *The End of the House of Lancaster.* New York: Stein and Day, 1967.

Sumption, Jonathan. *Pilgrimage: An Image of Medieval Religion.* London: Faber, 1975.

Tanner, Norman P. *The Church in Late Medieval Norwich 1370–1532.* Toronto: PIMS, 1984.

———, ed. *Heresy Trials in the Diocese of Norwich, 1428–31.* Camden 4th ser., vol. 20. London: Royal Historical Society, 1977.

Thornton, Gladys A. *A History of Clare Suffolk.* Cambridge: Heffer, 1930.

Vauchez, André. *La sainteté en Occident aux derniers siècles du moyen âge.* Rome: Palais Farnèse, 1981.

Warner, Marina. *Alone of All Her Sex: The Myth and Cult of the Virgin Mary.* New York: Vintage, 1983.

Workman, Samuel K. *Fifteenth Century Translation as an Influence on English Prose.* Princeton: Princeton University, 1940.

ABOUT THE TRANSLATOR

Sheila Delany received her Ph.D. in English and Comparative Literature from Columbia University. She is currently Professor of English at Simon Fraser University in British Columbia, Canada. In addition to *A Legend of Holy Women*, she has published five other books. Her most recent works are *Medieval Literary Politics: Shapes of Ideology* and *Telling Hours and Other Journal Stories*. Professor Delany's study, *Chaucer's Legend of Good Women: The Naked Text*, is forthcoming from the University of California Press.